Racing the Street

RHETORIC AND PUBLIC CULTURE: HISTORY, THEORY, CRITIQUE

Series Editors: Dilip Gaonkar and Samuel McCormick

Racing the Street

Race, Rhetoric, and Technology in
Metropolitan London, 1840–1900

———

Robert J. Topinka

UNIVERSITY OF CALIFORNIA PRESS

University of California Press
Oakland, California

© 2020 by Robert Topinka

Library of Congress Cataloging-in-Publication Data

Names: Topinka, Robert J., 1984- author.
Title: Racing the Street : Race, Rhetoric, and Technology in Metropolitan
    London, 1840–1900 / Robert J. Topinka.
Description: Oakland, California : University of California Press, [2020] |
    Series: Rhetoric & public culture: history, theory, critique ; vol. 3 |
    Includes index.
Identifiers: LCCN 2020008839 | ISBN 9780520343603 (cloth) |
    ISBN 9780520343610 (paperback) | ISBN 9780520975057 (epub)
Subjects: LCSH: Mass media and race relations—England—London—
    History—19th century. | City and town life—England—London—
    History—19th century. | Technology—Social aspects—England—
    London—History—19th century.
Classification: LCC DA125.A1 T66 2020 | DDC 305.8009421/09034—dc23
LC record available at https://lccn.loc.gov/2020008839

Manufactured in the United States of America

29 28 27 26 25 24 23 22 21 20
10 9 8 7 6 5 4 3 2 1

For Charalambous Frank Topinka, my Bambos, forever

CONTENTS

ILLUSTRATIONS

ACKNOWLEDGMENTS

I owe more debts of gratitude than I can repay, but for a start I would like to thank the University of California Press, the Rhetoric and Public Culture: History, Theory, and Critique series editors Samuel McCormick and Dilip Gaonkar, and executive editor Lyn Uhl for their interest in this project. Thanks also to Enrique Ochoa-Kaup for guiding me through the process.

I have been lucky to have generous mentors at each level of my university education: David Houston Wood converted me from football player to scholar at the University of Wisconsin–La Crosse; at the University of Kansas, Frank Farmer and Dave Tell welcomed me to the world of rhetoric; at Northwestern University, Janice Radway pushed me further than I thought I could go, and Angela G. Ray showed me what scholarly rigor means—I hope I've approached her high standards in this work.

I extend special thanks to Dilip Gaonkar for sharing his unique brilliance over many meetings and more coffees. Dilip possesses the singular ability to identify the kernel of insight in any work, extract it, amplify it, and return it in a form the original thinker could not otherwise have imagined. Dilip revealed to me where my project could go, and this book represents my best effort to fulfill that potential.

I am also grateful to Haixia Lan and Mary Morzinski at the University of Wisconsin–La Crosse; Amy Devitt, Dorice Elliott, and Geraldo U. de Sousa at the University of Kansas; and C. Riley Snorton (now at the University of Chicago), Robert Hariman, Sylvester Johnson (now at Virginia Tech), Charles W. Mills, Penelope Deutscher, and Carl Smith at Northwestern University. I am particularly grateful to Christopher Herbert, whose important work on Henry Mayhew made this project possible, and whose exacting standards sharpened my thinking.

I also wish to acknowledge the research resources at the Northwestern University Library, the British Library, the LSE Digital Library, and the Beinecke Rare Book and Manuscript Library at Yale University.

The best part of graduate school is graduate cohorts; the worst part is the scattering that follows the schooling. From the University of Kansas, shout out to Jason Barrett-Fox, Nathan Clay Barbarick, Kundai Chirindo, Eric Hood, Lauren Kiehna, Kristen Lillvis, Ann Martinez, Jeremy Miller, Gaywyn Moore, Daniel Rolf, Samantha Bishop Simmons, and Jana Tigchelaar. At Northwestern University, J. Dakota Brown, Patricia Anne England, Elisabeth Hoberman Kinsley, Ruth Mary Martin, Robert Elliot Mills, and David Miguel Molina—hugs. Special thanks to Jason Barrett-Fox, Robert Mills, and Elisabeth Kinsley for reading portions of this project and doing their best to improve it.

I owe infinite gratitude to my parents, Ralph Topinka and Mary Jo Bernhardt, who have shown me that being thoughtful can also be a way of being good to people. Thanks for listening to my big questions, and thanks for not answering them—you kept me searching. Thanks to big sisters Emily and Katie for teaching me that it's OK to be a chicken.

Before I could complete this project, I became a father twice over, and lost my firstborn son. Such a loss is beyond sublime—impossible to comprehend—and I've often felt I might fall from face of the earth. I owe the deepest thanks I can possibly give to Alexandria Innes, my partner, friend, companion, and often my sole comfort. Many people claim they don't know where they'd be without their partners; I know I wouldn't be here anymore without mine. Neither would this project, which has benefited from her insight and intellect, and her generous willingness to read every word and to guide every stray thought. To Andri, then, and, to my boy, Marios—I love you more than I love anything. To Bambos, even the pain of missing you can't match the love I will always have for you.

Introduction

A Genealogy of Race as Technology

"World-Wide Circulation," reads a billboard on a London street in 1877. The font size on *circulation* approximates the size of the torsos of the two "ladder-men" who stand below the announcement, busily pasting an advertisement for a new Madame Tussauds exhibition featuring the musician William Fish, who died a decade before his waxen resurrection. It is a striking image, taken using the Woodburtype process, which required only a few seconds' exposure to capture and, crucially, preserve for posterity luminously high-definition images of bodies in motion. A century and a half later, these ladder-men appear on page and screen in hauntingly rich detail and deep dimensionality; they could be steampunk hipsters in post-trendy Shoreditch.

There are times when it is best to deploy a "hermeneutics of suspicion," to critique, for example, the photographer John Thomson's claim that he brought to bear more "precision" on street life than had hitherto been technologically possible, to locate images in the contextual contours of visual culture, and so dispel the false apprehension that we are penetrating the mists of the past.[1] But there is also a time to greet text and image at the level of its presentation. In this case, we might marvel at the city street as a site of the changing same. Like nineteenth-century ladder-men, we move in thoroughly globalized and heavily mediated scenes, confronted at every corner with simulacra of public culture circulating through streets and on signs.

This image of "World-Wide Circulation" appears in John Thomson and Adolphe Smiths' 1877 *Street Life in London*. Back from a tour of Asia, where he photographed landscapes and headshots to index the typical features of the races to be found in Thailand, Laos, Cambodia, and China, Thomson hitched his global imaginary to his camera, claiming to capture photographically the "true types of the London poor" in their typical habitat, the street. Thomson believed technology allowed him to update Henry Mayhew's "ante-dated work," *London Labour and the London Poor*, a copious mid-century account of London's streets composed primarily of text, with only sporadic visual representation in the form of engravings from daguerreotypes. This early photographic process required minutes-long exposure time, making it useless for capturing street scenes. Mayhew had coaxed his "true types" into Charles Beard's studio, where they were encouraged to adopt typical poses. Afterward, Beard embellished his engravings with the accoutrements of street life—a brick wall behind a costermonger, a pile of oranges in his cart—so that the lithographic reproduction could represent the reality of the street to Mayhew's audience of middle-class readers, literary figures, and governmental operatives.

It would take little effort to question the reality of these representations, to unmask the many biases smuggled into their production, reproduction, and reception. But we might also pause to consider how Thomson's project echoes Mayhew's, how both hitched technology to a global imaginary in order to reckon with the street, and how race secured that hitch. In the first pages of his 1851 *London Labour and the London Poor*, Mayhew claims the world is composed of "distinct and broadly marked races," the "wanderers and settlers," "the vagabond and citizen," the savage and civilized. Although he contradicted, modified, and redeployed this claim in alternative racial registers throughout the four volumes of *London Labour*, this comment has become his epitaph in historical scholarship, no doubt in part because most readers do not venture beyond the first pages of the four-volume work, but also because it indicts Mayhew as a Victorian racist obsessed with "pyramidal skulls" and other clumsy ideologies of the racist past. Of late, scholars have expressed increasing frustration with such citations. Elsewhere in the text, however, Mayhew produces arresting and highly original insights; why obsess over the cliché?

Indeed, by the mid-nineteenth century Mayhew's racial framework had long settled into cliché. Another question, though, might be why such an original, if minor, figure as Mayhew would deploy clichés. And why does Thomson redeploy them decades later in his work on photography? Why, in 1865, did Joseph Bazalgette include a reflection on civilization and savagery before, of all things, a proposal for engineering works in London's sewers? And why do these clichés continue to appear over and over again, such as in 1903, when the American travel writer Jack London would compare the streets of East London to "Darkest Africa"? Or in 2009, when Salvation Army Captain Nick Coke would describe walking in the East End "down Mile End Road toward Whitechapel," where he "sense[s] their presence among the people milling around the busy street and market. Look closer and I observe them living in the shadows: innocent men, women, and children terrified of the authorities. . . . As much as this sounds like something from early Salvation Army history, it is not 1865—this is Whitechapel in 2009. Those of us who live in London's East End are only too aware that 'darkest England' is still well and truly with us. The 'shadow people' are irregular migrants living in the UK."[2] From a rhetorical perspective, a cliché becomes a commonplace, a reservoir of the ordinary forces not only shaping the present, but also animating as stowaways the ideas and practices of the past.[3] For two centuries and counting, liberal-minded reformers, with an eye on improving a society cross-cut by channels of "World-Wide Circulation," have ventured into the dark heart of London's streets, rendering in text and image the shadowy figures populating the street, a scene where the abstract operations of global networks manifest in the bodies of "true types" whose ambiguous racial status confounds London's status as a command center of civilization.

Instead of dismissing clichés, we can consider them not as manifestations of moribund ideologies but as novel approaches to technology. Mayhew in 1851, Bazalgette in 1865, Thomson in 1877, and Coke in 2009 approached the street technologically—with pen, camera, or both in hand—and as a technology, a material infrastructure of circulation with global scope. This global scope, in turn, demands a response that race fulfills by recuperating the excesses of this circulation, gathering these shadowy and wandering "true types" into a manageable framework. From a media archaeological perspective, which encourages attention to how media technologies determine situations, the street appears as a technological medium of circulation with worldwide scope. The scope of this circulation poses difficulties for liberal governance. This situation demands a response. For the last two centuries, the principal response has been racist. In globalizing scenes of street-level excess, race acts as a technology to gather and sort objects and bodies into hierarchical frameworks.

Racing the Street traces a counter-history of race as a technology of gathering, assembling, and networking the modern city. Studies of race, particularly those focused on the nineteenth century, tend to assume that race excludes, segregates, and others. By conducting an original genealogy of the nineteenth-century London street, this book provides an alternative view. It demonstrates how race offered a technological solution to a problem of local governance, namely, the need to gather the teeming particularities of street life and street culture into one manageable framework. Race as a technology gathers, sorts, and assembles particularities into manageable networks. In rhetorical terms, race responds to a crisis in metonymy; as the relationship between part and whole breaks down, race supplies resources for the canon of arrangement. To trace this genealogy of racial arrangement, *Racing the Street* compiles a wide archive of materials, many of which have yet to receive scholarly commentary, including parliamentary records, committee reports, periodical press accounts, sensationalist pamphlets, ethnological society debates, early criminological scholarship, lithographs, photographs, photographic technology including archival equipment, and engineering documents. Henry Mayhew's *London Labour and the London Poor* provides the entry point and organization behind this archive. Although Mayhew is considered a minor figure in Victorian studies—a curio of racist Victorian social investigation literature— this book argues that *London Labour and the London Poor* offers an unrivalled archive of the modern street, approaching and at times surpassing Walter Benjamin's *Arcades Project* in scope and ambition. Crucially, *London Labour and the London Poor* and the archive I assemble around it reveals that racism was invented, developed, and deployed to gather, sort, and assemble the people, animals, commodities, waste, traffic, and often illicit forms of commerce that circulated on the nineteenth-century street. The nineteenth-century street served as the basic unit of the urban network, but also proved to be the site most recalcitrant to that network's completion. Race offered not only an ideological but also a rhetorical and technological response to this paradox of the street. This genealogy of the modern street recovers a material and rhetorical history of how modern liberal governance and its racial, technological, and global-imperial aspirations were assembled.

WHITHER THE CRITICAL OBJECT

Increasingly, scholars in rhetoric, media studies, and literary studies are rejecting existing poststructuralist, post-Marxist, and deconstructionist models of critique in favor of a range of approaches inspired by media archaeology, object-oriented ontology, and actor-network theory. These diverse yet related forms of new materialism are challenging assumptions across disciplines. In Victorian studies, scholars now declare that "context stinks!" as they tear down the old gods of critical theory, replacing a focus on representation and the text with networked assemblages and nonhuman actors.[4] In rhetorical studies, a decades-long materialist rhetoric debate between Marxists and poststructuralists has been hijacked by new materialists, who claim that a humanist bias has blinded scholars to a material world of quasi-agential objects. Instead of uncovering, unveiling, and demystifying, scholars now trace networks, identify connections, and describe relations among objects and actors, both human and nonhuman.[5] Yet this new materialist venture to unseat the human subject risks forgetting the ways in which the modern human achieved subjecthood by casting racialized others into objecthood.[6] Racialization thus involves converting a subject into a problematic object to be recuperated in racially hierarchical zones of governance.[7] In this sense, new materialism has created an impasse for scholars interested in the ways in which humanity inscribed itself in a racialized and quasi- and non-humanity.[8] *Racing the Street* provides a route out of this impasse by historicizing the descriptive move as itself a response to political imperatives. Indeed, nineteenth-century Londoners were concerned with a range of human and nonhuman actors, objects and things (from immigrants to the crowd and from cholera to the manure or "street mud" clogging every corner). Describing the relationships among these various actors was a pressing rhetorical and political concern. This book, therefore, follows the call one rhetorician has issued to examine rhetoric as concrescence,[9] but it does so without sacrificing questions of power and structure as they shape the history of urban modernity. Instead, *Racing the Street* argues that assembling the social requires deploying power through race as a technology of urban governance. If, as many media archaeologists now argue, the network is the primary modern technology, then race is not only a form of domination and exclusion but also a secondary technology of describing and gathering, sorting and assembling.

In suggesting that we take Thomson's photographic interest in "worldwide circulation" at its word, I am motivated by what Diane Davis calls the "*non*-hermeneutical dimension of rhetoric," which deals "not in signifying meaning" but "in the address itself, in the exposure to the other."[10] The other can be human or nonhuman, object or animal. Davis, along with Nathan Stormer and his notion of rhetoric as taxis or arrangement, Thomas Rickert and his attunement to rhetoric as an ambience rather than a system of signs, and Debra Hawhee and her rhetorical bestiary, all participate in the increasingly expansive and diverse project of new materialism.[11] Feminist new materialist approaches associated with Diana Coole and Jane Bennett have developed an influential critique of the subject-object dualism undergirding Cartesian reason, recuperating objects from the non-agential world and recovering "lively" or "vibrant" matter. As a dominant strain of so-called speculative realism, object-oriented ontology claims to radicalize this approach, treating objects not only as vibrant but as recalcitrant to human-centered ways of knowing.[12] This recalcitrance of the object encourages a kind of ethical deference to inscrutable objects that allows nonhumans to flourish.

The tensions between Bennett and object-oriented ontology, and indeed among competing strains of speculative realism, are legion. However, one key difference between Harman and Bennett is crucial for this project's consideration of race as a technology in a world of circulating objects and actors, both human and nonhuman: where Harman emphasizes the recalcitrance of objects, Bennett highlights the relationships among objects. As a rhetorical inquiry, and therefore an inquiry into "figures of entanglement," *Racing the Street* follows the route Bennett takes when she argues that all bodies "are inextricably enmeshed in a dense network of relations" in which vibrant matter and agential objects play a crucial role.[13] Here media archaeology and actor-network theory (ANT) emerge as important approaches to networks of vibrant matter. Media archaeology highlights how media cultures are composed of sedimented and layered technologies; linear human progress thus appears as an accumulation of technological objects.[14] ANT defines itself against Bourdieuian models that treat power as an established force rather than something assembled in dispersed networks of human and nonhuman actors, encouraging scholars to trace how objects, actors, and ideas gather in the assembly of the social.[15]

MODERNITY, RACE, HISTORY

Antiracist theory has long recognized what is at stake in the imbrication of the human and the nonhuman, the subject and the object. Frantz Fanon argued that the global-imperial scale of racial domination demands an approach he names as "sociogeny."[16] This form of critique would, as David Marriot suggests, reckon with "the role of race in bio-economic accounts of the human."[17] Fanon's sociogeny, therefore, entails a "sociodiagnostic" that directs attention not only to the human but to the physical and material ground upon which an account of the human is raised. In short, then, race extends into the material world. As Sylvia Wynter explains, modern race "was therefore to be, in effect, the nonsupernatural but no less extrahuman ground . . . of the answer that the secularizing West would now give to the Heideggerian question as to the who, and the what we are."[18] Wynter's identification of this extrahuman ground of race requires, as Katherine McKittrick has shown, a reconsideration of "racialized geographies."[19] Indeed, Fanon's famous encounter with the frightened French boy who cries "Look, a Negro!" occurs on a Parisian street, where "the whiteness that burns" Fanon also forces him to reckon with this spatial location, asking, "Where am I to be classified? Or, if you prefer, tucked away?"[20] Fanon's description of how his body is "given back to him" by this little boy's racism is an account of the lived experience of blackness in the imperial metropole, of the "two frames of reference" that shape the identity of racialized others.[21] But this parable of modernity and its alterity also discloses the material spatialization of racism: Fanon finds himself "completely dislocated" by the whiteness he meets on the street, which decomposes his "*self* as a body in the middle of a spatial and temporal world" organized by a "schema . . . that does not impose itself on me" but instead composes the "definitive structuring of the world."[22] This racial schema, then, saturates the "extrahuman ground" of race. *Racing the Street* conducts a genealogy of street-level technologies that gather and sort the "extrahuman ground" staging the racial assembly in nineteenth-century London. This project thus attends to technologies of identification (as opposed to identity) in a scene of urban sublimity. Hence the word *racing* in this book's title does indeed modify its object: the project is concerned with the racing of the *street*, and through it the biopolitical city.

This is, of course, not to suggest that attention to technologies of identification ought to occasion a rejection of any attention to identity, or to the many racialized others haunting modernity. Indeed, the specter of the racial other hovers over technologies of gathering, sorting, and assembling. As I show in chapter 1, for example, Kant positions the putatively chaotic and irrational state of "Black Africans" as the absolute embodiment of both sublime incomprehensibility and abject deficiency with respect to reason. Kant's very notion of sublimity—and with it his understanding of how civilization might order and structure its progress from savagery—is shot through with revulsion for the "pure" racial other embodied in "Black Africans." Similarly, as I demonstrate in chapter 4, Francis Galton's technological approach to typifying the human body relied on a racial imaginary: Galton insisted that not only do the fingerprints "of Negroes betray the general clumsiness of their fingers" but that the prints themselves—their arches, loops, and whorls—"give an idea of greater simplicity," a claim Galton adhered to despite his self-confessed inability to submit this claim to "scientific measurement." Here alterity haunts classification itself. This project therefore investigates what Ann Laura Stoler has described as a tension between "incorporation and distancing" in the colonial project, a tension that manifests in the metropole as well as the colony.[23] As Ann McClintock has shown, Victorians—and in particular male Victorians—managed divisions internal to British society by "projecting them onto the invented domain of race."[24] This book thus foregrounds Mayhew as a minor protagonist in the narrative of whiteness and its projection of race onto the "extrahuman ground" of material space. Crucially, though, this "invented domain of race" was not external to the metropole. Indeed, as Cedric Robinson has argued, "Racism ... was not simply a convention for ordering the relations of European to non-European peoples but has its genesis in the 'internal' relations of European peoples."[25] Here Robinson highlights not only how class divisions accrue racial significance but also how "the development, organization, and expansion of capitalist society pursued essentially racial directions."[26] Robinson's notion of racial capitalism thus identifies a dynamic tension between incorporating and distancing, differentiating and interrelating. Racial capitalism also animates street scenes. As I describe throughout the book, a series of informal street markets sourced their stock—often illicitly—from colonial trade routes. Race thus gathers and assembles the far-flung in metropolitan space, implicating circulatory networks in racial imaginaries.[27] This coordinating and condensing function of race requires further attention. Ruth Wilson Gilmore highlights this need to examine incorporation alongside distancing in her famous definition of racism as "the state-sanctioned and/or extra-legal production and exploitation of group-differentiated vulnerabilities to premature death, in distinct yet densely interconnected political geographies."[28] The final clause of this definition is crucial: race not only others, it also incorporates the other into a network of interrelation and differentiation.[29] *Racing the Street* attends to these dense interconnections on the space of the street, providing a genealogy of how racial technologies gather, sort, and assemble the human alongside and among the extrahuman and the nonhuman.

This genealogy of racial technologies draws on new materialist approaches, but it also demonstrates the importance of remembering that race often endows objects with their vibrancy. As we defer to objects and their entangled relations with one another, we risk sacrificing a reckoning with power in favor of a recounting of its many relationships. As Kyla Schuller has argued, the new materialist claim to restore vibrancy to matter rests on the assumption that modern thought has always treated matter as if it were inert; however, this narrative "fails to recognize the structuring role of the intertwined ideas of vital matter and inert matter in the deployment of biopower over the last two centuries."[30] Indeed, as Schuller argues, the "dynamics of matter" served as "the ontological basis for race" in nineteenth-century racial thought.[31] Schuller provides an account of how race identified the body's capacity for culturally appropriate affective performance and logical reasoning, plotting a trajectory from the most inert (or the most racially "backward") to the most vital (or the most racially "advanced"). To ignore this genealogy of the inert and the vibrant, Schuller suggests, is to reanimate racial thought.

Although the trajectory from savage to civilized is crucial to nineteenth-century thought, it does not always map quite so neatly onto theories of matter and its relative vibrancy, as Schuller implies, and indeed racial thought included competing conceptions of linear progress and its relationship to race. As always, there are multiple controversies to be restored to genealogies of power. Entanglement is a more apt figure to describe the relationships among human, nonhuman, and object that nineteenth-century racial thinking sought to unpick. Here Edward Burnett Tylor's theories of race are instructive. Like his contemporaries Marx, Herbert Spencer, and Auguste Comte, Tylor developed a theory of the fetish—or of an agential object—in order to reckon with the exposure of the human to an urbanizing, industrializing, technologizing, and colonizing West. Although he is something of a forgotten figure, Tylor was the most influential anthropologist of the nineteenth century, and a major influence on such figures as Durkheim, Boas, Malinowski, and Freud. Tylor's signal preoccupation was with animism, the idea that souls or spirits animated elements of the natural world, which he approached through his "theory of the survivals." He defined survivals as the "processes, customs, opinions, and so forth, which have been carried on by force of habit into a new state of society different from that in which they had their original home, and they thus remain as proofs and examples of an older condition of culture out of which a newer has been evolved."[32] There are two key things to note from this definition: The first is that the "theory of survivals" is also a theory of race, but it is a theory that stretches to include *every race* within one human species. This is key, because Tylor argues against degenerationism, the nineteenth-century conservative Christian doctrine holding that non-Europeans had *degenerated* from the state of perfection Adam and Eve embodied. The second is that his theory of survivals linked "primitive" culture to European society, foregrounding the entanglements between savage and civilized. Of course, his theory assumed Europeans had progressed further than so-called primitives, but it also suggested that "animism" and "fetishism" had a biological rather than religious basis—to fetishize was the instinct of the underdeveloped human, to be countered by culture, or the increasing advance of civilization. Freud's *Totem and Taboo* follows this same basic argument but suggests that civilization displaces rather than erases the fetish. Nevertheless, Tylor "shared with Darwin the desire to put humans in the biological and material world."[33] Animism was the basis for a global theory of entanglement—what a speculative realist might call a "flat ontology"—that linked humans, nonhumans, and objects in a social scene cross-cut by connections with global-imperial scope.[34]

Reckoning with the manifold connections between bodies and technologies, objects and actors is crucial for a genealogy of modern race and racism. As Achille Mbembe has argued, race has long haunted the potential fusion between capitalism and animism in modernity.[35] Although Mbembe suggests that this fusion is nearly complete under neoliberalism, his project also participates in a larger effort to recover the *longue durée* of race and racism, rediscovering, in the process, the racial project of modernity. Such approaches take various forms, from discussion of the resuscitation of nineteenth-century theories of animism in new materialism, to Charles Mills's examination of how racism is built into the foundational contract of liberal governance, to Ann Laura Stoler's genealogies of colonial "racisms of the state," to David Theo Goldberg's genealogies of racism and the rise of the nation state.[36] Despite their differences, these approaches all reject a view of racism as an ideology, a set of biases wielded by individuals or groups seeking to sustain power. Instead, race is at once constitutive of modernity in its imperial and colonial iterations and a contingent collection of materials, practices, actions, and structures. Building on these approaches, instead of speaking of racial formations, we might speak instead of race *in* formation.[37] This book thus approaches race as a technology, asking, as Wendy Hui Kyong Chun suggests, not *what* race is but *how* it operates, how it intervenes in social arrangements, how it recuperates excess as hierarchy.[38] Viewing race as a technology reveals how it persists even as racist ideologies subside. Hortense Spillers's notion of pornotroping, for example, identifies how racism's historical weight is made present in cultural tropologies first forged in the violence of slavery.[39] Although tropes are techniques of rhetorical invention, they can function to reanimate the past. Race as a technology persists in the tropes that sustain modern social arrangements.

Race and racism, therefore, must be approached as at once quasi-universal features of modernity but also as historically specific and culturally contingent. As Eric King Watts has argued, race has long been crucial to biopower, which makes efforts to expunge racist ideologies without attending to racist genealogies of governance a misguided endeavor.[40] Thus Darrel Wanzer-Serrano critiques Michael Calvin McGee for highlighting fragmentation as if the "modern/ colonial" era were marked by homogeneity, suggesting that we must account for and critique "epistemic coloniality."[41] Many important contributions to the study of rhetoric and race therefore adopt a historical or genealogical approach to race in formation, developing what Lisa Flores has called "historical racial rhetorical studies."[42] Kirt H. Wilson's study of reconstruction and segregation in the post–Civil War United States, Josue Cisneros's genealogy of the US-Mexico border, Wanzer-Serrano's discussion of the history of the Young Lords in New York, and Bryan McCann's study of the overlaps between responses to gangsta rap and the rise of War on Crime discourse all seek to recover the genealogies of race and racism and the varied responses to these formations.[43] Following Wanzer-Serrano's decolonial critique of McGee, I show in what follows that race is precisely an effort to recuperate homogeneity in the face of fragmentation; to assume such concerns are unique to the present moment is to naturalize the historical victories of race and racism. This has severe repercussions for a genealogical rhetorical method, which is also to say it has severe repercussions for any rhetorical study that would grant the significance of the rhetorical situation and rhetorical context.

To trace how these fragmented materials, practices, actions, and structures gather into race, I rely on a genealogical approach to assembling the social. By taking the street as my archive—the scene of collision between abstract forms and particular phenomena—I describe both the role of race in securing liberal governance during its nineteenth-century ascendancy and the discursive resonances of race in formation. With this approach, I contribute to the project of sketching the racial contours of modernity without reducing race to an ideology. If race were an ideology alone, it would be enough to agree with those who dismiss Mayhew's racism as a relic of the nineteenth century. But we would still be no closer to accounting for the durability of race as it survives from the age of liberalism to our neoliberal moment. Drawing on Foucault's notion of technologies of governance, I examine race as a technology rather than an ideology, a set of techniques, practices, and materials that function to make the particular body recognizable, analyzable, and archivable within the totality. Where disciplinary power targets the individual isolated in the panoptic gaze, attempting to produce the disciplinary subject in advance, biopolitics targets the shared field of interaction that sustains flows of people, goods, and capital, making it possible to manage risk, promote health, regulate circulation, and harvest profit.[44] Approaching race as a technology of governmentality has the virtue of opening the question of how race assembles, gathers, and networks rather than others, excludes, and oppresses; how it brings things into relation in a field of shared interaction rather than fragments fields into stable categories of domination.

This admittedly counterintuitive approach to race stems in part from this study's focus on mid-to-late-nineteenth-century London, a city emerging as a command center of a global empire, where the key concerns revolved around global flows of people, goods, and capital in contrast to the much-studied United States, where race and racism sustained settler colonialism and slavery, and thus functioned to segregate, exclude, and expel. This is not to deny, of course, the British Empire's complicity in these projects. Instead, my purpose is to highlight how race functions not only in the founding moment of biopolitics as a caesura between who must live and who must die, but how race also surfaces in the ongoing biopolitical project of managing mobility and sustaining circulation. As a biopolitical technology, race not only excludes and others; it also functions to include, to gather, to assemble into a field of shared interaction—crosscut, of course, by unequal power dynamics. From this perspective, technologies of race emerge as constitutive features of the expanding totality within which governmentality operates. As I show throughout *Racing the Street*, the story of modern racism is not complete without an account of racial technologies deployed on the street, the paradoxical scene where particularities escape abstract totalities, where these totalities in turn produce new forms of particularity, and where networks at once find their structure and site of incompletion.

THE MODERN STREET AND THE MINOR ARCHIVE

As London's population rapidly expanded over the course of the nineteenth century, the paradoxical status of the street troubled the status of London's urban network. The desire to manage and regulate this networked city generated efforts to gather the teeming particularities of the street into an abstract field that would provide the target of application for governmentality. Yet, as recent work on the status of the Victorian city has shown, the urban network was in a recognizably incomplete status in nineteenth-century London.[45] Indeed, no centralized form of representative government existed in London until the formation of the London County Council in 1889. As John Stuart Mill remarked in 1851, "There is no local government of London. There is a very badly constituted and badly administered local government of one section of London."[46] The need to bring London's disparate governing structures—and the material city that they managed—into one communicative network was a recurrent theme in the public sphere.

Although contemporary theorists increasingly argue that we need to recover a vocabulary that can describe how humans and nonhumans gather in the networked assembly of the social, in nineteenth-century London—where the profusion of the social was unavoidable—the word was also readily available: *communication*. The word *communication* meant discursive communication, as when the Metropolitan Sanitary Association declared in 1866 that its primary function was "To bring into friendly communication members of different vestries, of boards of guardians and others, so that the practical experience of every single district may be brought to bear upon all."[47] But communication could also mean material connection, as when the Metropolitan Board of Works in 1864 identified one of its goals as "securing a complete system of railway communication for its inhabitants, with the greatest advantage to the public and least interference with public or private rights."[48] Communication included both discourse circulating in media and objects and places connected by technology.[49] To communicate was to operate in a discursive and material network that united the parts of the city into an interconnected totality. The desire to complete the connections sustaining the communicative (in the double sense of the word) urban network generated attempts to gather the particularities circulating throughout that network into an abstract totality that, in turn, provided the target of application for governmentality. As I argue in what follows, the street both structured that network and staged its unraveling.

In *Racing the Street*, I describe the gathering of particularities into an abstract field, where abstraction is not a flight from material reality but a factor crucial to its comprehension as a scene of circulation. Although I refer to abstract vision when the object of analysis suits visual metaphors—as when, for example, James Pennethorne offered a vision of a new street system in London, or when photography made the particularities composing the photograph visible in new ways—I prefer the language of gathering, not only because it emphasizes the materiality of the particularities to be gathered but because it suggests that abstraction is plastic and pliable: As objects gather together, they constitute a new archive. The contours of the archive expand, stretch, or dissolve along with the contours of the gathered objects. To gather an abstract field is to produce the field in the form of the gathering. The work of abstraction requires not only such familiar components as representational distance but also some means of approaching materiality, of getting close to the flux and flow of the phenomenal world.

The abstract field sustaining London's urban network was partly planned in parliamentary and committee reporting and partly imagined in the public sphere—the London rather than the national public, although the tensions between the local and the transnational resonate in the London public in ways that the word *network* captures better than *nation*. But the abstract field providing the target of application for governmentality also included a working infrastructure that staged a city's heaving traffic—the stones crushed by poor-law laborers into an even size of "3 in. wide, 9 in. deep, and from 9 in. to 15 in. long" so that they could be fitted together, the gaps between them filled in with "stone lime grout" to form a street that ran over telegraph wires (from the 1840s), over train lines (proliferating in the same decade), and under electric lamps (from 1875).[50] Projecting an abstract field that would make the material metropolitan network manageable required gathering those stones, wires, train lines, and street lamps along with the people, goods, and traffic that moved over, across, and under them.

Racing the Street gathers its archive at the level of the street, at once the basic structural unit in this communicative network and the scene of that network's undoing. To explore this dynamic, I examine not only the discursive but the material scene of the street, its curbstones, cameras, pushcarts, carriages, clothing, lighting, shop windows, advertising, sewers, train tunnels, street crossings, feces (human and animal), water, wood pavements, MacAdamized pavements, granite pavements, market stalls, and more. I do not pretend to provide an exhaustive account of the nineteenth-century London street, but I do aim to show why an exhaustive account would be impossible now and was impossible then, and to explore how that very impossibility exorcised a host of urban actors.

As these urban actors of governmentality discovered, the street structures the networked totality, but it is also the source of the excess that overwhelms any abstract framework that would gather the street into a totality. To the extent that this claim is true, the street places governmentality's target of application in motion: This target is the totality—a projection of an abstract field of shared inter-action, where abstractions are not arid impositions imposed upon a fertile world but frameworks for gathering particularities in scenes of worldwide circulation. In chapter 3, for example, I offer Petticoat Lane as one such plane of immanence where the potentials of abstraction in the form of James Pennethorne's urban planning were unleashed to gather the particularities of the street, including Jews, Lascars, and Sunday Markets, into a manageable totality. Yet the particularities found on the street flourish (or search for ways to do so) in a field that abstraction can never fully capture, even as actors working toward abstraction seek to exert control over the conditions of the field—say, by building Commercial Street to "ventilate" Petticoat Lane, as I describe in chapter 3 as well. I thus seek to remain attendant to the controversies and contradictions surrounding the managing of the urban network and the objects, ideas, and actors that coursed through it, recovering in the process a genealogy of the modern street. Without accounting for the street, no genealogy of the racial, technological, and global-imperial aspirations of modern liberal governance is complete.

Racing the Street thus turns to the street for an archive of modernity. As an archive, the street provides "a transcript of dynamic simultaneities," the staging ground of "discourse ecologies" that emerge from the interconnection of technology with image and infrastructure, flowing or gridlocked traffic, and embodied movement or congestion. I refer to street *scenes* in order to describe these "dynamic simultaneities."[51] Adopting a Deleuzian idiom, we might say that the street is a scene of emerging intensities. These intensities emerge in the tensions between abstraction and particularity. As these tensions resonate, they produce the "conditions of emergence, not of the categorical, but of the unclassifiable, the unassimilable, the never-yet felt," which

Brian Massumi has famously theorized as affect.[52] As I explore through the theory of the sublime in chapter 1, *affect* describes the uncategorized experience of intensity— the unfolding of events, the excess of the yet-to-be-named, the paradoxical emergence of phenomena for which no rules or structures exist. The street stages these intensities: it is a scene of paradoxical unfoldings, of events that escape and exceed existing structures even as they emerge from those structures.

As I explore through photographic technologies in this book's final chapter, the archive of the street promises a "galaxy of . . . cultural inscriptions," but this promise requires some standardized format—a reproducible vision of the totality—to gather the galaxy, to map it and make it navigable.[53] The street archive thus promises a fugitive totality, one that forever defers completion. Indeed, as I will argue in chapter 1, one of Mayhew's most original insights was to recognize the impossibility of his own project, to reckon with the inevitable failure of his attempt to account for the totality of London's streets and street laborers. Through Mayhew, one can recover a glimpse of this fugitive totality by returning to the scene of the chase, to those moments where his target eluded his grasp. Mayhew's failures, then, constitute his most valuable insights. Chapters 1 and 2 foreground Mayhew's search for solutions to London's problems, following his references and concerns into a broader archive of the London street. Chapters 3 and 4 also attend to solutions proposed to London's problems, but move beyond Mayhew both thematically and temporally, extending the genealogy of London's streets beyond the 1850s—by which time Mayhew had completed the bulk of his investigations—and up to the turn of the century.

If the street generates an archive of modernity, Mayhew offers an archive of the minor. In contrast to accounts that treat as paradigmatic of urban modernity the Haussmanization of Paris and the merciless imposition of an abstract vision on urban space, an analysis of Mayhew can recover something of the hesitations between the allure of the total view and the thrill of the street.[54] In Mayhew we can discover no victory of the totality, and indeed there was no Haussmann of London. Although Mayhew's work draws on major figures of the day—many of whom, including Charles Dickens, Mayhew knew personally—Mayhew was a minor figure who assembled a minor approach to the street. He hovers somewhere between Dickens and William Haywood, the author and the engineer, the aesthetics of the novel and the aesthetics of governance. This book seeks in part to recover Mayhew's text as a crucial if minor index of modernity, but also, more importantly, to make its minor status central to its methodology: to read Mayhew is to recover one route through the broader—and never complete—archive of the modern street. Mayhew's work, then, is historically and conceptually significant as the most thoroughgoing (and contradictory) inquiry into urban sublimity in the modern era.

Relying on Mayhew to recover a minor archive requires retreading the discursive route Mayhew took on the way to producing one of the most fantastically flawed texts of the nineteenth century. Just as he hesitates between abstraction and particularity, Mayhew hesitates between discursive and generic conventions: As a project, *London Labour and the London Poor* is not a periodical press account, a parliamentary report, a novel, a sensationalist pamphlet, a statistical inquiry, or a sociological investigation, but it adopts and drops all of those generic conventions at various times.

Indeed, the version of *London Labour and the London Poor* that survives today bears the scars of a harshly competitive publishing world. The idea for what would later become *London Labour* began as a series of weekly dispatches for the *Morning Chronicle* that began in September 1849. Mayhew's reports appeared three times a week until April 1850, when publication was reduced to once a week. Publication ended abruptly in the midst of public controversy that first began when Mayhew claimed the editors were censoring his interviews. Then, at a public meeting of tailors, Mayhew criticized the *Chronicle* for publishing an article praising the exploitative "contracting" system of clothes production that Mayhew had denounced in his *Chronicle* letters—and that a clothing firm advertising in the *Chronicle* happened to use.[55]

After this public separation, Mayhew turned to his next project: *London Labour and the London Poor*. This new project began as a weekly publication, which was repackaged into monthly issues and finally into book form. Volume 1 was published in 1851. Mayhew halted his ongoing investigations and writing abruptly in 1852 when his printer filed an arcane lawsuit, halting his cash flow, but an incomplete version of Volume 2 was still released in 1852.[56] In 1855, with the aid of his brother, Augustus, and working with a new publisher, Mayhew resumed his investigations. His plan was to complete volume 2 and issue a third volume, which was to be composed of expanded versions of his *Chronicle* letters on street entertainers along with the material from his new investigations.[57] Although a completed version of volume 2 was released in 1856, his plans for a three-volume set were scuppered by the sudden death of his new publisher in the same year. In 1861–1862, yet another publishing company published the four-volume set on which most scholarship (this book included) focuses. Volumes 1 and 2 in the 1861–1862 edition were relatively unchanged from the 1851 and 1856 works, respectively, but Mayhew was apparently out of the country during the publication of the 1861–1862 edition. As a result, volume 3 is a loosely edited compilation of incomplete material, expanded *Chronicle* reporting, and interviews conducted between 1855 and 1856, and volume 4 is primarily composed of contributions from other writers. A second edition of the entire four-volume set was released in 1865.[58] By this time, however, Mayhew had begun his slow descent into anonymity and penury.

Despite his relatively anonymous death, Mayhew's work provides unique insight into his time. Indeed, by virtue of being caught between promoting social reform and publishing quickly and remuneratively, Mayhew was also uniquely tapped into his historical moment—and, as I will suggest in chapter 2, self-consciously aware of the need to assess one's historical situation. Although he is cryptic about his sources, he clearly draws on a variety of discursive currents, absorbing and processing insights from political theorists such as John Stuart Mill, ethnologists such as James Cowles Prichard, and literary figures such as his friend Dickens. He was also a key figure in London's periodical press—a cofounder of *Punch* and *Figaro in London* and of course a leading correspondent with the *Morning Chronicle*. Mayhew thus survives adjacent to some of the foundational texts of Victorian scholarship. As a result, he has been routinely cited but rarely read: He typically appears to provide a bit of character to a passage of historical context in a text ultimately concerned with a more canonical figure, or he is summoned only to be dismissed as an example of Victorian racism and slum fetishism. And perhaps he was both of those things. I am interested, however, in his minor status: He was no Dickens, and he lacked the institutional status of an Edwin Chadwick or the systematic approach of a Charles Booth, but he hesitated between the discourses those figures have come to stand for, illuminating a discursive space that the study of single figures that stand as metonymies for larger discourses forecloses. To follow Mayhew is to enter a profuse network of nineteenth-century discourses and to discover a chorus of voices, many of them from street laborers whose ideas, actions, practices and habits are recorded in no other archive. Mayhew attempted a total account of London's streets, and although he failed, his failures also indicate directions for inquiry. I have followed these directions in the four chapters that follow.

Each chapter begins with a paradox emerging from encounters with material objects on the street and proceeds to explore technologies imagined, debated, and developed to respond to that paradox. Objects include both humans and nonhumans interacting in complex and often inscrutable ways to shape the rhythms and spaces of the street: costermongers, their carts, and the cartways that predominate in their close-knit neighborhoods (chapter 1); sewer tunnels, cholera, sailors, and urban scavengers (chapter 2); and doorways, shop windows, cobblestones, horse manure, paper sellers, photographs, mass-market periodicals, sex workers, and Jewish immigrants (chapters 3 and 4).

Chapter 1 begins where Mayhew began, with a sublime encounter with London's streets. I read sublimity not as an encounter with one large, awe-inspiring object, but as a crisis of metonymy resulting in a breakdown in the relationship between the part and the whole. Mayhew describes as sublime his encounter with forms of excess on the street that troubled his frameworks for knowing and understanding London. Mayhew saw his inability to gather the crowds, markets, and mess of the street into one intelligible framework as a problem for urban governance. He registered this sublime encounter with London's streets as a practical and technological problem, and he therefore deployed race as a technology to solve this problem. Race restores metonymic coherence by assembling the parts into a whole that can be taken in at one view. Race thus equipped Mayhew with a means of gathering that which exceeded the established vision of the city—the streets and street people of London—into a view of the metropolitan totality. Viewed at the point of its application, where it describes and sorts the teeming street-level actors into a manageable assembly, race becomes a technology rather than an ideology, a radically open response to external conditions rather than a set of fixed internal preconceptions. As I argue throughout *Racing the Street*, the street was a key target for racial technologies. This chapter thus introduces the material street as a scene of encounter through a discussion of what Mayhew calls the "side-bone streets" that branch off the "fish's spine" of Drury Lane. These streets communicated materially with major London thoroughfares, but the crowds of costermongers, sweepers, and sex workers who lived upon them exceeded Mayhew's grasp of London as a symbolic totality. I contextualize Mayhew's attempt to grasp that totality through a discussion of the civilizational stakes of sublimity in Kant and Edmund Burke's influential theories of the sublime, which, along with Mayhew, I consider in relation to John Stuart Mill's theories of representative government. The sublime both identifies a crisis in metonymy and encourages a response to the crisis. I thus suggest that the sublime generates an aesthetics of governance that intervenes in material forms of rhetorical arrangement. The chapter closes with an example of how this aesthetics of governance is tested in Mayhew's discussion of the London Dock, which is a scene that combines the excess of the streets with the excess of the seas, the wasted lumpenproletariat with the wealth of empire. In this scene, Mayhew responded to a sublime encounter by turning to race to theorize the totality. This chapter therefore demonstrates how the questions new materialists ask about objects and non-human actors are crucial for rethinking rhetorical concerns around the range and scope of public life.

Chapter 2 continues to follow Mayhew's attempts to apprehend the material and symbolic scope of London's street network, this time by focusing on a particular case study in technical engineering: Joseph Bazalgette's 1860s renovation of London's sewer network, which I consider in the context of Mayhew's assessment of London's sewer technology and its relationship to the tidal Thames. I show how Mayhew reckoned with the streets as part of a larger street-sea-sewer network with global-imperial scope, and indeed how Bazalgette intervened in London's sewer technology to establish new channels linking London's streets and sewers to the seas. In Mayhew's investigation of the sewers, he folded race as a technology into his discussion of sewer technology. He attempted to assess the status of the material forms comprising the sewer infrastructure and the bodies of the workers scraping a living from the waste in those sewers. Through this assessment, Mayhew sought to characterize the workers as types—an organizing principle of race—and to use those types to track the social and moral trends shaping civic life in London. What Mayhew discovered in London's sewer technology was that the metropolis was in a state of paradox—at once civilized and savage, wealth-producing and waste-producing, moving toward progress and plagued by regression—and that assessing the status of typical bodies in their relationship to the street-sea-sewer network was a necessary task for establishing a totalizing framework that would enable proper management of the city. Instead of studying the representational rhetorics of race, then, this chapter identifies race as itself a response to rhetorical contingency.

Chapter 3 develops an original argument that updates familiar themes of urban studies and the spatial turn in rhetorical studies: large-scale urban planning, street improvement, and slum clearance. Typically, scholars argue that urban planners impose a totalizing, abstract vision onto the teeming particularities of lived experience in public space with the stated goal of clearing congestion and improving circulation and with the ulterior motive—stated or unstated—of clearing undesirable people from the urban core. I argue, though, that studies of these themes have routinely overlooked one central paradox: congestion moves, circulating throughout the city in unpredictable ways. Indeed, urban planners were often well aware of this paradox. Rather than *imposing* an abstract vision of space that existed entirely outside of lived experience, urban planners, managers, and other reformers attempted to *assemble* an abstract vision of space by gathering mobile particularities into a vision of the totality, which was at once abstract and grounded in lived experience. I explore the paradoxical movements of congestion and their repercussions for abstract visions of space through the case of one street, Petticoat Lane. In this chapter, then, the technology is the material stuff of the street itself. I build a street archive of parliamentary reports, press accounts, novels, transcripts of public debates, and more that covers the history of Petticoat Lane from 1840 to 1890. I reveal that Petticoat Lane was at once a space of intense congestion and intense movement, a cloistered community and a cosmopolitan collection of strangers. Two metropolitan types—the Jew and the prostitute—bring these tensions into focus. I show how attending to the movements issuing from apparent forms of immobility reveals a parallel form of circulation that shadows the circulation that abstract space promotes, always exceeding the latter's perspective and thus prompting it to expansion.

Chapter 4 returns to the theme of the relationship between racial types and technologies through a media archaeology of street photography. With good reason, study of visual culture has tended to focus on visual representation. This chapter adopts a media archaeological approach by centering on visual technologies. Instead of attending to visual culture by analyzing the rhetoric of particular photographs, the chapter demonstrates that the public repercussions of photography were first worked out in non-photographic visual technologies, particularly lithographs, which could be mass printed long before photographs, as the latter could not be printed in mass circulation periodicals until the end of the century. This chapter thus tracks the development of photographic technologies and the deployment of those technologies by a variety of institutions and actors, including cheap street photographers whom Mayhew encountered; the satirical illustrated periodical *Punch*, that "British institution" where a photographic public sphere was sketched and imagined long before photography could be mass produced; and Francis Galton, who advocated the use of composite photography by ethnologists and anthropologists to capture the racial type. The chapter concludes by comparing Mayhew's reliance on daguerreotypes to John Thomson and Adolphe Smith's use of Woodburytype photographs in their 1877 *Street Life in London*, which they explicitly advertised as an update on Mayhew's work. I focus in particular on the appearance in both *London Labour* and *Street Life in London* of "Ramo Samee," the name for an Indian street performer who was both a historic individual and a racial type. As Ramo Samee's case shows, photography at once captured the individual and dispersed the individual into a scene of racial types organized in an abstract field of mediated interaction. The street was both the scene where this field expanded and the target of application for ethnological, criminological, and sociological investigations into mobile bodies. Although scholars typically argue that street photography was a mere precursor on the way to cinema, which first captured the motion of the modern street, I show how photography was in fact developed, described, and deployed precisely in order to trace the contours of the body in an animated scene of mobility. So-called still photography is, in fact, always in motion. By gathering the particularities of photographed details into an abstract archive that was in principle limitless, photography offered a technological solution to the paradox of the street, the foundational structure of the totalizing urban network and the scene of emerging particularities forever frustrating that network's completion.

I conclude by reflecting on the technological formation of modern power and on the fundamental role race has played in that formation. For too long, studies of power in the nineteenth century have remained lodged in an approach adapted from Foucauldian notions of disciplinary power. From such a perspective, everything appears to be a symptom of the panopticon, a sign of a system that fixes, isolates, and locks in place, rendering every object and actor subject to an all-seeing gaze. The nineteenth century, though, was characterized not by fixity but by mobility, not by isolation but by circulation. Controversies and competing approaches arose around the material movement of bodies and commodities, dirt and disease, waste and wealth, images and ideas. A media archaeological approach focused on material interventions into human and nonhuman urban actors can recover a genealogy of the modern city street. The nineteenth century was the founding century of the modern era in all its imperial reach, global scope, and transnational connectedness. By studying the incomplete formation of the urban network—and the continual frustration of that project at its point of contact with the street—I restore the controversy to the rise of modern power and its global-imperial ambition, revealing how racial technology responded to the paradoxical status of the street, the site that structured the network and staged its unraveling.

Sublime Streets, Savage City

Metonymy, the Manifold, and the Aesthetics of Governance

In 1851, the same year in which Mayhew published the first volume of *London Labour and the London Poor*, the Metropolitan Sanitary Association proposed that the water supply of London be taken out of the hands of private companies and placed under public administration. The *Economist* responded with a furious critique, claiming that public ownership of water would irrigate a slippery slope: If the government were to assume control of water, the *Economist* argued, they would soon assume control of every necessity of life, and then "Land must no longer be private, it must be public property," putting liberty itself under threat. Chastened by this perhaps unexpectedly virulent response, the Metropolitan Sanitary Association turned to John Stuart Mill, the preeminent political economist of the day, asking him "whether it is consistent with sound political economy, that the supply of water to London should be provided by companies trading for profit, and supplying only those who are able and willing to pay the local water rate?" In a letter to the public health reformer Edwin Chadwick, Mill explained that he would oblige the Association's request, writing, "I shall not give the Assn a *long* answer. If they want me as an authority against the nonsense of the Economist &c. they will get what they want."[1] And so they did. Mill's reply dispatches the *Economist*'s fears by pointing out that London's water supply was in monopoly control, and thus received no benefit from "the free agency of individuals" acting in a state of liberty, which exists only where there is free competition.[2] Breaking the monopoly would be impractical, though, Mill argues, because water is a fixed resource: No amount of individual free agency can generate more water. Free competition over water is impossible. The water supply thus falls well within the domain of government: "The cases to which the water-supply of the towns bears most analogy, are such as the making of roads and bridges, the paving, lighting, and cleansing of streets."[3] Like other resources necessary for metropolitan life, water cannot be privately produced, and therefore the "Government" must ensure that "these operations" be "adequately performed."[4] This suggestion that public administration ought to provide what private production cannot leads Mill to diagnose the central problem facing Mayhew's London:

> In the case of London, unfortunately, this question [of central governance of the water supply] is not at present a practical one. There is no local government of London. There is a very badly constituted and badly administered local government of one section of London. Beyond this there are only parochial authorities. The municipal administration of a town, whether great or small, ought to be undivided. Most of the matters of business which belong to local administration concern the whole town, not the separate parts of it, and *must be all taken in at one view, to enable any part to be well managed.*"[5] (Emphasis added.)

Mill's claim that the affairs of the whole town be "taken in at one view" was little disputed at the time. Yet combining the many parts of London into a whole that could be "taken in at one view" was easier said than done. In its comments on Mill's response to the *Economist*, the Metropolitan Sanitary Association seconds Mill's deflation of the *Economist's* hyperbole, but it also, in exasperated tone, explains that Mill's theoretically sound proposal ignores nearly insurmountable practical problems. Implementing an overarching government for the metropolis "will require the framing of a constitution for upward of two millions of people, a population equal to one-ninth of that of England and Wales, and exceeding the population of the whole kingdom of Scotland, and three or four time more than that of all Wales."[6] Although the government would only administer one city, the scope of the population it would be required to accommodate vastly exceeded existing municipal frameworks. The profusion of objects and actors on city streets overwhelmed any infrastructural or governmental technology that might be capable of linking part and whole. London thus suffered from a crisis of metonymy.

In 1849, two years before the *Economist*, Mill, and the Metropolitan Sanity Association would have their public dialogue, Mayhew began publishing in the *Morning Chronicle* the fieldwork he would later collect and expand upon for *London Labour and the London Poor*. His work shared in the same impulse to find some means of taking London in at one view. As I demonstrate in this chapter, the paradox propelling Mayhew's investigation surfaces in Mayhew's repeated turns to the category of the sublime, an aesthetic category with often overlooked ramifications for the governance of racialized civilizations. In his first published report, Mayhew wrote that since the "mere name of London awakens a thousand trains of varied reflections," he decided to ascend to the Golden Gallery of St. Paul's cathedral to obtain a "bird's-eye view" of the city:

It was noon, an exquisitely bright and clear spring day; but the view was smudgy and smeared with smoke. And yet the haze which hung like a curtain of shadow before and over everything, increased rather than diminished the giant sublimity of the city that lay stretched out beneath. It was utterly unlike London as seen everyday from below, in all its bricken and hard-featured reality; it was rather the phantasm—the spectral illusion, as it were, of the great metropolis—such as one might see it in a dream. . . . But as the vast city lay there beneath me, half hid in mist and with only glimpses of its greatness visible, it had a much more sublime and ideal effect from the very inability to grasp the whole in its literal reality.[7]

Mayhew adopted the sublime in order to pose Mill's solution as a problem: London was sublime—and, one might say, in response to Mill, ungovernable—precisely because of the inability to gather the "hard-bricken reality" of the everyday into one view that would "grasp the whole." Mayhew adopted the sublime as a name for that which exceeded such a networked whole.

Mayhew would thus leverage sublimity as a figure describing the overwhelming encounter with street scenes brimming with mobile bodies, moving objects, informal markets, narrow backstreets, and leaky infrastructures. In contrast to the Romantic pastoral sublime, his was a sublimity of the urban. Departing from the sublime of grand, singular objects, Mayhew developed a sublime of profuse and peripatetic objects and bodies, images and infrastructures. Conceptually, the sublime diagnoses the urgent need to corral this profusion of objects into the infrastructures of civilization.[8] Yet the sublime not only diagnoses an issue; it also demands a response to it. The sublime thus functions metonymically in two senses: First, it identifies a collapse in the relationship between part and whole. Second, it demands a catachresis, an invention of some means of gathering objects into a relationship of contiguity, thus repairing the breakdown between part and whole. A catachresis is a figure of rhetorical and technological response to a crisis of metonymy. Catachresis thus names a form of gathering human and nonhuman actors together in novel arrangements.

In this chapter, I examine how this sublimity of the manifold answered the crisis of metonymy, allowing Mayhew to develop an aesthetics of government that would, he hoped, secure the continued advance of civilization. In showing how Mayhew routed his aesthetics of government through race, I am also recounting tropes of Victorian racial thinking that now appear as clichés. Mayhew infamously opened *London Labour* with one such cliché, writing: "Of the thousand of millions of human beings that are said to constitute the population of the entire globe, there are—socially, morally, and perhaps even physically considered—but two distinct and broadly marked races, viz., the wanderers and the settlers—the vagabond and the citizen—the nomadic and the civilized tribes."[9] This passage is routinely quoted as evidence that Mayhew was a typical Victorian racist.[10] Instead of pursuing this familiar path and treating racism as an ideology, I will argue in this chapter that Mayhew employed race as a technology to solve the problems that arose in his sublime encounters with London. Rather than critiquing clichés at the level of representation, I recover how these racist clichés once functioned as catachretic responses to material urban excess. A catachretic moment, a living tendon binding part and whole, fossilizes into cliché only if its bind endures. The durability of a cliché is therefore a measure of how effectively a catachresis responds to material concerns. A cliché, then, is not evidence of a symbol wrung dry of significance but of a durable rhetorical form capable of gathering objects and actors together. Racist technology persists in the form of governmentality itself. Approached from this perspective, clichés offer an encounter with what Eelco Runia has called historical presence, or the "unrepresented way the past is present in the present."[11] Drawing on Vico's notion of topics as places housing repositories of time, Runia argues that topics harbor as stowaways forms of historical presence.[12] This approach suggests a metonymic as opposed to a representational approach to history, an attention to the material forms that become contiguous in a particular *topos* as opposed to the referential chain attached to the signifier.

Postfoundational and deconstructionist approaches to discourse theorize catachresis as the figure of the founding moment of signifying systems: by naming the unnamed, catachresis at once calls a signifying chain into being and signals a space beyond the system of signs. Thus Derrida positions catachresis as the figure of the constitutive outside.[13] In a rhetorical approach, Ernesto Laclau has called catachresis the "zero point of signification" and the "common denominator of rhetoricity as such."[14] I am similarly interested in the ways in which catachresis gestures to a kind of outside, or to what I am describing here as forms of urban excess. However, instead of examining how catachresis provides the ontological basis of discourse or establishes chains of signification, I am interested in how catachresis folds material objects and actors into relationships of contiguity. For example, when Hortense Spillers describes how chattel slavery perpetuated itself in part through "the moral and intellectual jujitsu that yielded that catachresis, person-as-property," she demonstrates how catachresis enfolds human and material worlds in ways that sustain durable structures of power.[15] Rather than theorizing catachresis as a kind of founding moment, then, I position catachresis as a figure for an ongoing encounter with excess that generates attempts to gather excess into a manageable framework. Clichés take shape as durable responses to catachretic moments. Catachresis graduates to cliché only after a series of leaps into the unknown.

Although the clichés of history—like Mayhew's distinction between wandering and settled tribes—yield little to symbolic readings and representational critiques, they often harbor stowaways of historical presence. In recovering Mayhew's response to his sublime encounter with London in 1851, I am beginning a genealogy of race as a technology of gathering, sorting, and arranging in response to a crisis of metonymy. This historical form of race endures not as symbol or representation but as a technological response to the sublime demand for order and arrangement. Viewed at the point of its application, where it assesses, apprehends, and comprehends the sublime encounters on London's streets, race becomes a technology rather than an ideology, a radically open response to external conditions rather than a set of fixed internal preconceptions. As a technology, race assembles the bodies of the city into "one view," a totality of particularities that becomes the target of application for governmentality.

I begin by sketching Mayhew's complex deployment of race in *London Labour* before proceeding to Mayhew's description of one street upon which he used race both to discover a complex social organization and to chart the ways in which that organization might come undone. I then turn to Kant's and Burke's theories of the sublime, drawing out their comments on the civilizational stakes of sublimity—which threatens reason's grasp of the totality. Next, I consider the sublime aesthetics of governance through Kant's and Burke's shared notion that sublime encounters pose a civilizational test, demanding the expansion of reason's grasp of the totality and therefore promoting progress, a notion that resonates with Mill's argument that modes of governance must target the totality of a given civilization and must be appropriate to the state of progress of a given civilization. The sublime thus programs the subject for civilization. I close with Mayhew's discussion of the London Dock, a scene that combines the excess of the streets with the excess of the seas, the wasted lumpenproletariat with the wealth of empire. In this scene, Mayhew responded to a sublime encounter by turning to race to theorize the totality, providing a case study of race as a technology of urban arrangement.[16]

RACE AND THE STREET IN MAYHEW

Despite Mayhew's claim to grapple with the "giant sublimity" of London, Gertrude Himmelfarb criticizes historians who fail to note Mayhew's diminishing object of enquiry, which shrinks from the entirety of the laboring classes of London in his *Morning Chronicle* reporting to the "street-folk" in the pamphlet series that would become the perhaps misleadingly titled *London Labour*. Mayhew is to blame for the historians' mistakes, according to Himmelfarb, since his "profusion of statistics" and ethnographic accounts "had the illusory effect of suggesting a profusion of people."[17] Mayhew estimated the total number of "street-folk"—those people obtaining their living from the street—at fifty thousand. The number is far smaller than the total number of laborers in London, to be sure. However, these fifty thousand people were left unaccounted for by official statistics, including the 1841 and 1851 censuses and other government reports, which, as Mayhew lamented, "ignore the very existence of such a class of people" as costermongers, the sellers of fruits and vegetables who were the largest subclass of street folks.[18] It is hardly "illusory," then, to suggest that fifty thousand uncategorized, uncounted, and, from the perspective of governance, unknown street folk constituted a profuse object of inquiry. Indeed, their status as unaccounted masses is precisely what made the street folk so profusely sublime: They were the yet-to-be-assembled excess, existing outside extant frameworks of knowing, understanding, and governing London; not only that, but they were *wandering*—hard to pin down in their perpetual mobility and thus recalcitrant to a civilization of settled tribes supported by the stable categories that provide government with its target of application.

Mayhew's object of inquiry may have diminished in quantitative size, but it increased in sublimity. And as the size of the population under study diminished, so Mayhew's attention to race increased. Indeed, Mayhew turned from class as an analytical category in his *Morning Chronicle* reporting to race in *London Labour*. In the *Morning Chronicle,* Mayhew wrote, "I shall contemplate two distinct classes, vis., the *honest* and *dishonest*-poor."[19] In *London Labour*, by contrast, he proposed to contemplate "two distinct and broadly marked races, viz., the wanderers and the settlers—the vagabond and the citizen—the nomadic and the civilized tribes."[20] In the *Morning Chronicle,* Mayhew wrote, "I shall consider the whole of the metropolitan poor under three separate phases, according as they *will* work, they *can't* work, and they *won't* work."[21] In *London Labour*, race inflected these categorizations. Mayhew divided the street folk into "(1.) Those who are *bred* to the streets. (2.) Those who *take* to the streets. (3.) Those who are *driven* to the streets."[22] In the *Morning Chronicle,* then, Mayhew's categorizations turned on the relationship between the poor and labor. In *London Labour*, Mayhew turned to the relationship between the body and the street. He began to rely on race to assess bodies on the streets, which in turn allowed him to develop a categorized archive of those bodies that might be submitted to the "one view" sustaining metropolitan management. Race thus satisfies the demand for totality that governmentality issues. This is how race operates as a technology rather than an ideology of governmentality.

Mayhew's deployment of race, though, is subject to the same inconsistencies as the rest of his project. The first category—those "who are *bred* to the streets"—is a racial category in the commonplace contemporary understanding of race as based on biology and heredity. Indeed, Mayhew parsed the "*bred* to," "*take* to," and "*driven* to" categories into "race, organisation, and circumstances," which would seem to preserve only one category—the biological—as one of "the three common causes of the social and moral differences of individuals."[23] Yet, in the same passage, he further parsed these categories into conditions, writing, "none of us are proof against the influence of these three conditions—the *ethnological*, the *physiological*, and the *associative* elements of our idiosyncrasy."[24] As is so often the case with Mayhew, the categories do not quite align: The first "*bred* to" category fits well with the category of "race" and the "ethnological" condition. The final "driven to" category fits with the category of "circumstances" and the "associative" condition. But it is unclear how the "*take* to" category fits with "organisation" and "physiological" elements. Indeed, physiology would seem to be a biologically racial category, as when Mayhew described the "pyramidal skulls" of the wandering tribes in the opening passage distinguishing the wandering and settled tribes (but nowhere else in *London Labour*). If physiology is a racial category, it is unclear what Mayhew meant to distinguish when he aligned "race" with the "*bred* to" and the "ethnological" condition. One solution would be to claim that by race Mayhew meant nation, and by ethnology he simply meant the studies of the various nations of the earth. This would leave "*driven* to," "circumstances," and "associative elements" as class categories, but it would still not resolve the tensions in the "*take* to" category and its alignment with physiology. To make matters even more complicated, Mayhew elsewhere used race and class almost interchangeably. To cite just one example, in the same paragraph Mayhew claimed, "the dustmen are, generally speaking an hereditary race," and "dustmen, as a class, appear to be healthy, strong men."[25] Dustmen are at once a race and a class, where race is hereditary and class—in another category confusion—is defined physiologically.

Clearly, any search for a stable definition of race in *London Labour* will be in vain. Even in his most strident claims, Mayhew was ambivalent: When he claimed that there existed two distinct races—the wanderers and settlers—he suggested that they were distinct when "socially, morally, and *perhaps even* physically considered." Mayhew was at once certain that race offered him a key tool and uncertain about what exactly race was. This ambivalence, however, is precisely what makes the text so significant for the history of race in its relationship to governmentality: for Mayhew, race was an open space of invention rather than a closed site of predetermination. Race was thus radically open for Mayhew in the strict sense of the term: the definition was subject to questioning, revision, and complication at its very roots. What is consistent is not how Mayhew defined race but how he used it: as a technology for assessing the relationship between a body and its world; or, more specifically, between a *laboring* body (with a heredity, a physiognomy, and a set of everyday practices organized around work or at least the search for sustenance) and the street.

Indeed, given that the street and the street people were entirely absent from existing municipal frameworks, we can hardly expect Mayhew to have readymade categories to apprehend the particularities of the street world and organize them into a comprehensive framework. Race, therefore, was not an extant formation but a technology applied to encounters with embodied forms of excess. As a technology, race "seeks out and utilizes material that seems uncategorized in order to . . . eliminate or manage potential challenges to the social and political organization of a society," as Falguni Sheth argues.[26] Sheth's argument that race is a technology clears the way for adapting Friedrich Kittler's description of the functions of media technology to the functions of race: media technologies process, store, and transmit information; they assess, archive, and circulate knowledge. Indeed, race operates in precisely this way: processing or encoding bodies (through physiognomy, phrenology, or skin-color bias), transmitting information about those bodies (by, say, aligning characterological traits to the shape of the skull or the slant of the jaw line), and storing information about bodies (a bias, after all, cannot operate without drawing on an archive of information).[27] Like any technology, race entails its own techniques, sets of practices for modifying, adapting, and implementing technologies. Through the techniques they require and make possible, technologies fold "time, space, and actants,"[28] mediating relationships between places, times, and things in the world. Technologies thus gather around them a "whirlwind of new worlds," new ways of perceiving, communicating, and, in this case, gathering forms of excess into an expanding field.[29]

Attending to race as a technology can therefore help sketch the contours of techniques and their technologies as they operate in the service of governmentality. Sheth suggests that race primarily targets "the unruly," and indeed those who deploy the techniques often begin there, as Mayhew did with his wandering tribes. But race as a technology does not only target the unruly. Particularly in cases where race is deployed to manage rather than eliminate material that seems uncategorized, race cannot help but reconfigure the system of categorization itself. When the unruly enters the system, we can hardly expect the system to be unaffected. Indeed, if race is a technology for managing systems, then race is also a condition of systematicity. As Mayhew suggested, "none of us are proof against the influence of these" racial conditions. The twin outlooks of race—toward that which exceeds the system and toward the internal management of the system—is analogous to the twin outlooks of the sublime—toward that which exceeds ways of knowing and understanding and toward the expansion of those ways of knowing and understanding to include the excess. I wish, however, to press beyond this analogy to argue that theories of the sublime provide the programming required to deploy race as a managerial technology. As the sublime programs the human by propelling an expansion of the techniques and technologies of knowing and understanding, race enters into the very structure of the program, in the materiality of *taxis* or arrangement itself.[30] The sublime programs the mind to deal with excess, and race is deployed as a technology wherever excess is confronted. Before elaborating this argument by developing a theory of the sublime, I must begin with the scene of excess that generates the sublime encounter. I thus turn to Mayhew's account of excess on an anonymous street near Drury Lane in order to trace how it leads him to race and the sublime.

INTO THE FISH'S SPINE: INVESTIGATIONS
ON AN (UN)RULY STREET

In one of his investigations of crossing sweepers—an occupation that attracted his attention at several points over the course of *London Labour*'s four volumes—Mayhew asked two young crossing sweepers, both members of a "gang of boy crossing-sweepers," to conduct him to their lodgings.[31] The two sweeps were Gander, nicknamed "Goose," the sixteen-year-old captain of the gang, and Harry, dubbed the "King" of the sweeps by his colleagues for his remarkable tumbling ability (although "Goose" still outranked "King"). They readily obliged. Mayhew described his approach to their street, writing: "The boys led me in the direction of Drury-lane; and before entering one of the narrow streets which branch off like the side-bones of a fish's spine from that long thoroughfare, they thought fit to caution me that I was not to be frightened, as nobody would touch me, for all was very civil."[32]

Drury Lane, the general scene for this tour of the sweepers' particular street, had been a slum since the eighteenth century, notorious for its prostitution. The area around Drury Lane is also the scene for Hogarth's famous etching "Gin Alley," which foregrounds a drunken, bare-chested woman dropping her baby over a public bannister. The comparison of the street where Goose and King lived to the "side-bones of a fish's spine" evokes the density of London's streets and emphasizes their networked relationships. Drury Lane is the chord supporting these offshoots, which are circuited both to Drury Lane's traffic and commerce—both licit and illicit—and through Drury Lane to the wider urban street system. These side-bone offshoots, then, were intimately linked to the basic skeletal structure of the street network, yet anonymous enough to go unnamed, and distant enough from Mayhew's vision of the city—his own schematic and proprioceptive map of where to go and where not to go in London—that Goose and King "thought fit" to assure Mayhew that "nobody would touch" him upon the street, for all "was very civil." Thus when Mayhew wrote of the side-bone street, describing his entrance to it, "The street itself is like the description given of thoroughfares in the East," he was not merely imposing a racist and colonialist view onto the street—although this is certainly a statement that Edward Said's orientalism thesis would cover—he was also searching for terms that would reflect how Goose and King viewed their own street, which, as they recognized, existed in a world apart from Mayhew's London, where the civility of a street presumably required no additional remark.[33]

After comparing the street to a thoroughfare in the East, Mayhew proceeded to describe the spatial arrangement of the street, writing that "Opposite neighbours could not exactly shake hands out of the window, but they could talk together very comfortably."[34] The comparison to the East, then, was less the imposition of a pre-calibrated view of "the other" than a search for the terms appropriate to describe this fish-spine side-bone of a street where only crossing sweeps and costermongers lived, and where they worked in such close proximity that even within their private homes they remained in public space. Mayhew, then, turned to the archive of travel writing and ethnology—the street was like a "*description* given of thoroughfares in the East"—not to collapse the street into racist stereotype but in order to trace its contours. Mayhew continued, writing, "As I entered the place, it gave me the notion that it belonged to a distinct coster colony, and formed one large hawker's home; for everybody seemed to be doing just as he liked, and I was stared at as if con[si]dered an intruder."[35] Once again, Mayhew routed his description of the street through a colonial perspective, referring to the street itself as a colony, and, in his description of everyone "doing just as he liked," echoing ethnologic reports emphasizing the savage's inability to sublimate desire or stem libido.[36] Yet Mayhew's turn to ethnology, colonial discourse, and ultimately race to describe the street—problematic as it is—did not provide an excuse for him to ignore the street, or assume he understood it without observing it, as one might expect someone operating from the basis of crude stereotypes to do. Indeed, Mayhew's observation that he was "stared at as if con[si]dered an intruder" revealed a level of self-reflexivity: he did not presume ownership over the street, but recognized that he was, in this "distinct coster colony," decidedly an outsider, and indeed an intruder. He thus relied on Goose and King for access rather than assuming it was his privilege to enter the street. In his sensitivity to the unequal power dynamics at play in his visit to a street where all was "very civil" yet where he recognizably did not belong, Mayhew practiced an ethnography that in many respects adheres to contemporary ethical standards.

Mayhew's description of the side-bone street demonstrated in microcosm the method he brought to the entire project of *London Labour and the London Poor*. As in the opening lines of text, he announced his intention to describe a scene unknown to the reading public, governmental officials, and other members-in-good-standing of London's civil society, and to unite this unknown scene within the city into a complete vision of London. On the side-bone side street, this meant drawing on "descriptions" of thoroughfares in the Far East to develop an adequate description of the thoroughfares around Drury Lane. To describe the members of the unknown city, then, Mayhew relied on race, which offered a means of uniting the particularities of the city into a totality.

This passage also reveals how Mayhew's approach to race drew on ethnological studies of the peoples of the earth. Finding some means of uniting the global panoply of humanity into one vision—a large-scale version of what Mayhew attempted on the streets of London—was the goal of James Cowles Prichard, the preeminent English ethnologist at the turn of the century (whom Mayhew cites), and Edward Burnett Tylor, who took Prichard's mantle into the latter half of the nineteenth and into the twentieth century. Prichard and Tylor both sought to account for the status of humanity on a global scale by assessing each culture's relationship to civilization, a word that both described the most economically, culturally, and (particularly for Prichard) morally advanced cultures on earth and designated a teleological goal toward which all cultures ought to find ways to advance. Civilization referred, therefore, both to a status and a telos awaiting fulfillment. Describing a culture or group as savage, then, was to locate them further away from that achievement, but not to disqualify them from it. Nor was the repercussion of such a description only to other the savage; indeed, for Mayhew, Prichard, and especially Tylor, who would formalize the point in his theory of survivals, not only was the savage element never expelled from civilization—never radically other—but the savage was also constitutive of civilization, both as a step on the way to its full achievement and as an active variable within any given civilization, whether "preying upon it," as Mayhew remarked, or returning in the terror of the sublime encounter, which robs the civilized subject of reason, returning the civilized to a savage state.[37] This is an important point often missing from accounts of what would later be called scientific racism: in its dominant forms, scientific racism viewed all races as capable of progress; there were no *fixed* races. To be sure, there existed a strain of polygenesist thought arguing for the biological fixity of race and suggesting that black people, for example, were a separate species. To resist this view, however, Darwinians rejected the term *anthropology*, which the polygenesists advocating fixity adopted, and formed an unlikely alliance with Christian ethnologists, with whom they shared a view of all humans as one species continually progressing, although they differed on the origins and causes of that unity and progress.[38]

Thus when Mayhew distinguished between wandering and settled tribes, or described the side-bone street by comparing it to the street in the "Far East," he was not being racist in the contemporary conventional meaning of the term as treating the inhabitants of the street prejudicially because of preconceived notions about their fixed biological or cultural inferiority. In fact, he was doing precisely the opposite: He entered a scene where his knowledge and understanding were completely lacking, and he attempted to generate a vision of a particular street— only one side bone in the metropolitan skeletal structure—by learning as much as he could to develop new frameworks that would accommodate the lives of Goose and King, and the children, old men, and costermongers—men and women alike—who lived nearby. He relied precisely on *race* to generate that vision. Race provided Mayhew with a technology, a means of *processing* the appearance of bodies in space by assessing their relationship to civilization (the street reminded him of "descriptions of thoroughfares in the Far East"), of *storing* or *archiving* information about those bodies (everyone was doing "just as he liked," as ethnological scholarship suggested they would), and then of *transmitting* that processed information as part of a larger assessment of how the savages of London's streets might advance to a higher state of civilization. Race thus functions as a technology.

To move from processing and archiving the street through race to transmitting information about it, Mayhew combined the model of descriptions of thorough-fares in the Far East with careful attention to the relationship between the street and bodies doing just as they liked. He proceeded from his general statements about the Far East and the coster colony into minute descriptions of the particularities of life on the street Goose and King called home. In all of these descriptions, Mayhew used the physical arrangement of the street—that side bone where neighbors could nearly touch hands through opposite windows—to render a detailed phenomenology of the relationship between the people, the pavements, the street, and the houses that lined it. In the course of a few paragraphs, Mayhew accounted for nearly every physical feature of this street so narrow that, "were it not for the paved cartway in the centre . . . would be called a court."[39] Indeed, the cartway was key: the costermongers' carts contained their shops, their stock, and their livelihoods. The costermongers' commercial pursuits left their mark every-where Mayhew looked: Costermongers' carts were parked "before most of the doors," and it was possible to "guess what each costermonger had taken out that day by the heap of refuse swept into the street before the doors."[40] The "parlour-windows of the houses" had "wooden shutters, as thick and clumsy-looking as a kitchen flap-table," painted a color that had turned into the "dull-dirt colour of an old slate" with age.[41] These shutters were used not for security but to "chalk the accounts of the day's sales."[42] Mayhew was also attuned to the social life of the street: "Doorways were filled up with bonnetless girls"—a sign that they were prostitutes—"and youths in corduroy and brass buttons . . . were chatting with them" and "leant against walls as they smoked their pipes, and blocked up the pavements, as if they were proprietors of the place."[43] Near these posturing adolescents, "little children formed a convenient bench out the kerbstone" and "men were seated on the footway, playing with cards which had long turned to the colour of brown from long usage."[44] In the midst of this commercial and social inter-action, domestic life carried on in public, as "women were seated on the pavement knitting, and repairing their linen."[45] Once repaired in public, the linens were also dried in public, as "from the windows poles stretched out" from which "blankets, petticoats, and linens" were hung to dry, "so numerous" that "they reminded me of the flags hung out at a Paris fête."[46] Mayhew's first impression of the street may have been that everyone was doing "just as he liked," but as he proceeded to note the details of the street—paying close attention to pavements, windows, cartways, and kerbstones—he began to recognize social, cultural, and economic dynamics: he saw courtship, claims to power over public space, social interaction across the generations, the pre-planning and organization that the street trade required, and a form of domesticity sustained in public. From the general view he brought to his task—a view steeped in ethnology, colonial discourse, and the vision of race undergirding both—he began to assemble into a totality the particularities of the street, searching the material stuff of the street for a vision of the "very civil" world it supported.

By routing his assessment of the civility of the street and the bodies who populated it through race, Mayhew attempted to bring the side-bone street into a vision of the metropolitan totality. Race thus offered the condition for uniting the total with the particular and the techniques required to accomplish this unification in practice. Uniting the particular with the total allowed Mayhew to gather the profusion of urban objects and actors into a shared field of metonymic contiguities: a new metropolis in which the side-bone streets could be understood in their relationship to unquestionably civilized thoroughfares. As such, race held promise for any attempt to resolve the paradox of the modern city, which in turn, required assessing the status of the street. The modern city functions through a total network, one that gathers all the particularities of the city into one system. The street is at once that basic structure of that network— the bones comprising the spinal cord—and the scene that sustains the bodies, commerce, and traffic that exceed the network, overrunning its boundaries and leaking into the spaces between channels. The street is at once the system and the glitch.

THE SUBLIME PARADOX

Race offers a technology for gathering new forms of embodied excess into the categorizable archive, corralling excess into domains that can be targeted by governmentality. The category of the sublime describes this encounter with the yet-to-be-categorized; the sublime "is always that which is in excess of any kind of limit or boundary," the "category for a power or 'greatness' that is beyond categorization."[47] Yet, paradoxically, the recalcitrance of the sublime to categorization only consolidates the desire to categorize. The sublime is a terror-inducing encounter with that which exceeds all existing ways of comprehending the world, where the terror inspires a scrambling, fumbling effort to modify existing modes of comprehension to include the sublime encounter in what Kant calls the totality of reason. For Kant, precisely because sublime terror threatens reason's ability to grasp the totality, it prompts reason to expand, thus securing reason's perpetual progress. The stakes of the sublime encounter are therefore civilizational: fail to respond to sublimity, and civilization declines as the ability to expand reason degrades. Indeed, both Kant and Burke insist that savages do not experience the sublime because the affective charge of the sublime that so threatens civilized reason already governs the savage. Lacking reason's demand to categorize, to submit the excess into the totality, the savage does not experience terror in the face of excess, makes no effort to expand reason, and therefore suffers stagnation.[48] Yet the sublime encounter also returns the civilized to the savage state where affect overpowers reason, where formless excess reigns over the categorizable totality. Sublimity, therefore, secures civilizational progress only by threatening its undoing.

The sublime tension between excess and totality surfaces in Mayhew's project from the very beginning of his *Morning Chronicle* reporting, where Mayhew argued that London had a "sublime and ideal effect from "the very inability to grasp the whole in its literal reality."[49] The motivation for Mayhew's inquiry, then, was an effort to discover a sense of the "whole" or the totality. Unlike in Romantic iterations of the sublime, the form of excess Mayhew encountered did not emerge from beyond a frontier, or through an encounter with a natural force surpassing human capacities.[50] Instead, urban excess was intensive rather than merely extensive. From atop St. Paul's, Mayhew was less troubled by his inability to see the boundaries of the city—the point at which the city stopped and nature began— than he was by his inability to grasp the whole of the city in one vision, to unite the city's teeming particularities into one view. London was sublime, according to Mayhew, not because it was one large and overwhelming object, but because to encounter London was to encounter proliferating particularities that could not be grasped in one vision of the totality.

Although Mayhew twice documented street booksellers carrying copies of Burke's *A Philosophical Inquiry into the Origin of Our Ideas of the Sublime and Beautiful*, his use of the sublime aligns more with Kant than with Burke.[51] Where Burke catalogs sublime objects—the ruined city, stars arrayed in the vast night sky—Kant insists that sublimity arises in the encounter rather than from the object itself. Naming the sublime object, as Burke does, presupposes its apprehension. Yet the very inability to apprehend the object and arrange it in the totality that reason constrains us to seek is what induces sublime terror. Here technology enters Kant's account, offering a means of submitting objects into the totality, but not of satiating the anxious desire sublimity arouses:

> Telescopes have put within our reach an abundance of material to go upon in making the first observation [that infinitely large objects can become small under observation], and microscopes the same in making the second [that infinitely small objects can become large under observation]. Nothing, therefore, which can be an object of the senses is to be termed sublime when treated on this footing. But precisely because there is a striving in our imagination towards progress *ad infinitum*, while reason demands absolute totality, as a real idea that same inability on the part of our faculty for the estimation of the magnitude of things of the world of the senses to attain to the idea, is the awaking of a feeling of a supersensible faculty within us; and it is the use to which judgement naturally puts particular objects on behalf of this latter feeling, and not the object of the sense, that is absolutely great, and every other contrasted employment small. Consequently it is the attunement of the spirit evoked by a particular representation engaging the attention of reflective judgement, and not the object, that is to be called sublime.[52]

Instead of the sublime object, Kant offers the sublime encounter. If imagination strives toward "progress *ad infinitum*" and reason "demands totality," then the encounter with that which exceeds the totality interrupts progress, prompting reason to expand. The telescope and the microscope are therefore secondary technologies responding to the primary technology of the imagination-reason circuit, which sublime terror powers. The terrifying encounter with limits of totality—an encounter with reason's failure, and therefore the undoing of progress—paradoxically secures reason's expansion and progress's continuance. As Paul De Man writes in his reading of Kant's sublime, "It is the *failure* of the articulation [or comprehension] that becomes the distinguishing characteristic of the sublime."[53] De Man describes this constitutive failure as the distinctive aporia in Kant's theory, the moment where the theory of the sublime unravels. But the theory of the sublime is in fact a theory of the constitutive function of unraveling; reason's failure paradoxically protects progress. Hence Kant's insistence on primary and secondary technologies: the telescope and the microscope resolve certain instances of what Kant calls the "mathematical sublime," where an object's magnitude surpasses (or fails to register in) comprehension, but these resolutions do not exhaust the impulse to totality. The aporia De Man identifies is, therefore, sublimity itself: the constitutively unreachable, unassimilable, and unmanageable, which forever recruits new technologies to satisfy the impulse it continually stimulates, *ad infinitum*.[54] Hence it is perhaps less that the sublime trains the reasoning subject to grasp totality than it is that the sublime trains the reasoning subject to think metonymically.[55] The subject must scrutinize the relationship between part and whole even if that very act of scrutiny implies that the whole is incomplete. To strive for totality implies that it does not exist.

The terror of the sublime encounter with such a fugitive totality—and the technologies recruited to surmount that terror—provides the affective charge that powers the progress of civilizations. Although this question of sublimity and civilization is less often commented upon, Kant devotes an entire section of his treatise on the sublime and beautiful to a taxonomy of national characteristics, in which he classifies humans on a hierarchy ranging from white Europeans, yellow Asians, black Africans, to red American Indians, offering suggestions on modes of governance best suited to the affective status of each race (Africans, for example, do not submit to training of their reasoning faculty, but can be made into effective servants with physical training, including beatings).[56] Indeed, Kant expressed no opposition to the transatlantic slave trade until a decade before his death when, in the draft notes for *Towards Perpetual Peace*, written sometime between 1794 and 1795, he suggested that the transatlantic slave trade might threaten a cosmopolitan moral order.[57] However, his concern was not for the slaves but for their seafaring European captors whose greed might tempt them to violate the laws of commerce, a well-regulated market being a condition of progress.[58] Kant's primary concern, then, was not with protecting human captives but with commerce; his opposition was to the slave trade, not slavery as such. Yet Kant cut the bulk of even this tepid opposition to the slave trade from the published version of *Towards Perpetual Peace*. Although some have offered this mid-1790s unpublished opposition to the slave trade as evidence that he changed his views on race, Kant republished in 1798 his infamous *Anthropology from a Pragmatic Point of View*, which offers an extended argument for a hierarchy of human races, and in 1799 he republished three essays similarly arguing for a hierarchy of races, with white Europeans at the top and Africans and Native Americans at the bottom.[59] Indeed, for Kant, Africans and Native Americans were both "born slaves," and he speculated in lecture notes that "all races will be wiped out, except for the white."[60] For Kant, then, Africans and Native Americans were relegated to what Fanon called the "zone of nonbeing," where the black (and, in this case, indigenous) subject remains "imponderable" and therefore unqualified to advance from the terror of sublimity to the stability of reason.[61]

The key point is not that Kant's personal views were racist—which they certainly were—but that the sublime is ultimately a racial encounter, one that both indexes the progress of a race and threatens to undo whatever progress has been achieved. Thus we should take Mayhew's reference to London's sublimity not as mere literary flourish but as an aesthetic encounter opening a methodological imperative to grasp the totality in order to fulfill civilizational demands. For Mayhew, the primary sublime question, then, is what sort of totality London presents, and therefore what sort of governance is appropriate to it. Race offers a secondary technology to resolve this sublime question.

The aesthetics of racialized governmentality are sublime. Indeed, in *Considerations on Representative Government*, Mill returns to two crucial points: first, civilizations, to be governed properly, must be governed as a totality, as "so complex an object as the aggregate interests of society," a standard that requires it "to enumerate and classify the constituents of social well-being."[62] Second, once enumerated and classified, this totality must be governed in accordance with the level of progress achieved, which requires that modes of governance "be radically different, according to the stage of advancement already reached" by a society.[63] Race both indexes this status and offers a technology for status assessment. Mill returns over and again to the need to match governance with civilizational status. Mill writes, "A rude people, though to some degrees alive to the benefits of civilized society, may be unable to practise the forbearances on which it demands."[64] Representative government, Mill argues, can promote progress only once the precondition of order has been satisfied: "A people who are more disposed to shelter a criminal than to apprehend him; who, like the Hindoos, will perjure themselves to screen the man who robbed them, rather than take trouble or expose themselves to vindictiveness by giving evidence against him . . . require that the public authorities should be armed with much sterner powers of repression than elsewhere, since the first indispensable requisites of civilized life have nothing else to rest on."[65] To promote the progress civilization requires, a "despotic" government must first tame "savage independence."[66] As Mill writes, "Nothing but foreign force would induce a tribe of North American Indians to submit to the restraints of regular and civilized government."[67]

These references to the savage state quickly become repetitive—as Mill acknowledges—but this is only because they are crucial to his argument. A civilized society requires a different form of governance than a savage one, and race is a requisite technology for assessing the status of the society and thus diagnosing the apposite form of governance for it. Race charts the status of the society and assembles the particular interests of the society into a total framework. Both civilized and savage societies must be governed according to their racial status. Race introduces distinctions, but not only as a practice of othering; it also gathers, unites, and assembles particularities. It offers Mayhew a resolution to sublimity precisely because it provides a framework for metonymic thinking: the profusion of parts can be linked to the racial whole, or what Mill calls the progress of civilizations.

Race thus emerges as a catachresis in Mayhew's method, a figure for explaining whatever exceeded his understanding. London's sublimity troubled this gathering not only because of the scale of the city or because of the intensity of its street activity, but also because it proved difficult to assess the civilizational status of London's streets. Mayhew thus lamented the status of the costermongers, the street traders whose consciences "are as little developed as their intellects; indeed, the moral and religious state of these men is a foul disgrace to us, laughing to scorn our zeal for the 'propagation of the gospel in *foreign* parts,' and making our many societies for the civilization of savages on the other side of the globe appear like a 'delusion, a mockery, and a snare,' when we have so many people sunk in the lowest depths of barbarism round about our very homes."[68] In staking this claim, Mayhew's reasoning mirrors Mill's: "That [the costermongers] are ignorant and vicious as they are, surely is not their fault."[69] They had not yet established among themselves the Order that is prerequisite for Progress; nor had they acquired the faculties required to sustain progress. In a remarkable moment of self-reflection and sympathy late in the first volume of *London Labour* that comes a mid an extended dilation on his race theory, Mayhew sounded out the implications of the theory of progress, government, and race that we can find in Mill:

> I am conscious that it is this active and directing power, not only over external events, but over the events of my own nature, that distinguishes me as well from the brute of the fields as it does my waking from my sleeping moments. I know, moreover, that in proportion as a man is active or passive in his operations, so is his humanity or brutality developed; that true greatness lies in the superiority of the internal forces over the external ones; and that as heroes, or extraordinary men are heroes, because they

overcome the sway of one or other, or all, of the three material influences above named [race, organisation, and circumstance], so ordinary people are ordinary, simply because they lack energy—principle—will (call it what you please) to overcome the material elements of their nature with the spiritual. And it is precisely because I know this, that I *do* know that those who are bred to the streets must bear about them the moral impress of the kennel and the gutter—unless *we* seek to develope [sic] the inward and controlling part of their constitution.[70]

This passage not only reveals how race theory can be promoted in the service of paternalistic sympathy, but how the theory of the sublime programs the subject for civilization. Sublime encounters spark a circuit that charges the "internal forces" of imagination and reason to overcome "external" forces of excess or terror. But such encounters do more than that too, because the excess of the sublime opens a battle between passivity and action, between submission to terror and its overcoming. The savage is not equipped for this battle, but if "*we* seek to develope the inward and controlling part of their constitution"—to activate their imagination-reason circuit—then the savage would begin to advance toward civilization. For Mayhew, race assesses the status of the laboring body in its relationship to the street world, and the results of this assessment, in turn, require that the race of those "*bred to the streets*" be gathered into the totality that sustains the progressive achievement of civilization. The street, then, becomes the scene of the sublime encounter, where excess populations can be submitted to the totality.

SAVAGE AFFECTS AND SUBLIME CROWDING

On the side-bone side street where Mayhew used race to uncover a complexly organized social world, the street revealed itself to be equally the staging ground of order and disorder. After describing the street in careful detail, noting how its curbstones gave children a place to play, the doorways a place for adolescent flirtation, and the windows a place to manage business, Mayhew described how those same street features could promote disorder on the street. Finding himself observing an ongoing "row," Mayhew described how "from a first-floor window a lady, whose hair sadly wanted brushing, was haranguing a crowd beneath, throwing her arms out like a drowning man, and in her excitement thrusting her body half out of her temporary rostrum as energetically as I have seen Punch lean over his theatre."[71] The unintentionally comic woman in the window was accusing a crossing sweep of having physically abused another woman on the street; the crossing sweep "had his defenders," one of them a woman who "answered the lady in the window by calling her a 'd—d old cat.'"[72] During this exchange, Mayhew observed how the street become suddenly alive with a new energy, as "this 'row' had the effect of drawing all the lodgers to the windows—their heads popping out as suddenly as dogs from their kennels in a fancier's yard."[73] The same street that could host a "very civil" social scene could also channel a scene of rioting and rowing that reduced its characters to comic props at best and animals at worst.

The proximity of life on the side-bone street promoted what Burke calls the "contagion of our passions," which can quickly precipitate crowd formation.[74] Indeed, Burke closes his reflections on the sublime with what for him was the most fearsome sublime object of all: the crowd. He writes, "The shouting of multitudes has a similar effect" as storms, thunder, and artillery, "and by the sole strength of the sound, so amazes and confounds the imagination, that in this staggering, and hurry of the mind, the best established tempers can scarcely forbear being borne down, and joining in the common cry, and common resolution of the crowd."[75] This theory of crowd contagion appears in Mayhew's description of the vagabonds, who were the lowest of the street people, according to Mayhew, and who "form the most restless, discontented, vicious, and dangerous elements of society. At the period of any social commotion, they are sure to be drawn toward the scene of excitement in a vast concourse."[76] The street was the staging ground for sublime encounters with the crowd.

As Mayhew described it, the side-bone street channeled affects that in turn attracted more bodies to the street, further increasing the affective charge. The woman "thrusting her body" out of her window yelled, "The willin dragged her . . . by the hair of her head at least three yards into the court—the willin!"[77] Her shouting brought faces to windows and attracted passersby. A woman on the street replied by calling her a "d—d old cat," while the crossing sweep's wife called someone else on the street "'an old wagabones as she wouldn't dirty her hands to fight with.'"[78] In this street that Mayhew compared to the Far East, he found a felicity of crude expression that Burke identifies as the source of crowds: "the oriental tongues, and in general the languages of most unpolished people, have a great force and energy of expression; and this is but natural. Uncultivated people are but ordinary observers of things, and not critical in distinguishing them."[79] Burke suggests that speakers who, in line with reason's demand, offer careful distinctions, are unlikely to motivate passionate responses; but a rude, uncultivated tongue generates its force precisely from its inability to distinguish one thing from another.

Behind Burke's statement lies the broader theory of affect that supports Burke's and Kant's theory of the sublime: Savage people prefer similarity to distinction, making them susceptible to contagious affects of the kind that attract crowds, threatening liberal governance.[80] Similarities are immediately pleasurable, and there is great force in adding similitude to similitude, pleasure to pleasure. Hence the inexorable attraction of the vagabond to the crowd: the vagabond craves excitement, and the crowd not only supplies it but amplifies it. Higher-order pleasure, however, derives from making distinctions. Affective immediacy and affective mediation map onto the status of civilization: A civilized society cannot rely on similitude alone but must sustain itself through careful distinctions. Similitude,

after all, cannot sustain progress ad infinitum toward the absolute totality of reason, which comprehends phenomenal objects in a field of contiguities organized
by distinctions.

The affective charge of the sublime thus powers civilizations that have progressed sufficiently to respond to sublime terror with an expansion of reason. If
reason does not continue to expand, the subject regresses to the savage state.
Indeed, the savage is incapable of experiencing the sublime, according to Kant:
"Impetuous movements of the mind . . . can in no way lay claim to the honour of
a *sublime* presentation" if they do not stimulate the imagination-reason circuit,
which expands reason's claim to the totality: "For, in the absence of this, all these
emotions belong only to *motion*."[81] Motion, like similitude, feels good, and indeed
it is to be welcome in the interest of good health, but "[motion], in the last resort,
comes to no more than what the Eastern voluptuaries find so soothing when they
get their bodies massaged, and all their muscles and joints softly pressed and
bent."[82] The sublime channels the *motion* of affect by submitting it to a *way of
thinking*. Reason carves a space between affect and immediate experience (whether
of hope or terror) by introducing distinctions; in this same space, the mind carves
the totality into particularities without sacrificing the picture of the totality. Immediate affects—*motions*, as Kant calls them—fuel the sublime, which forces the subject to convert immediacy into distance and submit those formerly immediate
affects to the totality. Sublimity emerged in the street's overwhelming motion, in
the immediacy of its affect, and in its staging of contagious passions: the side-bone
street was crowded with costermongers' carts, everyone was doing "just as he
liked," and neighbors exchanged insults across the narrow gap between buildings
on opposite sides of the street.

The world of the street savage, as Mayhew described it, was one defined preem-
inently by immediacy and motion. This characterization appeared in its starkest
terms in Mayhew's strident opening distinction between wandering and settled
tribes, which he elaborated by explaining, "The nomad then is distinguished from
the civilized man by his repugnance to regular and continuous labour—by his
want of providence in laying up a store for the future—by his inability to perceive
consequences ever so slightly removed from immediate apprehension."[83] The
nomad is entirely subject to the immediacy of affective experience, and therefore
in constant motion in search of immediate satisfaction, a condition exacerbated by
the inability of the nomad to perceive anything beyond immediate apprehension.

To assess the status of these nomads in sublime motion on London's streets,
Mayhew relied on race, at times treating the latter as an outcome of class status.
Again, this is race as catachresis, a figure for corralling excess into an intelligible
framework. As Mayhew wrote, "the sweepers, as a class, in almost all their habits,
bear a strong resemblance to the costermongers. The habit of going about in search
of their employment has, of itself, implanted in many of them the wandering pro-

pensity peculiar to street people."[84] In his analysis of the preference for wandering among street people, Mayhew suggested that habit and custom could congeal into race: "After a girl has grown accustomed to a street-life, it is almost impossible to wean her from it. The muscular irritability begotten by continued wandering makes her unable to rest for any time in one place, and she soon, if put to any *settled* occupation, gets to crave for the severe exercise she formerly enjoyed."[85] This muscular irritability limited the range of available desires, and "the least restraint will make her sigh after the perfect liberty of the coster's 'roving life.'"[86] Mayhew returned to the same line of analysis when he argued that those "who find continuity of application to any task specially irksome to them, and who are physically unable or mentally unwilling to remain for any length of time in the same place, or at the same work . . . are vagrants in disposition and principle; the wandering tribe of this country; the nomads of the present day."[87] The technology of race as Mayhew applied it diagrammed the relationship of the body to its world. This diagram displayed how organization and circumstances generated physical habits and mental faculties and formed a particular physiognomic appearance. By diagraming the relationship between the body and its world, race deployed as a technology also promised a diagnosis of the status of civilization and its relationship to savagery.

The same premise that sustains this analysis—that savages languish in their state because they lack the ability to mediate immediate affect—also requires that those same savages, if equipped to do so, would progress from savagery to join the fold of civilization. To approach the sublime, then, was to approach the limits of civilization, both because the sublime encounter initially returns the subject to the savage state and because the constitutive failure to overcome the sublime places the totality sustaining civilization under radical pressure. Mayhew thus began by noting the sublimity of London as viewed atop St. Paul's, but, as his inquiry proceeded, he offered competing and contradicting diagnoses of London's functioning as a totality. His failure to comprehend London stimulated his repeated attempts to apprehend its teeming particularities. Rather than identifying Mayhew's failures and contradictions as the aporia of his project—as de Man does in his critique of the Kantian sublime—we ought to view his failures and contradictions as the moments at which the stakes of his inquiry come into clearest view.

One such moment comes in Mayhew's description of the London Dock, where he discovered a scene of sublime excess—both of want and wealth—that he resolutely failed to explain. Laborers who could not obtain work elsewhere migrated to the London Dock because there they could obtain employment "without either character or recommendation," a fact that attracted "the most incongruous assembly." Mayhew enumerates "decayed and bankrupt master-butchers, master-bakers, publicans, grocers, old soldiers, Polish refugees, broken-down gentlemen, discharged lawyers' clerks, suspended government clerks, almsmen, pensioners, servants, thieves—indeed, every one who wants a loaf, and is willing to work for it."[88] The London Dock appeared to Mayhew as a global panoply of bodies in pursuit of the work that eluded them elsewhere in London. In order to render this scene, Mayhew resorted to a moment-by-moment description of his experience of it, where he saw "now men with their faces blue with indigo, and now gaugers, with their long brass-tipped rule dripping with spirit from the cask they have been probing. Then will come a group of flaxen-haired sailors chattering German; and next a black sailor, with a cotton handkerchief twisted turban-like round his head."[89] This is a version of the free indirect style of the street that Benjamin celebrated in Baudelaire's *flâneur*, whose detached consciousness could penetrate the surface of bodies and things passing on the street. Yet Mayhew's attempt at detachment collapsed under the immediacy of the encounter: "now," "then," and "next," body after body overwhelmed any distanced analysis. This was a scene of pure apprehension, the move to metonymic comprehension perpetually deferred. The bodies were not all that overwhelmed Mayhew's sensorium: "On this quay" the air was "pungent with tobacco; on that it powers you with fumes of rum; then you are nearly sickened with the stench of hides, and huge bins of horns; and shortly afterwards the air is fragrant with coffee and spice."[90] This is the relay of a sublime encounter, an experience that so overwhelms the imagination that all one can do is fumble for adequate terms to describe it.

What primarily interested Mayhew were the bodies that populated the dock in a desperate search for sustenance: "The dock-labourers are a striking instance of brute force with brute appetites. This class of labour is as unskilled as the power of a hurricane. Mere muscle is all that is needed; hence every human locomotive is capable of working there."[91] Here Mayhew turned to a familiar trope—the unskilled laborer as locomotive, or as "human steam-engine, supplied with so much fuel in the shape of food, merely to set him in motion."[92] But Mayhew provided an unfamiliar turn on that trope: This type of laborer was as unskilled as a hurricane, an odd analogy, unless understood within the language of the sublime. Recall that Burke explicitly aligns the crowd with "raging storms, thunder, or artillery"—sublime forces that exert force indiscriminately. As Mayhew wrote, "one gentleman" whose job it was to dole out daily employment to the dock laborers "assured me that he had been taken off his feet and hurried a distance of a quarter of a mile by the eagerness of the impatient crowd around him."[93] The crowd of laborers—men defined by motion and paid to put objects in motion—were as unskilled as a hurricane and as powerful too, capable of picking up a man and moving him a quarter of a mile, but incapable of realizing that to do so was against their interests. As Mayhew wrote of these crowds of men in search of work, "In the scenes I have lately witnessed the want has been positively tragic, and the struggle for life partaking of the sublime."[94]

The London Dock was a scene of unmediated emotion and unchanneled motion, an overwhelming, incomprehensible, and therefore sublime scene. Although Mayhew rendered a rich description of the scene, he struggled to categorize it. The excess laborers from the street labor market were matched in their sublimity only by the excesses of the global market. Mayhew described the two competing sublime encounters in one space:

> The docks of London are to a superficial observer the very focus of metropolitan wealth. The cranes creak with the mass of riches. In the warehouses are stored goods that are as it were ingots of untold gold. Above and below ground you see piles upon piles of treasure that the eye cannot compass. The wealth appears as boundless as the very sea it has traversed. The brain aches in an attempt to comprehend the amount of riches before, above, and beneath it. There are acres upon acres of treasure, more than enough, one would fancy, to stay the cravings of the whole world, and yet you have but to visit the hovels grouped round about all this amazing excess of riches to witness the same excess of poverty. If the incomprehensibility of the wealth rises to sublimity, assuredly the want that co-exists with it is equally incomprehensible and equally sublime.[95]

The twin excesses—wealth and poverty—were alike in their sublime incomprehensibility. They were also alike in that they were routed through the streets and networked through empire to the global capitalist economy. Indigo, hides, coffee, and spice; German sailors, black sailors, master-butchers, and Polish refugees: Overwhelming wealth and wasted labor power, the twin products of a global market, discoverable only at the street level. The scene of excess was urban, but its reach was global, and attempting to apprehend the scene and its reach returned Mayhew to the natural, elemental forces typically associated with the Romantic sublime: the hurricane crowd of lumpenproletariat united on the street and connected by the chopping breeze to the wealth of the global market.

Describing this sublime encounter with the detritus of the street market and the riches carried in over the sea, Mayhew turned once again to race in its connection to technology. In an effort to explain the improvidence of the dock laborers, Mayhew resorted to the authority of the statistician George Richardson Porter: "'Previous to the formation of a canal in the north of Ireland,' says Mr. Porter, in 'The Progress of the Nation,' 'the men were improvident even to recklessness.'"[96] Here Mayhew likely referred to Porter's comment that this infrastructural technology "had the effect of bringing many places within the reach of inland collieries, which were formerly, in this respect, dependent altogether on supplies brought by sea."[97] In other words, technology established new links of communication, a more manageable network, and a surface of operation for governmentality that enabled the predictable flow of materials supporting manufactures. This technological fix sustained jobs, allowing the laborers the permanency required to develop providence, which Mayhew defined as "that power of projecting the mind into the space, as it were, of time, which we in Saxon-English call fore-sight, and in Anglo-Latin pro-vidence."[98] The sublime encounter programs the human for providence. Without the latter, Mayhew wrote, humans "are as much creatures of the present as beasts of the field—instinctless animals ... without the least faculty of provision."[99] Introducing distance into immediate sensation provides the space required to render a vision of the totality, a perspective from which to manage the sublime encounter.

The sublime demands a catachresis in the form of a novel aesthetics of governance, which in turn contours techniques of governance. By encouraging a technological response to terror, the sublime recruits novel forms of storing, processing, and transmitting data that would otherwise overwhelm reason, plunging the subject into the savage world of mere sensation. The sublime sustains the projection of a progressively expanding totality. Achieving this totality is a condition of civilization, but to achieve it requires race as a technology for gathering the particular into the total. The achievement also plays out as a recursive return to savage immediacy: The sublime begins in immediate terror and ends in the distance of the totality, but the ultimate recalcitrance of the sublime leaves open the possibility of the savage return. The techniques of government that the sublime encounter promotes are inevitably racial.

CONCLUSION

As I have argued in this chapter, race functions as a technology for gathering objects and actors into an arrangement of metonymic contiguity, which in turn becomes the point of application of governmentality. Race responds to the sublime paradox: It both names the excess and gathers it into the system, describing the contours of the civilizational totality while enabling its necessary expansion. The gathering and assembling function of race, its ability to unite the particular into the field of the total, satisfies the aesthetic demands of the sublime. This aesthetic response, which I have been describing as catachretic, adds another dimension to Foucault's enigmatic claim that "the modern State can scarcely function without becoming involved with racism at some point."[100] Although this claim is usually elaborated as a theory of the founding moment of the state—as in the line of inquiry taken up by theorists of life and bare life—race has a long history of operation as what Foucault elsewhere has called technologies of governance. As Mayhew's reference to Porter and urban infrastructure suggests, race as technology combines with other urban technologies to establish the conditions for the encounters between a body and its world. In the next chapter, I turn to the technological conditions of the encounters between bodies and the infrastructural technologies of sewers, showing how Mayhew relied on race as a technology to gather London's many parts into a vision of a totality in a scene of technological change.

Race is a technology that is radically open when applied to the street. The paradox of the sublime explains why: The sublime programs the subject to make distinctions and sustains the imagination-reason circuit. Yet this sustenance relies on failure. The street remains recalcitrant to the urban communicative network, the meshwork of discursive and material connections and exchanges. But perhaps recalcitrance is the constitutive lack that the network requires to justify its expansion. After all, civilization—as managed by liberal governmentality—strives toward progress ad infinitum, an impossible goal, for to achieve progress—to arrive at the end of history—would be to undo the very possibility of progress that civilization requires. This is why the sublime paradox—the constitutive failure—turns out to be at the heart of reason, that stalwart of civilization. And civilization, in turn, does not so much expel the other and expunge emotions as it does engage in an endless search for new ways to incorporate savage affects into the totality. In the savage world, these interests remain undefined—they are a homogenous mass, a crowd of contagious emotions that attract like upon like. Liberal governance progresses insofar as it gathers these similitudes into a scene of distinction, proceeding by expanding the totality of particular interests that offers governmentality its abstract field of application. If the racial form of this gathering appears to us now as a series of clichés, this is only because of the inventive power of race as a catachretic response to the sublime paradox. Rather than dismissing critiques of Victorian racism as rehearsals of tired clichés, we can foreground the cliché itself as catachresis, and thus recover a genealogy of the enduring presence of historical formations.

Sewers, Streets, and Seas

Types and Technologies in Imperial London

"Every positive is negative": With this phrase, Kenneth Burke captures the paradox of *substance*, a term that suggests that a thing can be grasped only in its context—that is, only by what it is not. But *substance* has many resonances, including bodily ones, where it can designate "humours that ought to come to the surface; also matter deposited in the urine" and "the sediments, lees, dregs, grounds," a set of meanings Burke says "can admonish us to be on the look-out for what Freud might call 'cloacal' motives. . . . An 'acceptance' of the universe on this plane may also be a roundabout way of 'making peace with the faeces.'"[1] Indeed, making peace with the feces is a condition of obtaining civilization, which Freud defines as the coexistence of cleanliness, order, and beauty. The substance of civilization is defined by what it is not: filth, disorder, and ugliness. Feces are filthy, their circulation promotes disorder, and they are too ugly to appear in public. As Dominique Laporte argues in his *History of Shit*, "The necessary outcome of socially profitable production, [waste] is the inevitable by-product of cleanliness, order, and beauty. But that which falls out of production also must be put in to use; the gain-in-pleasure must be made to *enrich* civilization in a *sublimated* form."[2] For Burke, Freud, and Laporte, then, at stake in the sanitary imaginary is nothing less than civilization itself.

In 1848, a decade before the famous Great Stink of 1858, London's Health of Town's Association reported that Londoners were complaining that the numerous clogged drains in the metropolis "smell very strongly" and that the clogged drains caused problems for "surface cleansing" in London, where "even the best streets are very badly cleansed, but in the poorer streets it is bad indeed—horribly bad!"[3] The streets threatened the health of the population: "Where there have been deposits accumulating in the sewers, and the drains have been choked up," these blockages began producing in the inhabitants "a low depressing nervous fever, most like that which is described to be the form of jungle fever" or malaria, the disease that haunted the colonial project.[4] Clogged sewers were thus portals to the diseases of a less civilized world. But if there were a "perfect system of drainage and cleansing," then "there would be a considerable extension in the duration of the life of the inhabitants."[5] To achieve this biopolitical goal, the Health of Towns Association proposed in 1848 a new Health Act that would formalize "the fundamental principle of the supervision of the local authorities intrusted with the execution of the [Health] Act."[6] The sewer system, then, ought to be taken in at "one view," its parts gathered into metonymic relationships of contiguity. This "one view" would offer a field of shared interaction as a target for governmentality. Proper management of this field would thus sustain civilization in its march away from savagery and toward progress. Like Mayhew's sublime encounter with the manifold complexity of London's streets, the sewers presented a material and technological problem with ramifications for the racial status of mid-nineteenth-century London. This chapter recovers how race supplied rhetorical and technological resources for a sanitary imaginary under duress.

Civilization, for Mayhew and his contemporaries, named the shared social field within which they operated. Despite their difference, the theories of civilizational progress of J. F. Blumenbach, Edward Burnet Tylor, and Charles Darwin all suggested that civilization involved a progression from savage to civilized, a notion that paradoxically included savagery as the basis of civilization. Tylor formalized this paradox in his "theory of survivals," arguing that the primitive could persist in the civilized.[7] This latent savagery has its analogue in the sublimated sewage of the city. The Thames' tides connected London to global imperial trade, but they also returned the sewage to the city in an odiferous echo of the return of the savage to the civilized, eroding the grounds on which a distinction between civilization and savagery, continued progress and latent past, might be made. Faced with the promiscuous exchange of goods and a sublime profusion of mobile, laboring bodies at the London Dock, Mayhew cited Mr. Porter's call for a canal in the north of Ireland to improve civilization by improving the communications network. The imperative to channel sublime excess into a civilized communicative network acquired heightened urgency in the sewers, which not only coursed below the streets but connected to the Thames's tides, linking the foul to the fair and the streets to the seas. Actors of governmentality thus confronted a moving—a seeping, flowing, and leaking—target.

Infrastructural technologies frame the field of contiguities that the management of civilization requires. As Freud suggests, technology constitutes "the first acts of civilization."[8] Like Kant, Freud offers the telescope and the microscope as examples of civilizing technologies. Freud suggests that the telescope, which makes large things small, and the microscope, which makes small things large, together allow "man" to perfect "his own organs . . . removing the limits to their functioning."[9]

Technology is thus closely related to the project of sublimation, which Freud defines as the "renunciation of instinct."[10] As I argued in chapter 1, responding to sublime excess—and the return to savagery it threatens—requires not renouncing, suppressing, or repressing but a catachretic intervention that channels and diverts, networking excess into a metonymic field of contiguity. Technology sublimates by channeling excess back into the network, making it manageable.

This chapter argues that race responded as a secondary technology to this sublime imperative to channel excess. Rather than focusing on sewers as emblematic not only of the underground, and, symbolically, of what lurks submerged below consciousness, I argue that London's mid-century sewers in fact presented a problem of breadth rather than depth, horizontal scope rather than vertical submersion. After all, the sewers discharged into the Thames; sewage thus surfaced in the city's superhighway, ebbing and flowing with the tides. The cloacal clogging of streets and rivers is not a problem easily contained in the subconscious. I thus focus on two key figures, Mayhew, who conducted a typology of sewer workers, and Joseph Bazalgette, who, along with William Haywood, engineered a solution to London's sewer problems, achieving a constant flow of waste by constructing intercepting sewers that discharged waste into the Thames beyond the point at which the tides would return it to London.[11] Bazalgette and Mayhew approached the sewers through their nexus with the streets and the seas, and both summoned race to sketch the contours of a sanitary imaginary that might be capable of grappling with the status of London's civilization under threat from seaborne and sewer-bound forms of savagery. To the questions of what the sewer-street-sea nexus meant for London's status as a civilization and as a potentially manageable totality, race responded as a secondary technology. As I will show, race guided Bazalgette's assessment of London's progress to civilization and technology's ability to undermine or advance that progress. Mayhew similarly relied on race to rate progress, but he further adopted race to conduct a typology of sewer workers, assessing the relationship between body and technology. Mayhew therefore attempted to assess the sewer network as symptomatic of a historical situation composed of sedimented technologies, indicative types, and general trends. This chapter proceeds by examining the technological interventions into the sewer-street-sea nexus and its connection to civilizational progress, before moving to racial typology, which I argue functions as a mode of apprehending the historical situation, gathering far-flung actors and actions into a field of shared interaction.

SEWERS AND SEAS: CIRCULATION AND CIVILIZATION

"It is remarkable how little is said in the London historians of the *sewers*," Mayhew wrote.[12] Remarkable because, for Mayhew, sewers were a precondition of historical development. If London's historians had ignored the sewers as inert objects, the leaks, clogs, and smells of the sewers circulated in mid-century public debate. As London grew, so did the waste it produced, and the latter amounted, according to Mayhew's difficult-to-evaluate calculations, to forty million tons of human waste per year.[13] This human waste mingled with the fifty-two thousand tons of horse dung dropped annually, the dust from three and a half million tons of coal burnt annually, and the one hundred forty-one thousand cartloads of street dirt removed annually.[14] Together, the dung, dust, and dirt produced "street mud," a capacious title for any muck of whatever source found on the street. As Mayhew recognized, waste could quickly render the streets "filthy and impassable."[15] Mobility thus produced problems of scale and scope, as tons of waste traversed the city.

Despite the surface-level circulatory problems these inadequate sewers caused, scholars describing nineteenth-century London's sewers have tended to emphasize the association of sewers with the underworld, and thus the diabolical, the unknowable, and the obscured—a subterranean underworld lurking below the vertical city.[16] Yet the subterranean city is not the obverse of the vertical city, and sewers exist precisely to manage street-level circulation.[17] Although Mayhew almost never emphasized the vertical depth of the sewers, he did emphasize their horizontal scope: "Thus in the 'reach,' as I heard it happily enough designated, of each of these great sewers, the reader will see from a map the extent of the subterranean metropolis traversed, alike along crowded streets ringing with the sounds of traffic, among palatial and aristocratic domains, and along the works which adorn London, as well as winding their ramifying course among the courts, alleys, and teeming streets, the resorts of misery, poverty, and vice."[18] Yet despite the reach of the sewer network, "There is no map of the general sewerage of the metropolis, merely 'sections' and 'plans' of improvements making or suggested ... but did a map of subterranean London exist, with its lines of every class of sewerage and of the drainage which feeds the sewers; with its course, moreover, of gas-pipes and water-pipes, with their connection with the houses, the streets, the courts &c., it would be the most curious and skeleton-like map in the world."[19] Thus, Mayhew was confronted with something of a paradox. On the one hand, London's sewer network was immanent to the city itself. It covered streets major and minor, quiet and crowded, posh and poor. All of this would purportedly be clear for any reader gazing at a map revealing the "extent of the subterranean metropolis traversed," yet Mayhew also acknowledged that no such map existed. London's sewerage was in one sense coincident with the space of the city—and thus immanent to the urban sensorium—and in another sense unmapped and impossible to imagine.[20] Mayhew's task, then, became projecting such a map, if not by drawing one, then by gathering the sewer network into a field of contiguities sustaining shared interaction. As Jeff Rice has theorized, urban networks gather human and nonhuman actors into a "complex site of interactions" that continually reshapes and reforms itself as objects and actors enter and exit the networked assembly.[21] The tension in Mayhew's analysis is not in the distance between depth and surface, subterranean and vertical, but in gathering excess into a networked field of immanence. Instead of asking what lurked deep beneath the streets, Mayhew explored how far the street network and its subterranean sewer technology extended into a global imperial network. It was a question not of vertical depth but of horizontal scope. To the extent that the sewers were unknowable, then, it was not because they were underground, but because no one had assessed their relationship to the broader social field.

Mayhew set out to sketch such a field—to gather objects and actors into a space of contiguity—because the detritus of civilization threatened its continued functioning. The most pressing form this threat assumed was cholera, which raged throughout Europe in a series of epidemics in the nineteenth century and which was understood in the zymotic disease theory of the time to be spread by miasma, foul-smelling vapors that issued forth from circulating feces. Cholera, or Asiatic cholera, was also a species of imperial blowback, a disease that first "appeared in the environs of Calcutta" in 1817 and spread as "global movements carried a local gastroenteritis attack to Europe and America."[22] "Asiatic cholera," like "jungle fever," revealed that global trade networks exert their own ambivalent forces resistant to direct management. Victorian theories of dirt as a "*force*, active and transmissible," and also untraceable, or at least traced only with great difficulty, further heightened the stakes for managing networked linkages.[23] The problem was particularly acute when the subject was human waste, which was understood to produce miasma capable of permeating the urban milieu, corrupting the pure through "contact with impurity" in a runaway process of unmanageable corruption.[24] The difficulty of channeling the force of dirt or of containing miasmatic effluence signaled that "street mud" was more than matter "out of place": it was matter that troubled the very notion of place.[25] Street mud clogged crossings, impeding movement, but it also, paradoxically, circulated in a corrupting network with global scope.

This paradoxical connection between street mud and global colonialism accounts for Mayhew's seemingly odd attention to sanitation workers and sailing, a theme that he returns to over and over again. One street sweeper—a profession steeped in street mud—explained to Mayhew that he was "a sailor," first on the "Old Colossus" and then "the Old Renewa guardship," aboard which he "was at the taking of Algiers in 1816."[26] Another street sweeper "was in Cape Town, Table Bay" as a manservant before he "got tired of Africy" and returned to "see my native land."[27] A worker in London's street orderly system—the metropolis's first citywide sanitation system—was in "the East India Company's artillery, 4th company and 2nd battalion," and, as he explained to Mayhew, "Why, yes, sir, I saw a little of what you may call 'service.' I was at the fighting at Candahar, Bowlinglen, Bowling-pass,

Clatigillsy, Ghuznee, and Caboul."[28] A pure-finder, or collector of dog excrement
to be sold as manure, took to the streets because she was left destitute after her
husband sailed for Bombay on the cutter *Neptune*, got drunk, fell overboard, and
drowned.[29] One flusher-man, who unclogged the sewers, explained to Mayhew
that "I was brought up to the seas . . . and served aboard a man-of-war, the *Racer*,
a 16-gun brig, lying off Cuba, in the West Indies, and there-away, watching the
slavers. I served seven years. . . . It was a great change from the open sea to a close
shore—great; and I didn't like it at all at first."[30] "Shore" is nineteenth-century slang
for sewer, a coinage that sketches the material connections among streets, sewers,
and seas that facilitate circulation, opening the local street and its "close *shore*" to
the "open sea" and imperial networks. It was as if the sanitation workers were
equally caught up in the Thames's tides, thrown out into open sea with the flowing
and returning to the close shores with the ebbing. Projecting a map of London's
sewerage thus required Mayhew to deal not in depth but in scope, encouraging
him to imagine the immanence of the sewers in the same field as far-flung imperial
adventures.

Surveying this global scope was key to assessing London's civilizational status.
As Mayhew suggested, sanitary practices indexed a society's progress away from
savagery and toward civilization. He quoted a Metropolitan Commission of Sewers report that stated that a certain Dr. Paley instructed the travel writer J. L.
Burckhardt, on his journey to Africa, to take note of the sanitary habits of the
locals, because "the facts connected with that topic gave him more information as
to the real condition and civilisation of a population than most persons would be
aware of. It would inform him of their real habits of cleanliness, of real decency,
self-respect, and connected moral habits of high social importance."[31] What does it
say about Londoners, Mayhew then wondered, that "we drink a solution of our
own faeces"?[32]

TECHNOLOGIES AND TIME LAGS

Thus far I have been arguing that the street-sewer-sea nexus coordinated the sanitary imaginary, compelling Mayhew and others to approach waste and its circulation
as a problem with global scope. But this street-sewer-sea nexus surfaced as a practical problem as well. Given the Thames's status as an open sewer, a mid-nineteenth-
century Londoner would have been able to smell the difference between high and
low tide. This is a case of an odiferous assertion of "rhetorical ambience."[33] The sanitary imaginary therefore took form out of everyday experience and shaped engineering solutions. Thus, Bazalgette opened his 1865 report on the main drainage of
London with a reflection on the connection between sanitation and civilization,
cataloging the various methods of "obviating the dangers" of refuse, including those
of the "Jews," who "kept a furnace called 'Gehenna,' or 'Hell-fire,' constantly burning

in the Valley of Hinnom, into which" they cast their refuse and executed criminals, and the Parisians, who separate their "solid refuse" and remove it for "agricultural manure."[34] Waste removal was so important that "even the most savage nations are unable entirely to neglect these considerations," including the "Chinese," who, "sac-rificing . . . the delicacy . . . prized by more civilized nations, but with a sound appre-ciation of the value of town refuse, apply it in the most direct and rude manner to the production of their growing crops."[35] Although Bazalgette does not take the step to assess, as Mill does in *On Representative Government*, how to plot nations along a continuum from savage to civilized, this opening aside demonstrates that Mayhew and Bazalgette shared the sense that sanitation systems provided insight into the status of a civilization.[36]

Bazalgette therefore faced an engineering problem with civilizational repercus-sions. London's lack of central governance—a problem not remedied until the for-mation of the London County Council in 1889—made his task difficult. Until 1847, there existed eight commissioned bodies with jurisdiction over the sewers, each with their own (often conflicting) theories of sewerage, each using different mate-rials in the sewers, and none communicating in any consistent manner with any of the others. As Bazalgette wrote in 1865, until the 1847 creation of the Metropolitan Commission of Sewers, each body with jurisdiction over portions of London's sewerage "appointed its own officers, and carried out its drainage works, frequently regardless of the effects thereby produced upon the neighbouring districts, through which sewage flowed. The works were not constructed on a uniform sys-tem; and the sizes, shapes and levels of the sewers at the boundaries of the different districts were often very variable."[37] With the many Londons came many sewer systems.

Bazalgette thus faced an unevenly developed sewer system. The technologies available to manage sewage were unevenly in use, and old technologies were rou-tinely in conflict with new ones. Bazalgette thus adopted something of a media archaeological approach, attending to the sedimentation and layering of technolo-gies. As he explained, "Large sewers were made to discharge into smaller ones; sewers with upright sides and circular crowns and inverts were connected with egg-shaped sewers; and egg-shaped sewers with the narrow part uppermost were connected with similar sewers having the smaller part downwards."[38] In the irreg-ularity of the sewer network's spatial form, Bazalgette thus encountered a problem of temporal succession: Sewer technologies from different time periods coexisted in one network. Instead of progressing from an older to a newer network, old and new forms coexisted haphazardly in London's sewer system.

The problems of uneven spatial form and inconsistent temporal development combined to disrupt the functioning of London's sewer network. Although the pooling of feces in the Thames below Parliament during the Great Stink of 1858 is often cited as the motivating cause behind Bazalgette's renovation of London's sewer system in the 1860s, the Great Stink was only one moment in decades of uneven sewer development. Throughout the eighteenth century and into the nineteenth, London relied on a system of cesspools: Each house emptied its refuse from pail closets into cesspools, which were in turn emptied manually by nightmen. Joseph Bramas's water closet, which he patented in 1778, did not come into widespread use until the first decades of the nineteenth century, and it was initially a luxury item. However, an 1854 report on the cholera outbreak on Broad Street, an area where most of the houses were "let out in lodgings," provides some indication that water closet use was not limited to the wealthy. As the report stated, "the number of houses inspected has been 207, in which are situate 218 water-closets, most of them fixed over cesspools, 20 open privies, 88 dust-bins in yards . . . and 25 kept in kitchens under the stairs."[39] This focus on toilet technology in a report on cholera reveals the interconnection among sewers, circulation, and managing the city.

This report on the Broad Street cholera outbreak is also significant in the history of managing urban circulation. As we now know, thanks to Dr. John Snow's 1854 analysis identifying the Broad Street Pump as the source of the Broad Street cholera outbreak, consuming waterborne fecal matter causes cholera. It was not until some decades after his experiment, though, that Snow's theory displaced the zymotic disease theory, which held that airborne miasmas and effluvia issuing from contaminated water caused cholera. The zymotic disease theory granted nearly unlimited scope to the circulation of contaminants and offered little means of managing their circulation beyond promoting the movement of fresh air. Snow's theory provided a target for managing circulation: Control the movement of feces through watercourses, and the disease could be controlled. The time lag in the acceptance of Snow's theory has its analog in the time lag in the implementation of sewer technologies: From open privies to cesspools to water closets to drain pipes to intercepting sewers that carried sewage away from the city, London's sewer network moved unevenly toward more precise management of feces flow, which promised the successful sublimation of feces and the securing of civilization.

Yet even technological advances can create regressions elsewhere. The water closet, as its name implies, used water to flush waste directly into cesspools, obviating the need to remove waste manually from the pail closet in the house to the cesspool outside, but not the need to empty the cesspool manually. The water closet also vastly increased the amount of water delivered to the cesspools, which quickly began to overflow, their contents emptying into the streets. In 1847 the Metropolitan Commission of Sewers attempted to cleanse the streets by outlawing cesspools and requiring each house to install small-pipe sewers to channel sewage directly to underground sewers, which in turn emptied into the Thames. As a result, "in a period of about six weeks, thirty thousand cesspools were abolished, and all house and street refuse was turned into the river."[40] But, again, the Thames is a tidal river, and though the tide ebbs, it also flows, and the sewage left London with the ebbing only to return with the flowing. The Metropolitan Commission of Sewers succeeded in abolishing individual cesspools only by turning the Thames—the water source for the largest city in the history of the world to that point—into one large cesspool, forcing Londoners to "drink a solution of our own faeces."[41]

The sewers, therefore, were the site of real-and-imagined connections between London and its seaborne empire, and London's tidal links were the key focus of Bazalgette's renovations. Although he fine-tuned certain aspects of the sewer system, the primary purpose of Bazalgette's project was to lay intercepting sewers that discharged London's waste into the Thames at sufficient distance to prevent it flowing back to the city. In other words, Bazalgette did not so much entirely overhaul the sewer system as he did engineer a new interface between streets and sewers on the one hand and the sea on the other. He diverted London's sewage beyond its connection to the seaborne world, which returned both shit and savagery to London, corrupting civilization.

Bazalgette thus modified the relations of force among tides, sewers, and feces. This approach to renovation supports Latour's comment that technologies channel rather than influence action. In his famous analysis of the Berliner key, which has to be pushed through the lock on one side of the door and removed on the other (thus forcing users to lock the door behind them), Latour suggests that technologies can translate "a possible program relying on morality into a program relying on dire necessity: you might not want to relock the key, but you cannot do otherwise."[42] This anecdote offers a concise description of techno-modernity: Technology manages social bodies by structuring their actions. The target of this framing is not the moral action of the specific individual but the general tendencies of the member of a typical class or group. Technology introduces the typical subject whose actions are predictable and therefore manageable. Another way of describing the movement from cesspools to a jerry-built sewer system to Bazalgette's intercepting sewers is therefore a move from morality to force, or from a program that relies on individual action (personal cesspools and manual removal) to the force of a unified system that redirected sewage beyond the influence of the tides. The Broad Street example is again instructive, because a unified drainage system is precisely what the area surrounding the street lacked: A new sewer was built in the same year of the cholera outbreak near its source, but only "two applications have been made to drain into it," despite "a circular left at each house" urging residents to connect their houses to the drain.[43] Moral rhetorical suasion thus failed to implement the structural change required. When it came to matters of drainage and circulation, circulars requesting that individual houses connect their drains to sewers were insufficient. What was needed was not suasion that induced moral action but clever engineering and governmental enforcement combining to compel movement. Technocratic intervention can bypass moral suasion, but it requires a target of application. I turn now to describe the assembly of that target of application, which opens out of the coproduction of the particular type and the general trend.

TYPES AND TECHNOLOGIES

The scope of the imperial world made it difficult to describe the shared social field. As I will show in what follows, Mayhew's attempt to chart the relationship between sewer technology and typical sewer workers forced him to extend his imagination beyond the sewers and streets to the seaborne empire. Indeed, the global status of eighteenth- and nineteenth-century empire has, of late, brought renewed attention to Lukács's argument that the novel form recuperates the connection between the individual and the social, introducing totality into an alienated world.[44] Expanding the social world to include empire introduces new forms into the fold. Baucom, for example, argues that the spatiotemporal scale of transatlantic slavery and its system of lending, bond issuing, and insuring required theoretical realism, a means of imagining distant actions, events, and things in a shared social scene, which generated a kind of sea-borne image-scape.[45] The slave trade was therefore secured through a system of insured bonds, which mitigated the risks slavers faced and propped up a system of financial speculation on the backs of human cargo. Since its inception in fourteenth-century Italy, insurance has been a mechanism for reducing risks inherent to long-distance trade.[46] Insurance thus gathered a globally diffuse trade into a manageable and profitable totality. This system of insuring slavers against risk coincides historically with the life insurance business, which relied on tables drawn from the health of towns and sought to apprehend individuals as types with measurable risk. Mayhew's search for typical sewer workers thus extended the typological optic of life insurance—which was primarily sold to the middle classes—to society's human detritus, whose work put them in contact with society's waste.

Although typically associated with the cruel disciplinary regime of mid-nineteenth-century poor laws, Edwin Chadwick also recognized in life insurance and actuarial science a model for apprehending the social field by gathering observable instances of particular actions into a set of general trends. Archived and organized as indices of the general trend, formerly "circumstantial" particularities accrue significance as *cases*.[47] Chadwick presented life insurance tables as a privileged model for apprehending the particular in the form of the case, writing that "the value of any table of sickness or mortality is proportionate to the extent and accuracy of the information obtained relative to the class of persons from the number of whose casualties it is formed; and that the degree in which such a table is applicable to determine the number of casualties that may be expected to happen amongst another class of persons, must depend upon the similarity of circumstances under which the two classes are placed."[48] Life insurance tables made it possible to predict death at the level of a "class of persons" rather than the individual. Thus Chadwick argues that if "unnecessary injury" and "sickness consequent upon different sets of circumstances were accurately recorded" and examined as indicators of general trends, causes "not evident" on the level of the "single instance" would acquire causal significance at the level of the case, from which vantage "vicious peculiarities and habits" would indicate general trends common to a "class of persons."[49] Here Chadwick argues against targeting individual behavior for correction, suggesting a movement away from the individual subject and toward the type, from the subjectifying power of the disciplinary society toward the abstract biopolitical notion of the population. This also requires a rhetorical shift from discursive persuasion to the descriptive power of abstract insurance tables. Chadwick thus cautions against "inflammatory preaching" to counter "vicious peculiarities," recommending instead that the liberal statesmen "abstract from the clamour" in order to manage the social body.[50] This shift to abstraction paradoxically converts the peculiar into the typical. As Chadwick argues, "it is only from the most extended collection of facts, *in which the disturbing cases are merged in the most general effect*, that the general principles can be displayed with the certainty requisite for safe action."[51] Once facts are gathered at scale, then, what appears anecdotally to be peculiar emerges as typical of a larger trend. Accomplishing this conversion of a "disturbing case" to an index of a more "general effect" requires an abstract field—such as the life insurance table—that assembles material particularities in the form of the typical (and therefore predictable and manageable). Yet this abstract field only emerges tautologically, by collecting and recording the same particular instances that it claims to explain.

The street-sea-sewer nexus offered an initial structure to the abstract field for which Mayhew searched. Mayhew diagrammed the relationship between "disturbing case" and "general effect" in the sewers by attending to the assemblage of sewerage technologies and the various types to be working on them. Indeed, in all of his writing, Mayhew's interviewees tend to appear as types rather than individuals. He describes a female costermonger as a "fair type of the better class of trotter-sellers."[52] And an Irishman is rendered as one "who may be taken as a type of the less informed."[53] He even alerted his readers to his typifying practice with scare quotes, writing, "Of the third class, or the very poor, I chose the following 'type' out of the many others that presented themselves."[54] Assessing street laborers as types allowed Mayhew to link the street worker to the "general trend." He thus writes that street sweepers, "as a class, in almost all their habits, bear a strong resemblance to the costermongers. The habit of going about in search of their employment has, of itself, implanted in many of them the wandering propensity peculiar to street people."[55] Here Mayhew's language resonates with Chadwick's: both seek to identify that which is *peculiar* about the bodies under study, and both identify the peculiarities by registering them as indicative of general trends. For both Chadwick and Mayhew, the peculiar marks the typical. What struck Mayhew as most peculiar was the "wandering propensity" of street people—a trait they shared with savage "wandering tribes"—and a trait that made them analogous to street mud in the problem they posed for circulation. Mayhew understood that race offers a technology for apprehending particular "disturbing" instances and arranging them as indexes of historical progression.

By apprehending laborers as types, Mayhew sought to locate them within a shared abstract field, and thus to render them manageable within London's circulatory network. Race equipped Mayhew with a heuristic for typification (hence his suggestion that "wandering" is a characteristic of savages rather than what someone looking for work on the street would quite obviously have to do). Race also allowed Mayhew to reckon with the imperial scope of the street-sewer-sea nexus. At times, this registered at the level of the imaginary. He described, for example, a young boy working as a crossing sweeper who looked like "an Indian" because of the dirt on his face.[56] Mayhew thus imagines colonial residue in London's dirt. Yet Mayhew did not need only to imagine such connections.[57] He interviewed one street sweeper from Jamaica, and remarked upon the material connections between informal street economies and empire. For example, sailors in the East and West Indies shipping routes also sourced street trade in seashells, fish, birds, and even dogs, smuggling what items they could collect on their travels and selling them in London's streets.[58] In addition to smuggling, Mayhew discovered material connections to empire in the salvage trade: River finders and dredger men made money in the Thames not only by hauling up dead bodies (as did the Gaffer in Dickens's Our Mutual Friend), but by hauling up the detritus of imperial trade, including "tobacco, tea, spirits, and other contraband articles."[59] Similarly, as we have seen, many of these workers had connections to London's imperial network. As Mayhew suggests, many street orderlies also "have got engagements as seaman, their original calling."[60]

Confronted with the global links of London's sewers and the global mobility of sewer workers, Mayhew attempted a racial typology, one that would assess the relationship between laboring body and sewer technology, allowing Mayhew to recuperate the "disturbing effect" within the "general trend." Many sewer workers were either working illegally or with outdated technologies. There were three categories of sewer workers who occupied Mayhew's attention: the sewermen or sewer hunters, who scavenged illegally in the sewers for valuable items; the flushermen, who flushed blockages in the sewers, and the cesspool men or nightmen, who removed waste from cesspools. The relationship between the urban ecology and uneven sewer technologies made each job possible: the "gully-holes" on the streets above drained into the sewers below, and thus the sewermen profited from tradable commodities that became mixed with human waste. Their work was illegal, but they developed their economy in conjunction with sewer technology. The flushermen similarly developed along with the sewer technology, but their work of removing blockages that impeded sewer circulation was legally sanctioned. The cesspool men operated in a space that the sewers were intended to obviate: Above ground, removing waste house by house rather than as part of a citywide system, the cesspool men subsisted in an economy out of synch with the technological present of the sewers.[61]

Mayhew's method of assessing sewer workers resonates with Chadwick's advice for building insurance tables, with an emphasis not only on hours and pay but on indicative habits, physical appearance, health, and intelligence.[62] Mayhew indexed these categories to broader relationships between technology and its role in urban ecologies. In the lengthy quotation below, Mayhew described the sewer hunters (or "toshers") and how they earn their living by working within the technological network of the sewers:

> These "Toshers" may be seen, especially on the Surrey side of the Thames, habited in long greasy velveteen coats, furnished with pockets of vast capacity, and their nether limbs encased in dirty canvas trousers, and any old slops of shoes, that may be fit only for wading through the mud. They carry a bag on their back, and in their hand a pole seven or eight feet long, on one end of which there is a large iron hoe. The uses of this instrument are various; with it they try the ground wherever it appears unsafe, before venturing on it, and, when assured of its safety, walk forward steadying their footsteps with the staff.... Finally, they make use of this pole to rake about the mud when searching for iron, copper, rope, and bones. They mostly exhibit great skill in discovering these things in unlikely places, and have a knowledge of the various sets of the tide, calculated to carry articles to particular points, almost equal to the dredgermen themselves.[63]

These sewermen have thoroughly adapted to the ecology of London's sewer network—their clothes, their tools, and their mental faculties are all fashioned to negotiate the sewers. The same is true of the flushermen:

> The state of the tide ... compels the flushermen to work at every hour of the day and night. At all times they carry lights, common oil lamps, with cotton wicks; only the inspectors carry Davy's safety-lamp.... The flushermen wear, when at work, strong blue overcoats, waterproofed ... buttoned close over the chest, and descending almost to the knees, where it is met by huge leather boots, covering a part of the thigh.... The flushermen are well-conducted men generally, and, for the most part, fine stalwart good-looking specimens of the English labourer.[64]

The flushermen adapt their dress and their tools, including the Davy lamp, which was originally intended for use in coalmines, to deal with the inflammable gasses, and they adapt their schedule to accommodate the tide. They were also—somewhat surprisingly—good-looking and healthy.

The health of the sewer workers challenged the widely accepted zymotic theory of disease. Although they worked amid the effluvia and miasma thought to spread disease, Mayhew repeatedly reflected on the remarkable ability of the sewermen, flushermen, and nightmen not to be bothered by the smell of the sewers and cesspools and indeed to derive health benefits from their work. Describing one cesspool, Mayhew writes: "The smell, although the air was frosty, was . . . literally sickening. . . . The nightmen, however, pronounced the stench 'nothing at all'; and one even declared it refreshing!"[65] Mayhew claimed that this "scene was peculiar enough," but he subsumed the peculiarities, especially the surprising health of the nightmen, into the category of the typical.[66] Indeed, the health of the sewermen— their most peculiarly surprising feature—was also their most typical: "It might be supposed that the sewer-hunters (passing much of their time in the midst of the noisome vapours generated by the sewers, the odour of which, escaping upwards from the gratings in the streets, is dreaded and shunned by all as something pestilential) would exhibit in their pallid faces the unmistakable evidence of their unhealthy employment. But this is far from the fact. Strange to say, the sewer-hunters are strong, robust, and healthy men, generally florid in their complexion, while many of them know illness only by name."[67]

Mayhew marshalled this typology partly in refutation of the zymotic disease theory—if miasma and effluvia caused disease, then surely those who worked nearest the source of the miasma and effluvia would not be so healthy; they would not have escaped the cholera epidemic of 1848. Indeed, Mayhew discovered this peculiar healthiness in the nightmen as well. One nightman Mayhew interviewed "was a stout, hale-looking man, who had rarely known illness. All these sort of labourers (nightmen included) scout the notion of the cholera attacking *them!*"[68] What was most peculiar about them was most typical, and this peculiar typicality had its explanation in their material location as workers in London's sewerage technology.

Confronted with these peculiarities, Mayhew deployed race to identify types and to chart types as an index of progress, linking "disturbing case" and "general effect." As Bazalgette's opening discourse on sewers and civilizational development suggests, the scale of the risks Mayhew encountered registered at the level of the civilization. The schema by which Mayhew adjudicated the typicality of the peculiar scenes he encountered was racial: he attempted to assess the relationship between a body and its world, and to arrange that relationship on scale from savage to civilized. In describing a scavenging sewerman, Mayhew therefore wrote that he "is peculiar in showing the habitual *restlessness* of the mere labourer."[69] Mayhew's thinking on the type and the peculiarity is analogous to the form of thought James Chandler has described as characteristic of the case and its counterpart the anomaly, wherein "the case names not only the anomaly for a scheme or system, but also the scheme or system itself, as well as those processes by which anomalies and norms are adjudicated."[70] The historical situation, Chandler argues, emerges from deliberation over the norm and the anomaly is embodied in the case, which becomes a privileged site of assessing the historical moment. For Mayhew, the peculiar health of the sewermen becomes an index of the typical sewerman, which in turn offers commentary upon the risks London's sewers posed to its population and the possibilities of mediating those risks with techno-logical adjustments. The sewerman thus stood out in his particularity precisely because he embodied the typical restlessness of the street labourer apprehended racially as a member of the "wandering tribes" persisting among the settled and civilized. The peculiar thus becomes the typical, and the type registers the racial location of the body, providing an indicator of the "general trend" governing mid-century London and its leaky sewer system.

UNPLANNED OBSOLESCENCE: TECHNOLOGY AGAINST PROGRESS

Mayhew developed his typologies by assessing the relationship between the body and technology. Yet technological change always threatened to remake that rela-tionship. As one insightful nightman wistfully put it to Mayhew: "In time the nightmen'll disappear; in course they must, there's so many new dodges comes up, always some one of the working classes is a being ruined. If it ain't steam, it's some-thing else as knocks the bread out of their mouths quite as quick."[71] As this night-man recognized, technologies—such as steam—eventually overturn historical situations. But the nightman was no determinist: there are always "new dodges" coming up, not because technology distributes the labour force, but because tech-nology reformulates the peculiar relations of the labourer to the material world.

The question of typical bodies thus returned Mayhew to the technologies that framed the action of those bodies. In this sense, his method again mimicked insurance, which generalized from particular urban spaces in order to measure typical trends. Yet the insurance tables in use in Mayhew's moment abstracted from a historical space out of joint with the current time. Indeed, Chadwick argued that his contemporaries lacked the abstract knowledge necessary for proper governance because their knowledge was out of time and place: "Of the tables of mortality now in use, the oldest, and that which is most general adopted, is called the Northampton table," which was developed between 1735 and 1780, fifty-six years before Chadwick's writing.[72] Yet "a great improvement has taken place in the general mode of living among the people of this country even within the last twenty years," as the "higher classes are . . . less addicted to those gross sensual excesses which characterize people who, in the earlier stages of civiliza-tion, are not aware of the pleasures to be derived from useful pursuits."[73] Even the laboring classes, if not quite capable of sublimating sensuality into productivity along with the growing bourgeoisie, have learned to delay "immediate gratifica-tion,"[74] and the artisans "have acquired some notion that fresh air is conducive to health, and the streets where they live are less filthy and pestilential than for-merly."[75] Chadwick suggested that this racial improvement extended even to members of the aristocracy—bearers of timeless tradition—who had come to bet-ter understand their duty to the improvement of the "lower animals." As a result, Chadwick argued, "the satire of Swift is relevant only to bygone times."[76] Here race allowed Chadwick to chart the history of class. His claim was that the people of England had managed to suppress their latent savage tendencies, an advance that made generalizations based on mid-eighteenth-century Northampton obsolete and inadequate to the task of projecting an abstract field capable of gathering types in the historical moment of mid-nineteenth-century England. Anachro-nism was clogging the works of the technological and civilizational progress.

Mayhew faced a similar problem of anachronism in London's sewer network, where the coexistence of technologies from differing historical periods threatened London with the reemergence of latent temporalities in the present. In an era of Chartist demonstrations and revolutionary street fighting in Paris, Mayhew reflected on waste as a possible tool of street warfare, relating that during the English Civil War, "The mounds of rubbish" in London "were then kinds of street-barricades, opposing the progress of passengers, like the piles of overturned omni-buses and other vehicles of the modern French street-combatants."[77] These comparisons between Civil War–era London and the 1848 French Revolution and scavengers and mechanized street sweepers might appear to be minor asides. But the structure of the comparison, which emphasizes the street as a technological resource (whether of warfare or sanitation), the street as a spatial configuration, and the street as an index of temporality, turns out to be the organizing principle of Mayhew's writing on the sewers. In other words, Mayhew's investigation into the scope of London's street-sewer-sea nexus—including the uniformity of sewer technologies—and his investigation of its historical succession—including its his-torical roots—were intertwined. Spatial scope and temporal index combined to define the historical moment.

The street also staged battles between new technology and old labor. The street sweeping machines, for example, displaced the scavengers who sorted through London's street waste, but the scavengers did not acquiesce to the onslaught of progress: "In the first instance the machines were driven through the streets merely to display their mode and power of work, and the drivers and attendants not infre-quently came into contact with the regular scavengers, when a brisk interchange of street wit took place, the populace often enough encouraging both sides."[78] These scavengers, like London's sewer network, were caught between historical moments, on the cusp of obsolescence. Describing their division of labor, Mayhew writes that gang-work, or "Simple co-operation is of course the ruder kind; but even this, rude as it appears, is far from being barbaric. 'The savages of New Holland,' we are told, 'never help each other even in the most simple operations.'"[79] Thus the scavengers were anachronisms, and their habits were rude, but they were not quite savage. That Mayhew saw fit to distinguish their rude habits from the habits of the "savages of New Holland" reveals the imperial scope of the sanitary imaginary he brought to bear on his racial assessment of bodies at work in a changing techno-logical scene.

These competing temporal scales of progress and expansive spatial scopes of analysis thus posed problems for assessing London's progression toward civiliza-tion. These problems extended from the typical laborers to the very technologies on which they worked. On the one hand, Mayhew suggested that London—even more than modern Rome—continued the legacy of ancient Rome, writing, "The present system of sewerage, like our present system of street-lighting, is a modern work; but it is not, like our gas-lamps, an *original* English work. We have but fol-lowed, as regards our arched and subterraneous sewerage, in the wake of Rome."[80] London was thus modern but not original. Clearly, though, London carried the mantle of civilization handed down from the ancients.

On the other hand, this relationship with the Roman past also troubled London's present, making it difficult to apprehend the technological forms at work in the sewers. As Mayhew explained, "A few years back, the building of egg-shaped or 'oviform' sewers, was strongly advocated."[81] Oviform sewers drained more quickly than tubular sewers. Yet it was unclear how uniformly the oviform sewers had been deployed in London's sewer network: "What extent of egg-shaped sewers are now, so to speak, at work, I could not ascertain. One informant thought it might be somewhere about 50 miles," a number that pales in comparison to the "1100 miles" of sewers Mayhew claimed were underneath London's streets.[82] Thus the techno-logical present and past existed together within London's sewer network. Indeed, the connection with ancient Rome surfaced materially in the sewers, where one of Mayhew's interviewees related having discovered a flat-bottomed Roman sewer.[83] This inconsistency extended to the materials in use in the sewers, including the "very ancient" method of earthenware pipe, the more recent method of granite, and the modern method of brick reinforced with concrete.[84] This uneven and sedi-mented technological present made it difficult for Mayhew to apprehend the form of London's sewer network, wherein "no average size and no uniformity of shape can be adduced."[85]

Thus, as his investigation proceeded, Mayhew questioned London's status as Rome's successor in the modern age, noting that, of the 1,100 miles of sewers in London, "about 200 miles are still, in the year 1852, *open sewers!*—to say nothing of the great open sewer, the Thames."[86] Here Mayhew identified an anomaly that forced him to reckon with the historical situation within which he operated: That more than half of the sewers in 1852 London—the greatest city in the world, the center of the global empire, the site of such modern inventions as the gas lamp— were open sewers—that filth coursed through the wealthiest city on earth—called into question the status of the civilization that attempted to dominate its historical moment.

London's uneven technological infrastructure thus cast into doubt its status as the most modern city in a globalizing world. Mayhew's case study of London's sewer technology was also an encounter with his historical moment. As Chandler suggests, the anomalous case becomes typical once the deliberative judgment of historicism converts it into a symptom of more general trends. Open sewers were the anomaly within the empire, that which appeared *out of* place and thus required an assessment of what it meant for something to be *in* place in the given historical situation—London in 1852. Mayhew identified these open sewers as anomalous precisely because he judged them out of synch with general trends. The crucial point, though, is that the production of the typical case and the general trend (or historical situation) is simultaneous. Thus, as Chandler argues, "the case ... is the very form of 'deliberation.' It is always calling for judgment, and it is by virtue of judgment that it offers formal mediation between the particular and the general, between instance and rule, between circumstance and principle."[87] Historicist deliberation submits the particular to the general, and in so doing, creates both the general system and the means of recognizing the location of the particular within that system. Historicism resolves the sublime dilemma by inventing a new framework within which to assimilate the formerly inassimilable parts.

In this form of historicism, past formations come to be recognized as typical cases of a given moment, and these typical cases are seen in turn to generate new formations and new typical case studies. The typical case establishes causal links between old and new formations. The case acquires thus causal powers, offering an explanation for how one historical moment succeeds another. Historicism recognizes the "present as the future of the past."[88] By naming his historical situation London in 1852, identifying "the cultural conjuncture in terms of the chronological code," Mayhew was able to recognize the anomaly of the open sewers, to explain that they did not fit the historical situation.[89] The anomaly in this case names the system: by appearing out of time and place, it makes the proper time and place legible. Yet Mayhew was also aware that this process was tendentious: "It is not impossible nor improbable that in less than two centuries hence, we, of the present sanitary era, may be accounted, for our sanitary measures, as senseless as we now account" the sanitary technicians of the 17th century.[90] Here Mayhew drew out the implications of thinking in terms of historical situation. He not only recognized the "present as the future of the past," but reckoned with the future present's potential judgment of his moment.[91] Chandler's focus is on Romantic historicism, which deals with the succession of one age to another. But the spatial scope of London's sewers troubled any notion of succession from one age to another: It was not that London's sewers developed out of Roman sewers; Roman sewers were a functioning part of London's sewers. Instead of historical succession, Mayhew discovered the immanence of disparate temporalities in one historical moment. The diffusion of scope related directly to the diffusion of temporalities.

CONCLUSION

The layering and sedimentation of technologies at the interface between streets, sewers, and seas generated problems with imperial scope and civilizational stakes in nineteenth-century London. Types with connections to a savage world operated in a sewer network that was at once clogging the streets and connecting the city to colonial trade routes. The problem was compounded by the uneven succession of historical technologies coexisting in London's sewer network. Mayhew attempts to describe the typical sewer work as index of a general trend, sketching through this description an abstract field of shared interaction, but the ambivalence of Mayhew's historical moment troubled his efforts to open the field. The mutual predicates of type and trend thus plot civilization's progression, but the imperial scope of London's sewer connections undermined this progression. Race offered a technology to recuperate the abstract field that biopolitical management requires. However, the malodorous multitude circulating in the sewer system complicated any stable perspective of the city.

Although we might say, with Latour, that "context stinks!" (and sometimes quite literally), we also need to keep asking how *context works* without deploying it as a prefabricated explanatory category. As Carolyn Miller suggests, we can follow Latour's route out of the "text-context dilemma by turning texts into actants linked to other actants in complex chains of activity," but we also need to move beyond description to explain "the fact of association," to query its influences on "decision, adherence, and action."[92] Combining this perspective with Runia's notion of stowaways, we can see both how Mayhew, Bazalgette, and others used race as a mode of description and how that very mode of description begins to operate as a kind of contextual stowaway, shaping the form of association and structuring future associations. Instead of studying the representational or contextual rhetorics of race, then, this chapter has identified race as itself a response to rhetorical contingency. In other words, race was not a rigid abstraction imposed on vibrant human and nonhuman actors, but a mode of apprehending those actors and gathering and sorting them into a manageable framework. The metropolis was in a state of paradox—simultaneously civilized and savage, wealth producing and waste producing, moving toward progress and plagued by regression. Race as a technology intervened in this scene of contingency, assessing the status of typical bodies in their relationship to the street-sea-sewer network, and thus answering the biopolitical demand to establish a totalizing framework that would enable proper management of the city.

Moving Congestion on Petticoat Lane

Slums, Markets, and Immigrant Crowds, 1840–1890

Petticoat Lane was and remains one of the most famous street markets in London. Situated between the docks and the City—just north of the notorious Ratcliffe Highway, which helped bring maritime traffic from the Thames onto dry land—near such busy rail stations as Fenchurch Street and Liverpool Street, and home to the largest immigrant population in London, "altogether the scene" on Petticoat Lane, as Mayhew remarked, "is not only such as can only be seen in London, but only such as can be seen in this one part of the metropolis."[1] Petticoat Lane was remarkably peculiar, which meant that it could diagnose what was typical of the age, as I argued of the sewer network in the previous chapter. Crowds, markets, dirt, prostitution, crime, and foreign bodies were all commonly remarked-upon and widely lamented features of London's uncontrollable growth, and all of these features gathered on Petticoat Lane as nowhere else. Not surprisingly, then, Petticoat Lane and its immediate vicinity was the scene of a series of "street improvements" between 1840 and 1890, all of them aimed at clearing congestion and promoting well-regulated, citywide circulation.

In a series of reports to Parliament, James Pennethorne and other metropolitan improvers argued that "some thoroughfare should open" the area around Petticoat Lane "to public observation and wholesome ventilation."[2] Critiquing these plans, Lord Cowther acknowledged that "such an opening would much conduce to the improvement of health and morals of the district" and as such would be "a very valuable improvement with reference to that particular locality; but it does not appear to have that character of a general metropolitan improvement and increase of facility for traffic."[3] Cowther thus saw Commercial Street as a particular rather than a general improvement, local tinkering rather than the renovation of the metropolitan communications network. For Pennethorne, in contrast, Petticoat Lane might have been peculiar to one part of the metropolis, but it also contained the most general metropolitan problems in intensified form. This peculiarly problematic space, then, needed to be linked with the general metropolitan network. These competing perspectives on the relationship between the particularity of the street and the abstract vision of a metropolitan network index broader tensions in the planning, managing, and regulating of modern urban circulation.

In this chapter, I examine the history of Petticoat Lane in the mid-to late nineteenth century as a case study in the tension between the abstract and the particular as it manifests on the street. As I discuss in more detail below, abstract space is space rendered uniform in every direction and location by virtue of a long-distance view. Planning and managing a city—promoting "general metropolitan improvement"—requires just such a view. As Cowther's objection to Pennethorne's plan demonstrates, this abstract view promotes citywide circulation: It was not sufficient for Cowther that the opening would improve the health and morals of a particular district; it must also provide "general metropolitan improvement" by increasing the "facility for traffic." In other words, it had to support the citywide circulatory network.

Scholars tend to argue that nineteenth-century urban planning saw the uncontroversial rise of abstract space and the merciless imposition of this uniform vision over entire cities, leading to widespread slum clearance and increased policing of the working poor, racial others, and marginalized women. A focus on street-level circulation, however, can recover some of the controversies lost in this account. As I suggest throughout this book, the street is the structuring principle of the urban network and the site most recalcitrant to that network's completion. Streets are channels for urban circulation; they structure the urban network. But they are also the scene of illicit trade, crowded pavements, congested roadways, and promiscuously mobile bodies. Streets are at once the basic structure of the urban network and the most recalcitrant threat to it. As careful study of Petticoat Lane demonstrates, abstract space requires unimpeded movement and vision—"ventilation" and "observation." That which impedes movement and vision must be cleared from the system. Yet what appears to be immobile from the long-distance perspective of abstract space becomes highly mobile when viewed in close-up on the street: A costermonger's barrow blocks traffic, but it also attracts crowds, moves goods, and circulates money. I argue that the forces causing urban immobility in fact generate forms of mobility not immediately recognizable from the perspective of abstract space. This is not to say that the proponents of abstract space—planners, government officials, engineers, and others—were blind to the contradictions of abstract space. Instead, I am arguing that developing a perspective that would sustain abstract space involved various attempts to apprehend the forces of immobility, and that these attempts struggled to capture the movements these forces generated. Focusing on the movements issuing from apparent forms of immobility reveals a parallel form of circulation that shadows the circulation abstract space promotes, always exceeding its perspective and thus prompting it to expand its vision.

That immobility generates movement is paradoxical. Addressing this paradox, in turn, generated a number of hesitations, contradictions, and equivocations among those who actively advocated abstract space, those who questioned it, and those affected by it. The history of Petticoat Lane, the street that seemed to be everywhere in Victorian official discourse and yet nowhere in sharp focus—and indeed, widely referenced yet rarely investigated in current scholarship—provides insight into the various resonances of this paradox. To bring Petticoat Lane into focus, I have assembled an archive of materials including parliamentary reports, periodical press accounts, public pamphlets, essays, and novels that describe Petticoat Lane. Since archives are not ordered or searchable by street, I have read widely about the issues that surface most often in relation to Petticoat Lane—lodging houses, prostitution, theft, overcrowding, trade, and foreign migration—and I make use of some accounts that touch one these issues without explicitly discussing Petticoat Lane. With a few exceptions, however, I have conducted analyses of sources specifically addressing, describing, and analyzing Petticoat Lane. In this sense, this chapter offers an archive of one street from 1838 to 1892.[4]

The first half of this chapter describes abstract views of Petticoat Lane, and I begin with an outline of the history of material changes to the area. In this section, I use Pennethorne's arguments for Commercial Street—the eventual name for the "spacious thoroughfare" that would provide "ventilation" and "observation" to Petticoat Lane—to frame an intervention into spatial theory that replaces a focus on the tensions between representation and experience with a focus on networks and circulation. I then make use of such a focus in the following section, in which I show how street markets and the crowds they attracted congested Petticoat Lane, but how attempts to clear those crowds—specifically by a proposed ban on Sunday trading—confronted and ultimately tripped over the parallel circulation of the crowd.

In the second half of this chapter, I hew closer to a street-level perspective, focusing on parallel forms of circulation not readily apprehensible from the perspective of abstract space. I begin with Eliza Lynn Linton's advice to women walking in public, "Out Walking," as a means of analyzing the public appearance of prostitution, a much-discussed feature of Petticoat Lane. Along with the flaneur, the prostitute is one of the types most associated with unregulated movement in the modern city, but while flânerie is a vehicle for individual movement, the prostitute—and the venereal disease associated with prostitution—spins a "web of connection" linking social classes and city spaces. Yet one important and overlooked problem with prostitutes is that they often did not move—they idled. This was particularly so on

Petticoat Lane, where many of the prostitutes frequented overcrowded lodging houses and lingered near shop windows—spaces of licit circulation that provided cover for the illicit circulation of prostitution. I argue that it was precisely in this immobility that prostitution generated parallel forms of circulation. In the final analytical section, I attend to the relationship between immobility and mobility in Mayhew's account of Petticoat Lane. In direct contrast to the other accounts of Petticoat Lane, Mayhew recognized that Petticoat Lane was a space of movement. In this insight, only Israel Zangwill and his oft-overlooked novel *Children of the Ghetto: A Study of a Peculiar People* match Mayhew. Although full analysis of this novel is not possible here, I supplement discussion of Mayhew with reference to key moments in Zangwill's bildungsroman, focusing on how the movement of characters on, through, and away from Petticoat Lane structures the text. Together, Zangwill and Mayhew demonstrate that Petticoat Lane was both a cosmopolitan space and a ghetto. As a type, the Jew, like the prostitute, is paradoxically mobile and immobile. On Petticoat Lane, the wandering-yet-ghettoized Jew, along with other merchants, engaged in long-distance trade along colonial networks. The ghettos around Petticoat Lane thus required a close-up view of the street and one that could square that close-up with the scale of an expanding colonial empire. I conclude by considering how Petticoat Lane and other spaces that exceed abstract space prompt abstract space's expansion.

MATERIAL NETWORKS AND ABSTRACT SPACE

Scholars of space, spatial theory, and the rhetorics of space, particularly those influenced by the tradition Henri Lefebvre inaugurated, have long argued that the tension between the particular and the abstract—the "particular locality" and the "general metropolitan" network, in this case—is the basic and unresolvable tension of what Lefebvre calls the "production of space."[5] Indeed, a strain of cultural and critical theory has grown up around describing, characterizing, and critiquing this basic tension. Lefebvre's model has been singularly influential. His "trialectics" of space includes space as *conceived* by planners and managers, space as *perceived* in representation, and space as it is *lived* in daily life. Perceived space mediates both conceived and lived space. Conceived space (which Lefebvre also calls abstract space) and lived space, in turn, generate competing representations of space. Within abstract space, lived "space is crushed, vanquished by what is 'conceived of,'" but competing formulations of perceived space ultimately make it impossible for abstract space to secure permanent victory over lived space, and so the trialectics of space unfold.[6] This Lefebvrian thesis resonates throughout the various offshoots of the so-called "spatial turn." Even when not explicitly formulated against Marxist dialectics, such theories tend to introduce a third term into the dialectic in order to emphasize the distance between representation and experience and the peculiar ability of space to refuse synthesis. Michel de Certeau's distinction between strategies and tactics is another influential version: Planners and managers develop strategies from an abstract position—they see space as if from atop a skyscraper, viewing the total system rather than the particular movements of its users. The user of space relies on tactics, which exceed the strategic vision, both because they are invisible to it and because they cannot affect it—the jaywalker violating the rules of abstract space is invisible from atop the skyscraper, and the act of jaywalking does nothing to alter the strategic order: the street grid remains unchanged, as do the rules and regulations governing movement through that grid.[7] De Certeau thus modifies Lefebvre's pitched battle between abstract and lived space with a theory of how lived space in fact lives off abstract space, making tactical use of its strategic order. What unites these arguments, despite differences in vocabulary, is the argument that abstract space controls—or attempts to control—how things move in space by imposing a preplanned order built in representation rather than tested in experience.

Mary Poovey's description of the nineteenth-century production of abstract space—a term she takes from Lefebvre—encapsulates this thesis: "Modern space was conceptualized as isotropic (as everywhere the same) and as reducible (or already reduced) to a formal (that is, empty) schema or grid. Partly as a consequence, abstract space was symbolically and materially associated with homologies: seriality; repetitive actions; reproducible products; interchangeable places, behaviors, and activities."[8] Abstract space is a homogenous grid that is understood to channel the movements of people, commodities, and traffic in predictable and thus manageable ways. Describing this vision—and uncovering its constitutive contradictions—has been central to the work of scholars of nineteenth-century space. Such accounts, though, tend to replicate the terms of spatial theory: Abstract space attempts to dominate while users of lived space attempt to resist. The task then becomes to reveal the limitations of abstraction and uncover the potentials of resistance. Too often, though, such accounts cede ground to abstract space, treating it as an accepted concept rather than a contested controversy. By accepting abstract space as a concept, we "*use* power instead of *explaining* it."[9] This is how I draw on Actor-Network-Theory in this chapter: Instead of accepting abstract space as dominant, I am interested here in describing "the elements always present in *controversies* about" abstract space, in registering the "fabrication mechanism necessary to keep it alive" as a rhetorical ecology of circulation.[10]

Urban circulation brings the fabrication mechanisms of abstract space into focus. Scholars of nineteenth-century urban space have tended to argue that planners, managers, and government officials attempted to solve the problem of particular forms of congestion clogging their total systems by projecting an all-encompassing abstract vision of space that would simply flush particularities from the system. Richard Sennett has argued that Enlightenment planners thought that "if motion through the [urban] body becomes blocked anywhere, the collective body suffers a crisis of circulation like that an individual body suffers during a stroke," a vision nineteenth-century planners updated by imagining unimpeded movement as a form of protection from the congestion of the crowd.[11] The street is both the basic structure of the urban network—the veins moving blood through the body—and the site that hosts the congested traffic and crowds of bodies that clog the veins. Streets are thus the basic unit of abstraction and the scene of the irresolute and localized congestion and crowding that threaten the abstract order. This means that abstract space is caught between an overriding vision and one capable of recognizing and managing particularities within that system. Lord Crowther might well have been right in his prediction that Commercial Street would provide "ventilation" for circulation in the local neighborhood but not for the general metropolitan network, but how else to create a general metropolitan system other than by managing the movement of particular things?

If such an urban network is to be rendered as abstract space—as an isotropic, formal grid—then streets such as Petticoat Lane sketch the schematic and put it under strain at the same time. In the previous chapter, I argued that apprehending typical bodies in relation to historically situated technologies helped planners, managers, engineers, and critics project an abstract field of shared interaction, but that types and technologies were mutually entailing predicates. In other words, no prefabricated vision of an abstract field was imposed on bodies or on technologies; instead, describing those bodies and technologies assembled them into an abstract field, which was projected through the process of assembling. Abstract space is one such field projected in its assembly. In A Thousand Plateaus, Deleuze and Guattari think of space as a mutual "warding off" or mutual capture of striated space—or abstract, homogenous space—and smooth space—or the space of "smallest deviation."[12] Striated space is defined by "the requirement of long-distance vision: constancy of orientation, invariance of distance," and "the constitution of a centralized perspective," which combine to sustain a homogenous space that can be divided up, ordered, and regulated.[13] Smooth space, on the other hand, is "nonmetric, acentered, rhizomatic" and "a field without conduits or channels."[14] Without fully entering Deleuze and Gauttari's unwieldy theoretical vocabulary, it is enough to emphasize that striated space does not merely impose a representational order onto experience, as abstract or strategic space does for Lefebvre and de Certeau. Instead of imposing itself on smooth space, striated space carves channels (or striations) within the field of smooth space.[15] But smooth space, in turn, discovers new deviations amid the striations. In this sense, striated and smooth space share a field that opens up in the very process of mutual capture between striated and smooth space, between the carving of channels and the flowing of movements, performances, and actions that issue from those channels but also overspill them. Striated and smooth space are mutually entailing predicates: each makes the other possible. This dynamic of mutual entailment opens an abstract field of shared interaction in which long-distance views attempt to capture particularities, but in which particularities inevitably exceed those views, prompting further expansion of those views. I will not carry the language of striated and smooth space beyond this paragraph, but I will continue to argue that the network is an abstract field opened through this process of mutual entailment.

We can see this process at work on Petticoat Lane. Pennethorne and others viewed Petticoat Lane as a "field without conduits or channels" and argued that carving new conduits, such as Commercial Street, could clear Petticoat Lane's crowding and congestion. But by attending primarily to the total network of London (perhaps at Cowther's coaxing), Pennethorne risked missing what "can be 'explored only by legwork,'" including, in the case of Petticoat Lane, the various ways congestion moves.[16] Urban planners sought to structure London's urban space as a manageable network, a bounded space that would allow for communication between any two points contained in that space. It is possible, though, to distinguish between the actual network, or the network that materially exists, and the virtual network, or all those elements not yet assembled into the network's channels, including, in this case, Petticoat Lane. But the spaces beyond the network are not necessarily outside of it: Petticoat Lane was in the heart of London without being included in the network abstract space regulated. In the next section, I describe the yoking of Petticoat Lane to that network.

PETTICOAT LANE: THE HISTORY OF
A PECULIAR STREET

The street known as Petticoat Lane is in fact two intersecting streets, Middlesex Street and Wentworth Street. Middlesex Street runs north from Aldgate High Street, and splits in two just before Catherine Wheel Alley and Frying Pan Alley. The official Middlesex Street veers northwestward and terminates at Bishopsgate Street. Sandy's Row continues the original course of Middlesex Street, culminating at Artillery Lane, a street that reaches its end soon after at the intersection with Bishopsgate Street, just north of the official end of Middlesex Street. Wentworth Street begins as a narrow alley running eastward from Middlesex Street. It widens after Commercial Street—which did not exist before 1843—before turning into Old Montague Street after crossing Brick Lane. In this small section of Whitechapel, not much more than a square mile in size, Brick Lane and Petticoat Lane, two of the busiest markets in nineteenth-century London thrived (and continue to thrive today). These were markets for the poor, especially Petticoat Lane, where predominately Jewish (and some Irish) dealers sold old clothes, but also all manner of recycled tools, old metal, street food, cheap jewelry, cigars, curiosities, and other goods—some of them (or many of them, according to the market's detractors) stolen. Throughout the nineteenth century, the area around Petticoat Lane was home to the vast majority of London's growing migrant population, which by 1891 had reached a population of 219,523, 71 percent of which lived in Whitechapel, Mile End Old Town, Bethnal Green, and the City of London.[17] The confusion of streets, alleys, and courts surrounding Petticoat Lane in particular was also the site of the most notorious lodging houses of London, where "persons of all sexes are sleeping together,"[18] the scene of a "public promenade of prostitution,"[19] and the source of income for rag-pickers, rag-and-bone men, and pickpockets.[20]

Petticoat Lane was also in the region of "Oriental London," where, "in the crowded thoroughfares leading to the docks, in the lodging houses kept by East Indians, in the shops frequented by Arabs, Indians, and Chinese, and in the spirit houses and opium smoking rooms . . . one meets the most singular and most picturesque types of Eastern humanity, and the most striking scenes of Oriental life."[21] Middlesex Street, or Petticoat Lane, was only named Middlesex Street between Bishopsgate Street and Whitechapel High Street, but it connected to a physical line of street that continued to the docks, linking the street market to global trade. Indeed, Petticoat Lane proper also housed the great wealth of the East India Company's warehouses. Mayhew commented that "the contrast to any one who indulged a thought on the subject—and there is great food for thought in Petticoat-lane—was striking enough. Here towered the store-house of costly teas, and silks, and spices, and indigo; while at its foot was carried on the most minute, and apparently worthless of all street-trades."[22]

Although Mayhew celebrated the contrasts of Petticoat Lane, others saw them as impediments to well-regulated circulation in the city. Indeed, the crowds and congestion Petticoat Lane attracted intervened in the circulation of goods and capital from the docks to the City and the wealthy West End. This was the view of Pennethorne, architect, planner, and protégé of the prolific Regency planner John Nash. Nash was responsible for Regent Street, a stage for the display of state power and wealth. Pennethorne, in contrast, was more focused on circulation than representation. In reports to Parliament, Pennethorne wrote that the "communications and the means of drainage of" the area around Petticoat Lane "were defective; that it was inhabited, for the most part, by an exceedingly poor, and squalid, and immoral population; and that some thoroughfare was required that should open to ventilation and to the public eye the district in the immediate vicinity of Whitechapel, Spitalfields, and Shoreditch, as a remedy for the many moral and physical evils of which it was the centre."[23] Pennethorne proposed to create this spacious, ventilating thoroughfare "between the populous neighbourhood of Whitechapel and Spitalfields, and the docks and wharfs of the River Thames, by widening the northern and southern extremities of Leman-street, and by creating a new street from the northern side of Whitechapel to the front of Spitalfields church."[24] This new street, to be called Commercial Street, would bisect Wentworth Street and run directly parallel to Middlesex Street. The ventilation and observation was thus directed at Petticoat Lane.

Near Petticoat Lane itself, ventilation entailed observation: The street improvements would render the space visible as a totality rather than a cluster of markets, lodging houses, and immigrant crowds. For the metropolis as a whole, though, the street improvements would mean the unimpeded circulation of money, goods, people, and traffic. Together with the widened street from the docks to Whitechapel Road, Commercial Street would "take the entire traffic from the docks and the east of London, and deliver it to any part of London without passing through the city."[25] The street improvement would also resolve "complaints . . . made by persons wishing to proceed from the two railways in Shoreditch to the west end of London" by providing access from Shoreditch to the City Road, and thus to the West End.[26] Pennethorne envisioned Commercial Street as the missing link in a sea, street, and rail network that would facilitate the movement of people and goods throughout the city. It is worth quoting Pennethorne at length here to demonstrate his vision for the street:

> [Commercial Street] would afford the means of direct communication between the Regent's Canal Dock Basin and all the great dock establishments in the east of London, viz., the East and West India Docks, and the London and St. Katherine Docks, and the several railway establishments in the east, north, and west of London, viz., the Blackwall Railway in Fenchurch-street and the Minories, the Eastern Counties and Northern and Eastern Railways in Shoreditch, the Birmingham Railway in Euston-square, and the Great Western Railway at Paddington; it would also facilitate in an eminent degree the transit of passengers between one railway and another.[27]

The networking prowess of Commercial Street would make it one of the "greatest thoroughfares in all London."[28]

His argument ultimately proved successful, and Commercial Street was created as part of Pennethorne's broader plans for "Metropolitan Improvement," which included New Oxford Street, Cranbourn Street, and Endell Street.[29] Pennethorne obtained funding from the Commissioners of Woods and Forests under acts in 1839 and 1840 for the construction of Commercial Street from Whitechapel High Street to Spitalfields Church.[30] This portion of the street was completed by 1845.[31] By 1856, the street was complete and paved as far as Fleur-de-lis Street, and it was extended to Shoreditch High Street by 1858.[32] Between 1872 and 1876, the Metropolitan Board of Works built Great Eastern Street, which continued the line of Commercial Street from Shoreditch High Street to City Road, finally completing Pennethorne's original plan for a street connecting the docks and the eastern railways to the West End.[33] In 1883, the Metropolitan Board of Works "widened Middlesex-street to 40 feet between Whitechapel High-street and Wentworth-street in connection with the clearance, under the Artisans and Labourers Dwellings Improvement Acts, of an insanitary area known as the Goulsten-street, Whitechapel area."[34] In 1889, its first year of existence, the London County Council widened Sandy's Row, the street that continues the line of Middlesex Street to Artillery Lane.[35]

These public improvement projects were also slum clearance projects. Laying the new thoroughfare required clearing the overcrowded houses, which were "of the very worst description of property in London."[36] Indeed, according to planners, the "whole line" proposed for Commercial Street "is more or less, from the same causes, the constant abode of fever and other infectious disorders, which . . . will continue to be the case until these houses are actually thrown down."[37] And that is precisely what happened: In Whitechapel alone, 1,743 houses were pulled down just in 1851, and few houses were built to replace them.[38] Yet the emphasis on overcrowding and congestion along with spreading infection contained something of a paradox: Crowding prevented circulation and promoted it at the same time. In the next section, I trace discussions of Petticoat Lane as a site of the crowd, contagion, and the market in order to test the reach of paradoxically mobile forms of immobility.

MOVING CONGESTION: THE MARKET AND THE CROWD

To walk the streets was to risk encounters with illicit and ungovernable exchanges of all kinds. In nineteenth-century London, the street was also the market: Every street was a market or a potential market, every inch of pavement a place to make a sale. In a series of walks totaling forty-six miles, Mayhew counted 632 street stalls, or 14 stalls to each mile of street.[39] This figure does not include itinerant hawkers selling items without stalls. Nor does it include barrows, which were increasingly in use, a change "forced upon the street sellers by the commands of the police—that the men should 'keep moving.'"[40] The street as market conflicted with the street as vein in a circulatory network. The street sellers needed to "keep moving," because streets were meant for movement, and stalls, barrows, and carts simply got in the way. At the same time, though, they were mobile in a way that was difficult to track: A street seller might work a particular corner, but always without official claim to that corner, and many street sellers relied on changing locations as the tides of traffic increased or decreased. Street sellers did not fit into an isotropic, homogenous vision of abstract space. As a result, attempts were made to flush them out. As one street seller put it to Mayhew, "It's contrary to Act of Parliament to get an honest living in the streets now-a-days."[41]

On the one hand, street markets clogged the pavement, attracted crowds, resisted regulation, and therefore congested citywide circulation. On the other hand, street markets existed precisely to make things move. Street markets created a paradoxical problem for urban planners: Congestion *moves*. Immobility is in fact a form of shadow circulation. This paradox blurred the lines that structured abstract space. Street markets—or indeed the street as market—threatened well-regulated circulation of commodities, traffic, and bodies in the city. Petticoat Lane combined such threats in intensified form: Not only was Petticoat Lane a crowded street market, it was also famous for recycling stolen goods, and for attracting immigrants. As these foreign buyers and sellers crowded Petticoat Lane and its environs, they strained attempts to gather the street market into a vision of abstract space.

An article in the *Penny Satirist* captured the risks illicit circulation posed to licitly circulating bodies: "If any one desires to see the beauties of civilization," the author sardonically wrote, "commence at Petticoat-lane, and travel straight as you can go to Bethnal Green Church, then turn right towards Whitechapel-road, and bore your way right through to the London-dock, looking in at the lanes, alleys, blind courts, yards, and other civilized abodes of the greatest nation in the world."[42] This article addressed a middle-class audience with the presumed right to move throughout the city, in this case for the purposes of social investigation. But the paradox of immobilization through contact with illicit forms of mobility troubled this movement. The author took the recommended walk through the area around Petticoat Lane, popping in to observe nearby dwellings, where "the smell is that of a long imprisoned lukewarm corruption. Every article is impregnated with it."[43] Imprisoned in the "blind courts" of a cloistered slum created by the "lukewarm corruption" of an uncaring society, the articles in the dwellings began to smell like their social environs. Yet despite the smell of their long imprisonment, all of these articles "have passed through many a hand, been bought, sold, and exchanged like copper coins for many generations. They have been seized by the broker, knocked down by the auctioneer, bought by the Jew. . . . They are real *moveable* property. Fixtures there are none."[44] This emphasis on exchange and moveable property might seem to contradict the notion of the property's long imprisonment, but it also adumbrates the paradox of immobility through illicit or ungovernable mobility that is characteristic of the modern street.

Indeed, the emphasis on the smell of the long-imprisoned property already signals a circulatory relationship. According to the miasmatic theory of disease, poorly ventilated spaces generate putrid, disease-spreading miasma, which are sensible only by smell. An 1866 report on fever described miasma as the "exhalations arisen from crowding too many human beings in a close place."[45] An 1864 report on overcrowding claimed that lodging houses "are infested with that peculiarly fusty and sickening smell which is characteristic of the filthy haunts of poverty. There also lurk the germs of disease, which wait only for one last condition to bring them into frightful activity."[46] The "peculiarly fusty smell" is "characteristic"—or typical—of congested spaces that also portend ungovernable movement. Paradoxically, the transmission of disease issues from a scene of entrapment: close courts, cramped households, and cloistered slums were commonly viewed as sources of disease. Poor circulation created miasma, which then circulated in ungovernable and indeed invisible ways—sensible only to smell.

Even in this brief *Penny Satirist* article, the author encountered another such scene of mobility within immobility. Describing an attempt to avoid the ungovernable circulation of miasma, the author writes, "I called at a pawnbroker's, not to pledge, but just to see what was pledged; and oh! what a scene! to see it, was horrible—to smell it, worse—but to touch it was beyond my resolution. I kept my hands in my pockets, and compressed my lips."[47] Here the author sought to protect his body by avoiding physical contact with this ungovernable scene of circulation (which smelled worse than it looked, indicating its likely miasmatic properties). The diseased scene threatened to penetrate the body. Although the author of this *Penny Satirist* article presumed the right to move about the city, strolling through East End slums and poking around in lodgings and pawnbrokers, he also sought to protect his body from immobilization in a relationship of ungovernable circulation.

Urban planners, public commentators, and governmental officials sought to collapse this paradox of immobilization through ungovernable mobility by finding ways to render mobility manageable. In the case of Petticoat Lane, one early solution was simply closing the market. Under pressure from mounting public complaints, the City of London and Metropolitan Police collaborated to do just that in August 1858.[48] The attempt was warmly received in the periodical press, which quickly (and prematurely) labeled the effort a success. The *Daily News* and the *Morning Post* declared, "Petticoat-lane will soon be as open for traffic as any of the neighbouring thoroughfares,"[49] and the *Morning Chronicle* added that this opening was "a result for the attainment of which indirectly the Lord Mayor deserves the highest praise."[50] Petticoat Lane, according to both papers, was a public nuisance. The *Daily News* claimed, "not any part of" Petticoat Lane "can be called a common thoroughfare, although it is much frequented."[51] Instead, it is "a nest of above 500 wretched houses, built up in close courts and alleys, yards. . . . But very few of those houses are without the means of allowing those who enter them one way and require to leave by another from doing so."[52] Once again, the paradox of immobility through illicit mobility surfaced: Petticoat Lane was a "nest of wretched houses," but all of these close-built houses had second exits, implying that visitors to such houses often had reason for evading detection. Indeed, the *Daily News* claimed of Petticoat Lane that "a large proportion of the property which is daily stolen is there disposed of."[53] Hence Petticoat Lane could be both "much frequented" without any part of it being a "common thoroughfare": Congestion moves, but not in readily detectable or governable ways.

This illicit circulation of people and property created the obstruction that the police sought to remove. As the *Morning Chronicle* wrote,

The great obstruction to the traffic of the district, arising from the entire occupation of Petticoat-lane and some neighbouring thoroughfares, by dealers in old clothes, old tools, Birmingham jewellery, and other cheap merchandise of all sorts, who plied their occupations there from morning to night, to the complete exclusion of regular traffic, as the aggregation of so many buyers and sellers, fixed or peripatetic, upon one spot, rendered it utterly impossible for any respectable person to pass without making free use of his elbows to push his way through, or without finding himself, at the end of his struggle, minus his watch, his purse, or his handkerchief.[54]

This passage neatly captures the paradox of immobility through ungovernable and illicit mobility: Respectable persons could not pass through Petticoat Lane because dealers in cheap merchandise and pickpockets proliferated on that street. The dealers plied their trade from "morning to night," excluding "regular traffic," or traffic adhering to schedule. Respectable persons required predictable traffic patterns. As we have seen in the case of the free-roaming social investigator, ungovernable circulation also placed the body of the "respectable person" in risk of penetration, in this case by the fingers of pickpockets. To pocketed hands and pursed lips, we can add the swinging elbows to the armory of the threatened middle-class body.

This 1858 attempt to shut down Petticoat Lane—which, of course, failed—was not the first attempt, nor would it be the last. In 1850, Parliament considered an update to the Metropolitan Paving Act of 1817, or Michael Angelo Taylor's Act, which first established the requisite power for "seizing and disposing of [any] article obstructing" the streets.[55] Indeed, the strictures of the Michael Angelo Taylor act were such that street traders could be arrested "where the basket," barrow, or stall "extends only a foot over the pavement."[56] Street traders relied on no fixed address and thus were difficult to regulate; as such, they posed a threat to the well-regulated circulation of the city. Petticoat Lane and the markets nearby intensified this threat because of the crowds it attracted and because the most important day of trading on Petticoat Lane was Sunday rather than Saturday. This was true not only because the predominantly Jewish traders would not trade on the Sabbath, but also because many workers living in the area were not paid until Saturday night, leaving only Sunday for shopping.[57]

An 1850 parliamentary report from the Select Committee of the House of Lords on the bill "An Act to Prevent Unnecessary Trading on Sunday in the Metropolis," provides unique insight into the "Sunday question" and the varying viewpoints of street trade. In 1855, the Sunday Trading Bill was passed, banning all Sunday trade except "meat and fish sold before 9 a.m. and newspapers and cooked food sold after 10 a.m."[58] Although the intended purpose was to reduce crowding in streets on Sundays, the bill had the unintended consequence of summoning large crowds to Hyde Park—where the aristocracy took their Sunday rides—for three consecutive Sundays in the summer of 1855. On June 24, 1855, two hundred thousand people—including Karl Marx—attended a protest against the bill; the following week, one hundred fifty thousand more turned up.[59] The bill was withdrawn, but protesters gathered again the following week, some of them pouring into the streets of Belgravia where they "broke 749 window-panes."[60]

The fear of the crowd is palpable in the 1850 report. The Select Committee questioned a series of shopkeepers, street traders, magistrates, police officers— including Police Commissioner Richard Mayne—and concerned citizens. The magistrate Harry Chester described to the committee the bustling scene of these Sunday markets: "Persons who have not seen it, can have no idea of the crowd that now exists in some parts of London on Sunday; I never saw such a scene as I saw on Sunday week in Houndsditch, and in Lambeth, and in Westminster; there are complete fairs held there. If such a measure as in contemplation were carried out by the police, all that would cease; there would be no such scenes."[61] According-ing to Chester, the markets were out of control—to hold a fair on Sunday was to profane the Lord's day. This profanation stemmed directly from the overcrowding of the market. The crowd served as a conduit for emotion and desire, spreading ungovernable and un-Christian sentiments on the Sabbath.[62] One concerned citizen explained that overcrowding made it difficult for respectable people to move unimpeded through the streets, complaining, "When I was residing in Tyssen-street, and going down Brick-lane on Sunday morning, I was obliged to take my wife in the middle of the street, in consequence of there being so many costermongers and butchers with their stalls, that we could not pass without our shoulder knocking against the greasy meat."[63] The crowding of costermongers and butchers forced husband and wife to take a circuitous path in order to avoid bodily contact with the grisly and indeed gristly scene. Once again, respectable bodies developed tactics to wend their way through space without contacting any promiscuous congestion.

Despite the repetition of this theme of overcrowding contaminating respectable bodies, the value of this report lies in the diversity of viewpoints to be found in it. In addition to shopkeepers and street traders, who explain the necessity of shop-ping on Sunday, Superintendent of the City Police Charles George Hodgson explained the utility of the market to the committee, saying, "Sunday is the only day that they [the lowest orders] have absolutely at command. They resort to Petticoat-lane, as a place where they can get second-hand goods of a very cheap kind at almost any hour on the Sunday; Saturday night up to a late hour is taken up in receiving their pay, and drinking at public-houses, and so forth."[64] Although this was not a ringing endorsement of the market, Hodgson did recognize its util-ity to the "lowest orders," as he called them. And when the committee primed him to decry the "rioting occasionally taking place on the Sunday" in Petticoat Lane, Hodgson responded, "I can scarcely call them riots; we have occasional squabbles and conflicts amongst them, as we have in all crowded places."[65] Mayne, Hodgson's counterpart in the Metropolitan Police, took a similarly dim view of the committee's questions, tersely dismissing most of them. The committee asked Mayne whether he would find it difficult to enforce a ban on Sunday trading if it were added to the Police Act, and the sarcasm is hard to miss in Mayne's response: "No; if it were thought desirable to make the crying of oranges or apples an offence."[66] Although hated by costermongers for constantly forcing them to "move along," the police were perhaps less prone to exaggerate the purported evils of street trading than some parliamentary officials. More importantly for my purposes here, though, Mayne's indifference to the street sale of oranges demonstrates that whether something counted as illicit or ungovernable circulation was subject to contestation; there was no one definition or agreed-upon set of criteria for what was a nuisance and what was part of city life, what was an impediment to movement and what was not, what was proper or improper circulation. As a result, what looked like congestion, crowding, and crime to some looked merely like the "crying of oranges" to others—a mode of circulating goods and capital that posed little threat to the citywide order.

Nevertheless, Mayne and the proponents of the law banning street trade agreed that managing movement on the street required managing the crowd. The law would have granted police the power to flush the crowds by clearing away the trade that attracted them. The proponents of the law, then, saw the street as part of a total network of abstract space: A clog in one part of the system was like a clog in any other part; all that was needed was to flush it. Mayne, however, questioned whether crowds could be flushed so easily, citing the "difficulty of enforcing a law against unwilling persons."[67] When asked, "If the police were in crowded thoroughfares to stop parties so engaged, you think there would be excitement and confusion?" Mayne responds, "Very great, I think."[68] The crowd thus haunted both the vision of abstract space the law's proponents sought to promote and the practice of the police, who would have been tasked with enforcing the law on the streets. What was needed, then, was a means of restructuring the network itself, changing the very conditions of urban movement. Commercial Street, which was only partly constructed at the time of this report, would offer such a means: As a technology for opening and ventilating the congestion around Petticoat Lane, Commercial Street would obviate the need for the police to risk catalyzing the crowd by attempting to clear its members from the street.

As I argued in the previous chapter, updates in sewer technologies provided new channels for circulation, eliminating old forms of waste disposal that clogged sewers. Similarly, streets could clear out crowds by opening channels that would move people, preventing urban congestion before it started. The building of sewers was also part of the plans for Commercial Street. One parliamentary report outlining the benefits of Commercial Street explained that, "The drainage indispensably requisite for a good new street speedily effects the purification of the whole neighbourhood," since the "prevalence of some malignant disease" is "coterminous with the limits within which that defect" of poor drainage exists.[69] Commercial Street would thus purify all of the spaces immediately communicating with the new drainage system the street would provide. But such benefits would accrue not only because the area "coterminous with the limits" of poor drainage would improve, but because the new street would provide passage through that area: "It is almost unnecessary to remark that the remedy for this grevious evil will immediately follow the opening of new communications for greater convenience of public intercourse *through* the districts in which it exists."[70] A later report argued that the purpose of Commercial Street was "removing existing obstructions which now impede main lines of communication, through which most traffic is constantly passing, or for creating new and commodious thoroughfares in poor and populous districts, *by means of which additional facilities of intercourse may be afforded to the Metropolis in general,* while they would produce inestimable benefit by improving the health and moral habits of those districts in particular."[71] This passage explicitly linked the particular goals of Commercial Street with citywide circulation. By 1845, perhaps the report's writers had taken Lord Cowther's 1838 lesson to heart: Improving a particular district was not enough; the improvement must improve the "facility of traffic" for the metropolis as a whole. Arguments for Commercial Street thus emphasized its general decongestive powers. Securing the long-distance view of abstract space requires linking particular spaces to the citywide circulatory network: The abstract space of the city becomes isotropic once "facilities of intercourse"—or technologies of circulation—make any movement in any direction equally unimpeded.

Where bans on trading in Petticoat Lane failed to flush congestion, the restructuring of the street network hoped to succeed by expanding the scale of the operation. Rather than police forcing people to "move along" on the street level, Commercial Street would move things along by restructuring the urban network. In the previous chapter, I argued that Bazalgette's major innovation was to carve new channels in the network that linked London's streets and sewers with the Thames and ultimately the sea, bypassing the tides that returned expelled feces to London. Commercial Street was built to carve a new, aboveground channel in the network connecting the sea, the docks, the East End, the City, and the West End. Streets are technologies that make movement possible by creating new channels within the expanding field of abstract space. The tendency of abstract space is toward unimpeded movement in a fully visible field. Yet even as the scope of abstract space's vision expands, it is never merely a representation imposed upon another, separate space. This is true even in the extreme examples of abstract space, such as the Great Victorian Way, the Crystal Palace architect John Paxton's vision of a "ten mile 'girdle'" of glass and iron encircling London, combining a street with a railway and "tracks, incorporating shops and privates houses."[72] The Great Victorian Way, which was duly considered but never built, offered a sanitized, fully decongested vision of urban space, where movements would be entirely unimpeded and entirely visible. The Great Victorian Way was a technological dream: a world of glass substituting itself for the unwieldy material world of the street. But even this technological dream sought not to impose an order on the city but to capture its constitutive elements—railways, streets, shops, and houses—in a fully visible field.

Yet railways, streets, shops, and houses attract traffic, trade, and people, which participate in circulation and promote crowding. This connection between decongestion and re-congestion proved difficult to surmount. The same report that linked the particular improvement of Commercial Street to the increased facility in citywide circulation also argued that these same facilities created new forms of congestion. The ongoing construction of Commercial Street meant that nearby "Union-street East and Lamb-street, will be the only two vents for all the passengers and traffic accumulated in the spacious thoroughfare of the new street now forming up to Spitalfields church."[73] Thus the thoroughfare explicitly designed to ventilate traffic also accumulated traffic. Specifically referring to the renovations associated with Commercial Street, one author complained that, despite the clearances, "the poor are not removed. They are shoveled out of one side of a parish, only to render more over-crowded the stifling apartments in another part."[74] Thus the "spacious thoroughfare" named Commercial Street only exacerbated the overcrowding in adjacent streets, which led its planners to call for new vents. This is why, as theorists of urban planning often argue, the problem of urban traffic is unresolvable.[75] Creating new channels for traffic only attracts more traffic to those channels, creating new traffic problems, which require new solutions that only replicate the initial problem. This inextricable dynamic demonstrates that abstract space is not merely a representation imposed upon lived space, but an effort to capture the promiscuous movements of lived experience in a controllable form, and then channel those movements through uniform space. But these movements inevitably overspill their channels, creating, in turn, the conditions for a renewed effort at capture. Abstract space, then, is not merely an imposed representation but an attempt to assemble the particular elements of the city into a general metropolitan network.

Thus far, I have primarily described street improvement, slum clearance, and market policing. All of these are large-scale efforts to manage urban circulation by controlling and adjusting the citywide network. This is why it was crucial for Pennethorne to respond to Cowther's critique: He needed to prove he was improving the entire city, not just one street, and that his improvements would yoke particular problem areas to the network sustained by abstract space. In the remainder of the chapter, I focus on accounts that hew to the street level, revealing forms of circulation that escape the perspective of abstract space, even as these forms of circulation shadow the circulation abstract space promotes. I turn now to Eliza Linn Lynton's "Out Walking" and its advice for women dealing with street encounters with sexually aggressive men, which I contrast with Mayhew's account of the idle prostitute whose glance captures unsuspecting gentlemen as they pass by. Despite these differences, I argue that together these accounts demonstrate how the apparent congestion of the crowd both belied and promoted the exchange of commodities, bodies, and sex on the street.

OUT WALKING: IMPEDIMENTS AND ILLICIT CIRCULATION

One could argue that the repeated descriptions of crowds and congestion in the parliamentary reports and periodical press accounts I have cited thus far are merely examples of a moral panic—an ideological fixation on the poor as an aggregated threat.[76] It is worth remembering, though, that London was crowded indeed in the nineteenth century, and that making one's way through public space meant contending with the sheer phenomenological force of such crowding. Max Schlesinger's 1853 *Saunterings in and about London*, a book written in German for a German audience and translated into English after its unexpected popularity in England, describes contending with the London crowd:

> Strangers in London are not fond of walking, they are bewildered by the crowd, and frightened at the crossings; they complain of the brutal conduct of the English, who hurry their way along the pavement without considering that people who hurry on, on some important business or other, cannot possibly stop to discuss each kick or push they receive. A Londoner jostles you in the street, without ever dreaming of asking your pardon; he will run against you, and make you revolve on your own axis, without so much as looking round to see how you feel after the shock; he will put his foot upon a lady's foot or dress, exactly as if such foot or dress were integral parts of the pavement, which ought to be trodden upon; but if he runs you down, if he breaks your ribs, or knocks out your front teeth, he will show some slight compunction, and as he hurries off, the Londoner has actually been known to turn aback and beg your pardon.[77]

In a city as large and growing as fast as London, simply walking from place to place—which everyone, at some point, had to do—involved the risk of exposing one's body to unwanted physical contact. This bodily proximity was potentially a form of promiscuity, in both senses of the term: indiscriminate and unchaste. Indeed, the connection between sexual exchange and the crowd was a repeated theme of parliamentary reports on Petticoat Lane and Commercial Street, where the concentration of common lodging houses promoted outright prostitution and "frequent exchanges" of sexual partners even among married couples, at least according to outside accounts.[78] On Petticoat Lane, sex circulated amid the congestion of the crowd.

In his essay "On Duty with Inspector Field," Dickens follows Inspector Field and other police officers on their nightly rounds through low lodging houses, braving the "pestilent breath" that "issues from within" the lodging houses and confronting "crowds of sleepers" in "intolerable rooms" full of rats and "insect-vermin, but fuller of intolerable smells."[79] Inspector Field's tour concludes as the party make for Whitechapel to "unveil the mysteries of Wentworth Street" (or Petticoat Lane) only to confront a recalcitrant thief who refuses them entry into the sleeping rooms of the lodging house, whence they find themselves "shut up, half a dozen of us . . . in the innermost recesses of the worst part of London, in the dead of night—and not a man stirs."[80] As Inspector Field—the real-life inspiration for Inspector Bucket in *Bleak House*—shows the "secret working" of the street to Dickens and company, Dickens discovers the relationship between crowding, congestion, and circulation. Critiquing metropolitan improvements, including Pennethorne's plans for New Oxford Street, which were also part of his plans for Commercial Street, Dickens contemplates the crowd's movements: "Thus, we make our New Oxford Streets, and our other new streets, never heeding, never asking, where the wretches we clear out, crowd."[81] One place they crowd is the public street, where their movement brings bodily proximity and the promiscuity of unwanted—and unwashed—physical contact. Inspector Field routinely attracts such contact: "One beldame in rusty black has such admiration for him, that she runs a whole street's length to shake him by the hand; tumbling into a heap of mud along the way, and still pressing her attention when her very form has ceased to be distinguishable through it."[82] Desiring to touch the inspector even as her form can no longer be distinguished from street mud, this "beldame"—like the other "half-drunken hags" who frequent the lodging houses that Field inspects—is stuck in motion, a mise-en-scène of congested circulation, her uncontrollably desirous body contained in the mud yet moving through it, all while fully engulfed by it. Thus, promiscuous bodily contact circulates on the most congested streets, threatening the goal of unimpeded street-level circulation.

Although this problem was peculiarly intense on and around Petticoat Lane, it was also a general metropolitan problem. In her 1862 article "Out Walking," published in the periodical *Temple Bar*, Eliza Lynn Linton registered public norms of sexuality by advising young women how to comport themselves in the streets so as not to attract unwanted attention and thus to control as far as possible the promiscuity of public encounters.[83] Linton's article was published in the context of "intense debate in the *Times* and in the periodical press about men, women, respectability and streets in mid-Victorian London" that began when a certain "Paterfamilias in the Provinces" sent an angry letter complaining that his daughters had been followed by leering men on Oxford Street.[84] Obliquely referencing this controversy,

Linton asks, "Is the police of this great city of ours in such a shaky state that even daylight and the broadest thoroughfares do nothing for the better regulation of manners?"[85] This emphasis on daylight and broad thoroughfares suggests the importance of timing and spatial location as they relate to circulation. If women cannot move freely through broad streets in broad daylight—where ventilation ought to be most vigorous and observation most acute—then when and where could they move? Indeed, for "modest women" the stakes of urban encounters were such that they might find it necessary to remove themselves from circulation entirely if they "are continually spoken to as they walk alone."[86] Thus the "daily teachers, art-students, 'assistants' of every kind, readers at the British Museum, and the many other instances of unprotected womanhood abounding—creatures that now walk about daily in simple, unstained purity . . . would either shut themselves up for ever" or "harden into indifference" if "perpetually mistaken" for prostitutes.[87]

As Lynda Nead has argued, "Out Walking" provides "unequivocal affirmation of the routine presence of unaccompanied respectable women in the streets of mid-Victorian London," and it also indexes the relationship between female bodies and urban circulation.[88] Walking in the city as a woman, in Linton's view, was about being viewed, and about controlling the conditions of that viewing as much as possible. Women must not rely on men to judge them properly. After all, "how many men are physiognomists? And who among the ordinary loungers can distinguish attraction from solicitation, and discern the signs that label them distinct and apart? Not one in a thousand."[89] Physiognomy, the science of reading the face to discern type, was a widely used and widely discussed nineteenth-century technique for managing one's embodied encounters in urban crowds. The warrant for Linton's advice stemmed from the everyday breakdowns in the system of urban typology that physiognomy supported. Urban encounters were as much about labeling as they were about mislabeling types. The promiscuous circulation of bodies and commodities generated the errors endemic to urban labeling. These errors posed risks for "modest women" who risked becoming trapped in the street-level circulation of illicit sex.

Thus if "the broadest thoroughfares" could not regulate manners—as Pennethorne hoped they would—then women must develop new techniques for managing their urban encounters. Abstract space might support the carving of broad thoroughfares to regulate behavior, but its long-distance view could not fully predict what behavior these thoroughfares might in turn enable, or what techniques street-level users might be forced to adopt. Linton's description of these techniques reveals the complexity of bodily performance in public space:

> If she knows how to walk in the streets, self-possessed and quietly, with not too lagging and not too swift a step; if she avoids lounging about the shop-windows, and resolutely forgoes even the most tempting displays of finery; if she attain to that enviable street-talent, and pass men without looking at them, yet all the while seeing

them; if she knows how to dress as only a lady can, avoiding loud colours and too coquettish a simplicity as equally dangerous, the one for its assertion and the other for its seductiveness; if she has any thing of purpose or business in her airs, and looks as if she understands what she is about, and has really some meaning in her actions; if she has nothing of the gaper in her ways, and does not stand and stare on all sides, like a mark set up for pickpockets to finger,—she is for the most part as safe as if planting tulips and crocuses in her own garden.[90]

Linton describes an intricate bodily performance that wards of the various forms of immobility a woman moving through the street might encounter. Here we have a model of street behavior far different from that of the flaneur, who can be seen without risk and gaze with impunity, and who revels in the openness of the urban encounter, the erotic thrill of exchanging gazes with strangers, and the phantasmagoria of commodity exchange. So as not to be mistaken for the prostitute, who relies for subsistence on being seen, women must not exchange gazes with men or allow themselves to become caught up in commodity exchange. The flaneur opens himself to the city, while the "modest woman" finds the safety of her own garden in the streets through a complex urban dressage: She must walk while maintaining an even pace, muffling any noise, resisting commercial temptations, avoiding eye contact, dressing smartly, and moving with purpose. Women must perform respectability in their walk in order to control the terms of their circulation and avoid becoming mired in the illicit circulation of exchanged glances and saleable sex.

Commodified sex circulates as an undercurrent to well-regulated urban circulation of the kind that allows women and men to move unimpeded through broad, bright thoroughfares. This illicit sexual exchange mirrors the licit exchange of commodities. Linton nods to this connection when she doubts the ability of male physiognomists to "discern the labels that mark" prostitutes and modest women "distinct and apart." Later, she makes the analogy between women's bodies and commodities explicit: If a woman "does any thing to attract observation, she will most likely get more if than she wants. Now, can this be wondered at? . . . are men omniscient, and can always distinguish? Are we not perpetually having trouble about trade-marks and labels, so cunningly copied that no one not initiated can detect the true from the false?"[91] This analogy between women's bodies and trademark labels figuratively sketches the connections between prostitute's bodies and commodities. A particular danger arose around shop windows, where commodity displays attracted the gaze of passersby and arrested their progress through the streets. Indeed, on the street, the "brightest glare bursts forth" often enough from shop windows, where "boldness caries the prize" in attracting the eyes of passersby.[92] Linton thus warned against women "lounging around all the shop-windows: scanning *Punch* or the *Illustrated* as they stand with their faces against the glass."[93] The danger was that women's bodies might be mistaken for saleable commodities, that they might become immobilized on the street if they did not move through it at the proper pace.

In his discussion of prostitution techniques around Petticoat Lane, Mayhew similarly warned against this practice of lingering near shop windows, although his warning was to men who might find themselves victim to unwanted advances. "As soon as evening sets in," Mayhew writes, in the context of a description of Petticoat Lane, prostitutes "loiter at shop-windows and ogle gentlemen in public walks, making requests which might be expected only from long-hardened prostitution. Their nights are generally passed in a low lodging-house. They frequently introduce themselves with 'Please sir, can you tell me what time it is?' If they get a kindly answer, some other casual observations prepare the way for hints which are as unmistakeable as they are unprincipled."[94] Where Linton counseled women to avoid the gaze of men, Mayhew emphasized the direction of the prostitutes' gaze, who "ogle" unsuspecting gentlemen on public walks. For both Linton and Mayhew, the gaze was a means of communicating sexual desire, of making one's desire known and connecting one's desire to another body in public space. Indeed, the power of the gaze was so strong that it could impede one's progress through the city streets: if respectable women met the gaze of the leering man or the gentlemen that of the ogling prostitute, they could find themselves delayed or detained by unwanted sexual exchange.

The scene of the shop window thus materially manifests this close connection between bodily and commodity exchange. The prostitute (or male lounger) lingered by shop windows, hoping to catch the eye of unsuspecting gentlemen (or respectable women) in the reflection of the glass. Sexual exchange circulated in the mirror image of the shop window, which provided the cover of licit commodity exchange for the exchange of illicit gazes. Women who stood with their "faces against the glass" made themselves visible to men standing behind them, opening themselves to dangerous or perhaps desirable eye-to-eye encounters. Thus, the licit circulation of bodies and commodities made illicit forms of circulation possible. What Linton and Mayhew described as a trap—something that would arrest movement in the city—was actually a form of illicit, ungoverned, and potentially ungovernable movement. To walk in the city was to risk immobilization in a relationship of illicit circulation that shadowed the licit circulatory network. This paradox—immobility through mobility—is the constitutive paradox of the street in the modern city. These paradoxically mobile forms of immobility prompt the expansion of abstract space. Prostitution thrived on illicit street-level exchanges. In this sense, prostitution was part of a broader field of informal and sometimes illicit street markets.

Like the idle prostitute whose glance captures the unsuspecting gentlemen, the market crowds of Petticoat Lane were understood as a force capable of capturing and thus containing movement. In the concluding section to this chapter, I argue that Mayhew's insight was to recognize that Petticoat Lane was precisely a scene of promiscuous circulation, and building on this insight, his innovation was to attempt to apprehend the distance of that circulation without reverting to the long-distance view of established abstract space. If abstract space requires long-distance vision, then the global circulation of bodies and commodities, and their local appearance in crowded space, puts this vision under strain.

MAYHEW AND THE GLOBAL STRANGER: THE PARADOXES OF PETTICOAT LANE

Mayhew began *London Labour and the London Poor* with a focus on producing a "cyclopaedia of the industry, the want, and the vice of the great Metropolis," but as the inquiry proceeds, the street increasingly surfaced at the forefront of the project.[95] This is because, as Mayhew discovered, most of the London poor worked in the streets, finding ways to turn a profit with whatever meager resources they had available. In a brief excursus on the history of capitalism and the expansion of trade, Mayhew suggested that the market and the street existed in symbiosis: "Now, this extension of markets necessarily involved some machinery for the conveyance of the goods from one district to another. Hence, the pedlar was not only the original merchant, but the primitive carrier—to whom, perhaps, we owe both our turnpike-roads and our railways."[96] This is a surprising reversal of the typical account of modern space: Mayhew credited not powerful planners or virtuoso engineers, but the humble peddler, the "primitive carrier" whose footsteps were the original networking technology. The long-distance view of abstract space opened up through legwork: Around the market and the peddler an entire network of streets and railways sprang up.

This brief account of early capitalism resonates with Georg Simmel's famous account of the stranger, the potential wanderer who arrives today and stays tomorrow, never fully joining the indigenous community yet contributing to it and profiting from it. The archetypical stranger, of course, is the peddler or trader. The stranger-trader networks the local community to the circulation of necessary or desirable commodities, but this network strains the ties that bind the community. The generalization of the stranger is one definition of the modern condition, and in particular of the modern urban condition. One term for this generalization of the stranger that highlights its ethical potential is cosmopolitanism, which involves a drive toward "planetary expansiveness" combined with an ethical commitment to a "distanced attachment."[97] Indeed, as Amanda Anderson has shown, Victorians from George Eliot to John Stuart Mill argued that cultivating a detached perspective could induce moral sentiment lacking in "abstract forms of knowledge" and provide a perspective outside of one's own partial position.[98] Cultivating detachment was both a means of

binding oneself to others and distancing oneself from one's own biases; it was a tool
for ethical dealings in a world of strangers.

Anderson's emphasis on detachment resonates with my argument that abstract
space required long-distance vision to sustain expanding networks. Just as it is
possible to distinguish between actual networks and virtual networks—networks
in existence and networks in process of expansion—it is possible to distinguish
between actual cosmopolitanism as a "description of the actually existing, ineluctably mixed-up state of modern identity" and virtual cosmopolitanism as an
"unfulfilled task of planetary justice."[99] Cultivating a detached perspective supports the apprehension of identities mixed up in the transnational movement of
people. Such a detached perspective was particularly useful on Petticoat Lane,
where the overcrowding of migrant communities was seen to clog the urban network. Detachment is not a means of imposing order on the beliefs, ideas, and
practices of distant others, but a means of apprehending those beliefs, ideas, and
practices in their flourishing so at to better (and perhaps more ethically) manage
one's dealings with the other. Detachment thus opens a field of shared interaction.
Abstract space was not merely an imposition of an order but an attempt to coordi-
nate and regulate the circulation of "distant others" not yet bound to the network
of abstract space. Indeed, the paradoxical nearness of "distant others" makes cultivating a detached perspective increasingly important for managing one's dealings
in the city: Everyone in a metropolis is a stranger, a member of a group bound by
spatial proximity rather than shared origins. An underlying distance in origins
coexists with the close quarters of metropolitan life. Thus, the stranger and the city
embody the "unity of nearness and remoteness."[100] Detachment and long-distance
vision are crucial for managing urban space, but urban space also puts distance
and proximity under pressure.

Mayhew's account of Petticoat Lane addressed the ambivalence of this "unity
of nearness and remoteness." Middlesex Street—the north-south thoroughfare
that forms the heart of Petticoat Lane—is also the official boundary between London and the City. Petticoat Lane thrived quite literally in the shadows of the
world's most powerful financial center. As Pennethorne's arguments for Commercial Street demonstrated, Petticoat Lane's location between the docks, busy
rail stations, and the West End also made the area around Petticoat Lane crucial
for citywide traffic. The material nearness of this East End market to the city
center, though, was at times outstripped by its sensed remoteness in Mayhew's
account. Indeed, Petticoat Lane sounded foreign: "the whole neighbourhood
rings with street cries, many uttered in those strange east-end Jewish tones which
do not sound like English."[101] Not only the sound but "the savour of the place is
moreover peculiar. There is fresh fish, and dried fish, and fish being fried in a style
peculiar to the Jews; there is the fustiness of the old clothes; there is odour from
the pans which (still in the Jewish fashion) frizzle and hiss pieces of meat and

onions."[102] And the sights, of course, were remarkable as well: "The flaring lights from uncovered gas, from fatted lamps, from the paper-shaded candles . . . produce a multiplicity of lights and shadows, which, thrown and blended over the old clothes hanging up along the line of street, cause them to assume mysterious forms."[103] These sounds, smells, and sights are strange, peculiar, and mysterious: An ambient sensorium radically outside of yet fully within the metropolis. Mayhew was not alone in sensing strangeness not only in sight but in smell. In *Children of the Ghetto*, Zangwill's narrator emphasizes strange smells issuing from strange traders on Petticoat Lane: "Strange exotics in a land of prose carrying with them through the paven highways of London the odor of Continental Ghettos and bearing in their eyes through all the shrewdness of their glances the eternal mysticism of the Orient, where God was born!"[104] These "Hawkers and peddlers, tailors and cigar-makers, cobblers and furriers, glaziers and capmakers" unite nearness with remoteness, making their way through London bearing the scent of the Orient.[105]

As a scene, then, Petticoat Lane united nearness and remoteness. And what united all of these descriptions, of course, was the figure who embodied Petticoat Lane: the Jew. If the trader is one archetypical modern stranger, then the Jew, "cut from his origin yet not admitted to any other home," is the other.[106] As a type, the Jew threatens the modern world of strangers both because the Jew is too traditional and too modern. As Marx argues in his infamous essay "On the Jewish Question," "The Jew . . . can behave towards the state only in a Jewish way . . . by abstaining on principle from taking part in the historical movement . . . and by seeing himself as a member of the Jewish people, and the Jewish people as the chosen people."[107] In this argument, the Jew is a member of a tribe, and thus complicit in an anti-modern tradition that impedes the onward movement of history. But along with and in distinction to the Jew as tribesman exists the Jew as wanderer: instead of binding himself to tradition, the wandering Jew is "*too* autonomous"; his wandering portends the anarchical loss of control over modern circulation.[108] This fraught unity with and remoteness from modernity was the theme of Eliot's *Daniel Deronda*, in which the eponymous character must reconcile his deracinated condition with his newly discovered Jewishness.[109] In *Children of the Ghetto*, characters debate whether *Daniel Deronda* turned Jews into one-sided angels or accurately grasped the Jewish character. Ultimately, *Children of the Ghetto* leaves the debate unresolved, instead exploring Jews as "human paradoxes," caught between modernity and tradition on London's streets. "There were two strata of Ghetto girls," the narrator writes, "those who strolled on the Strand on Sabbath, and those who strolled on Whitechapel Road"—or those who assimilated and those who were traditional. The streets, then, indexed the tension between modernity and tradition that the children of the ghetto—second-generation immigrants—had to negotiate.

The ghetto, of course, is a trap, a way of containing illicit forms of circulation such as the paradoxical "wandering Jew," cordoned off in one corner of the city yet circulating globally. The narrative arc of *Children of the Ghetto* follows Esther Ansell's relationship with the ghetto from her "froom" East End youth to her fashionable adulthood as an adopted member of a wealthy West End Jewish family. When she ultimately rejects her new life and returns to her roots, she reenters Petticoat Lane, specifically Middlesex Street, and finds it a strange place:

> The well-known street she had entered was strangely broadened. Instead of the dirty picturesque houses rose an appalling series of artisans' dwellings, monotonous brick barracks, whose dead, dull prose weighed upon the spirits. But, as in revenge, other streets, unaltered, seemed incredibly narrow. Was it possible it could have taken even her childish feet six steps to cross them, as she plainly remembered? And they seemed so unspeakably sordid and squalid. Could she ever really have walked them with light heart, unconscious of the ugliness? Did the gray atmosphere that overhang them ever lift, or was it their natural and appropriate mantle? Surely the sun could never shine on these slimy pavements, kissing them with warmth and life.[110]

Here Esther does the legwork to explore a scene altered by the expansion of abstract space. The memory of her "childish feet" taking "only six steps" to cross the unaltered streets adjoining the "well-known street" of Petticoat Lane seems impossible upon her return. *Children of the Ghetto* was published in 1892, nine years after the widening of Middlesex Street and thirty-four years after Commercial Street was completed from Whitechapel High Street to Shoreditch High Street. Yet Esther's encounter with what we would today call the gentrification of her well-known childhood street also reveals both the incompleteness of abstract space, as the unaltered streets vengefully assert their narrowness, and the indeterminacy of Petticoat Lane. In her childhood, "the Lane" was coterminous with Jewish life in a Christian nation; as an adult, the Lane doubly signaled her alienation: It was no longer the traditional space she remembered—if indeed it ever was—and was no longer a space where she was at home. As she crossed the street to approach the house of a childhood friend, she noticed the suspicious gaze of a woman selling apples in the street, as "the apple-woman took her for a philanthropist paying a surprise visit to one of the families of the house." She had thus become a stranger in a strange land, which was also her homeland. She experiences this double alienation bodily as she marks the unity of nearness and remoteness with each step on Petticoat Lane.

The indeterminacy of strangerhood is also the theme of Mayhew's account of Petticoat Lane. Mayhew's experiences with and observations of strangerhood entailed concerns with the relationship between circulation and congestion. Like the gentlemen caught in the glance of the prostitute and forced into a relationship of illicit exchange, the customer's incautious glance risked the advance of unwanted exchange: "If once you look at the goods of a Jew pedlar, it is not an easy matter to get out of his clutches," Mayhew claimed.[111] Although Mayhew repeatedly noted that those who cast an "approving glance" at Jewish street sellers' wares would find themselves accosted and berated into buying, he also indicated that "this practice is less pursued now than it was, and it seems that the solicitations are now addressed chiefly to strangers. These strangers, persons happening to be passing, or visitors from curiosity, are at once recognised; for as in all not very extended localities, where the inhabitants pursue a similar calling, they are, as regards their knowledge of one another, as the members of one family. Thus a stranger is as easily recognised as he would be in a little rustic hamlet where a strange face is not seen once in a quarter."[112] In this description, Petticoat Lane becomes a premodern space thriving in the heart of the metropolis; a rustic hamlet where everyone knows your name, unless you happen to stroll in from the outside—perhaps from two streets over, in the City, or from a nearby train station—and then you will be accosted by merchants. This account also reverses the typical role of the stranger: Here the stranger is not the peddler but the customer. The stranger is not the one who brings goods to market, networking the hamlet to the world beyond, but the customer passing by. Petticoat Lane is both congested with crowds and trapped in time—a "not very extended locality" so sealed off as to become rustic.

But congestion, as I have argued here, circulates; immobility moves. Although the insight stands in seemingly direct contradiction to his vision of Petticoat Lane as a rustic little hamlet, Mayhew also recognized that Petticoat Lane was a space of circulation. The street name changes as it continues south, but Middlesex Street is on the same line of streets that connect the docks to dry land. As Mayhew's remark on the street seller who operated in the shadows of the East India Company warehouses suggested, Petticoat Lane thrived in the shadows of global trade. Not only did street traders operate in the shadows of the storehouses of colonial trade, they also profited from a system of circulation that shadowed colonial trade. Many of the commodities that circulated on Petticoat Lane were imported illicitly or informally through colonial trade routes, connecting Petticoat Lane to long-distance trade. The importance of importation is clear in Mayhew's list of available commodities on Petticoat Lane: "fruits, especially green fruits, such as oranges, lemons, grapes. Walnuts, cocoa-nuts, &c., and dates among dried fruits—shells, tortoises, parrots and foreign birds, curiosities, ostrich feathers, snuffs, cigars, and pipes."[113] Mayhew described in particular the circulation of shells, tortoises, parrots, and foreign birds from colonial outposts to "Shoreditch, Spitalfields, Whitechapel, Tower-hill, Ratcliffe-highway, Commercial Road East" and other East End markets.[114] The "supply of parrots, paroquets, cockatoos, Java sparrows, or St Helena birds, is not in the regular way of consignment from a merchant abroad to one in London."[115] Instead, birds find their way to the streets because "the commanders and mates of merchant vessels bring over large quantities; and often enough the seamen are allowed to bring parrots or cockatoos in the homeward-bound ship from the Indies or the African coast, or from other tropical countries, either to beguile the tedium of the voyage, for presents to their friends, or, as in some cases, for sale on their reaching an English port."[116]

Mayhew estimated that some three thousand birds were brought over annually in this way. The practice was so common that one merchant-seaman explained to Mayhew that when a ship could not dock off the coast of Sierra Leone, "the natives seemed to know what was wanted" from the vessel "as if by instinct . . . for they came off from the shores in their light canoes, which danced like feathers on the surf, and brought boat-loads of birds."[117] The practice was lucrative for street sellers and sailors alike: As the above-cited merchant-seaman related to Mayhew, "I would never go to that African coast again, only I make a pound or two in birds."[118]

Seaman brought seashells to London for the street trade in a similar manner. Jews also developed their own commodity routes, obviating the seaman as middleman and creating their own networks of exchange. One such example was the trade in tortoises: "Of live tortoises, there are 20,000 annually imported from the port of Mogadore in Morocco. They are not brought over, as the parrots, &c., of which I have spoken, for amusement or as private ventures of the seamen, but are regularly consigned from Jewish houses in Mogadore, to Jewish merchants in London. They are a freight of which little care is taken, as they are brought over principally as ballast in the ship's hold, where they remain torpid."[119]

It is impossible to know whether Mayhew's figures here are accurate because there are no sources of which I am aware on the informal trade in birds, shells, and tortoises between England and its colonies and among members of the Jewish diaspora. Yet this is precisely what makes Mayhew such an invaluable resource: Where other commentators saw only congestion, crowding, and crime, Mayhew sketched a transnational network of trade and commerce operating alongside formalized colonial trade. Mayhew, however briefly, in this case, attempted to develop a long-distance vision that would measure and perhaps (although he does not go so far here) manage this trade. Whether his figures are precise is less important than what the figures in fact show: Congestion moves, and its movement prompts the expansion of abstract space.

This movement was everywhere on Petticoat Lane, which was, of course, best known as an old clothes market. The old clothes moved through transnational networks of their own. "Rags are brought from France, Germany, and in great quantities from Belgium" and Denmark for sale on Petticoat Lane.[120] Merchants from Ireland also purchased wholesale textiles in Petticoat Lane and exported them to Dublin, and "bales of old clothes are exported to Belgium and Holland, but principally to Holland."[121] Petticoat Lane was a node in more local networks as

well: Sewer hunters would take recovered wares to Petticoat Lane, where merchants would purchase them, and ragpickers would search Petticoat Lane for any
rags discarded as unusable for old clothes.[122] Indeed, as Mayhew remarked, "there
is scarcely an article you can think of that lies in the street thrown away."[123] Despite
the emphasis parliamentary and periodical press reports sometimes placed on
Petticoat Lane's congestion, then, it was in fact a scene of intense circulation. As I
have argued, though, this was a form of circulation operating in the shadows of
licit circulation: seaman carrying their birds and seashells in addition to the official cargo, tortoises moving between Jewish families, recycled rags bought and
sold, and any and all waste recovered and recirculated. This is not to say that all of
this trade was illegal in the strict sense of the term—although Petticoat Lane was
known as a market of stolen goods—but that the long-distance vision of established abstract space could not apprehend this form of circulation, either in its
transnational reach or its local intensity.

The peculiar union of nearness and remoteness on Petticoat Lane escaped the
vision of abstract space. In escaping abstract space, though, it also goaded it to
expansion. Commercial Street, after all, was an attempt to bring the commodities
of the world in to London—to bring near that which was remote—and thus to
build a city for a world of strangers. Petticoat Lane was thus typical in its peculiarity. This uneasy location—escaping from an expanding abstract space—goes some
way toward explaining why Mayhew's account is seemingly so rife with contradictions: How could a rustic hamlet support so many transnational networks? How
could immobile spaces move so promiscuously? Mayhew was even inconsistent
with his description of strangers on Petticoat Lane:

> On one of my visits to Petticoat-lane I saw two foreign Jews—from Smyrna I was
> informed. An old street-seller told me he believed it was their first visit to the district.
> But, new as the scene might be to them, they looked on impassively at all they saw.
> They wore the handsome and peculiar dresses of their country. A glance was cast
> after them by the Petticoat-lane people, but that was all. In the Strand they would
> have attracted considerable attention; not a few heads would have been turned back
> to gaze after them; but it seems that only to those who may possibly be customers is
> any notice paid in Petticoat-lane.[124]

These visitors precisely conform to the model Simmel outlines: They arrived today,
and they will be staying tomorrow. Wearing "the peculiar dresses of their country,"
the Petticoat Lane people would clearly recognize them as strangers, but they
merely cast a glance at them as they passed, while the strangers themselves looked
only "impassively" on the hustle and bustle of Petticoat Lane that so fascinated
Mayhew. Unlike the prostitute capturing the gentleman's eye or the Jew trapping
the customer who glances at his wares, the strangers from Smyrna and the people
of Petticoat Lane reciprocated one another's glances, but the exchange was entirely

banal: Even habited in their peculiar dress—or perhaps precisely because they were habited in their peculiar dress—the foreigners were utterly typical. Yet in the Strand, they would have been objects of "considerable attention." Suddenly, the Strand—the most important east-west thoroughfare in the metropolis, the hub of theatre and nightlife, the home to the best writers and thinkers in England—was a rustic little hamlet, where cloistered locals gaped at newly arrived foreigners. Mayhew's two accounts of strangers on Petticoat Lane are thus in direct conflict, and even his concluding claim in the above passage that the immigrants from Smyrna did not attract notice because they were clearly not potential customers is undermined by Mayhew's argument in other passages that street sellers rely heavily on the custom of other members of their class, and indeed other street sellers. Yet these two accounts do not so much contradict one another as sketch two competing visions of abstract space. When viewed as a "peculiar" space to be absorbed into the abstract space of the larger metropolis, Petticoat Lane was a crowded, congested, and cloistered hamlet, where local markets looked like an impediment to citywide circulation, and where new faces attracted immediate attention. But when Mayhew considered how Petticoat Lane's congestion circulated—the transnational shipping networks that sustained the street sellers, the flow of migrants to the lodging houses, the movements of customers through the market—the rest of London seemed stagnant and sheltered. In the account of the strangers from Smyrna, Mayhew attempted to build a long-distance vision that would extend the logic of the circulatory networks of Petticoat Lane. This vision, of course, did not obtain the institutional or governmental support that Pennethorne's vision did, from which perspective Petticoat Lane was a congested space in need of clearance. But these competing accounts do reveal that abstract space is not merely a representation to be imposed but an attempt to expand a network over spaces that exceed it. For such an expansion to succeed, what is required is not an imposition of representation but an effort at inclusion within a network. This inclusion is also a capture: the forms of circulation that formerly shadowed the network that abstract space sustains are routed through the network and thus changed as their channels of circulation change. Yet new captures generate new movements, which in turn exceed the expanded vision of abstract space. And so the process of circulation continues.

CONCLUSION

I have argued here that congestion moves, and that this paradox makes it difficult to sustain any citywide network promoting unimpeded circulation. Impediments are not merely impediments; they are also movements. The abstract space that supports citywide networking is often associated with Euclidean geometry, empty grids, and thus with mapping, but the long-distance vision I have described is not exhausted by the cartographic imagination: that innumerable list of planners, engineers, architects, officials, periodical press writers, novelists, and bureaucrats who sometimes but not always combined to form the actors of governmentality also smelled, heard, and groped their way toward abstract space. The particularities that exceed and escape abstract space can be explored only by legwork. The knowledge gained in such explorations might help yoke the particular space to the abstract network, but this yoking in turn generates new particularities that issue from and exceed the channels, routes, and conduits of the network. This paradox of movement within immobility is also, then, the paradox of the street: The street is the technology that structures the network and the scene that ineluctably exceeds the network. Street crowds, street markets, and illicit street-level circulation shadowing well-regulated circulation overwhelm the actual network even as the street is proposed as a technological solution to the same overwhelming flowing, leaking, reeking, and clogging it supports.

Between long-distance vision and legwork, the street opens up as a field of shared interaction. Rather than accepting abstract space as a representational category imposed on lived experience, I have attempted to restore some of the controversy to its assembling, focusing on debates and inconsistencies among and within those we would typically align with the actors of governmentality—parliamentarians, officials, urban planners, the police, public order–minded press writers, and social investigators—and on the shadow forms of circulation that opened to those who did the legwork. In keeping with this effort to restore the controversy to abstract space, it is important to emphasize that the actors involved in assembling it were sometimes *but not always* the actors of governmentality. This mutability explains why the actors of governmentality are so hard to delineate—they are a series of types rather than a set list of individuals. Mayhew's work captures this mutability: At times his work promoted governmentality, at other times he fiercely critiqued it, and at still other times he attempted to develop new ways of apprehending the actors, actions, and objects involved in assembling the social. With Mayhew, the perspective tends to change with the object of study, and *London Labour's* repetitive organization means that Mayhew sometimes brings changed perspectives to bear on objects analyzed earlier and from a different perspective. Rather than call these contradictions, we might address them as different attempts at addressing the same problem. In this way, they become not contradictions but the controversies that arise through a series of attempts at describing scenes, sensations, events, and objects not yet integrated into abstract vision. Mayhew was thus able to describe Petticoat Lane both as a site of congestion and a space of circulation, and thus both reveal the logic of abstract space and do the legwork required to expand its vision to include shadow networks of global circulation.

4

Typical Bodies, Photographic Technologies

Race, the Face, and Animated Daguerreotypes

In *The Sign of the Four*, Sherlock Holmes and Dr. Watson must locate a pearl-thieving Englishman returned from India to London with his "savage" accomplice, the latter having left two traces at a murder scene: a small footprint and a poisoned arrow. With typical didacticism, Holmes alerts Watson of the need to distinguish "our savage" from "the Hindoo proper," with his "long and thin feet," and from the "sandal-wearing Mohammedan" with his "great toe well separated from the others" by the thong passing between them.[1] Pulling a "bulky" gazetteer from his shelf, Holmes notes that the "aborigines of the Andaman Islands" are recognizable by their "remarkably small" feet and their preference for "poisoned arrows."[2] After attaching the trace to the type, he relies on the gazetteer's description of the aborigines of the Andaman Islands and their "large, misshapen heads, small, fierce eyes, and distorted features," for a visual aid to guide his search through London's streets for the fugitive murderers. Having surveyed the scene and observed each trace detail, Holmes consults an archive in order attach the traces to the body that left them. The camera combines these functions in one technology—it surveys, captures, and archives. No wonder, then, that portable hand cameras—first commercially available in the 1880s—quickly acquired the moniker "the detective camera." It is also no surprise that Holmes routes his thinking racially, matching the trace to the typical and typically racialized body of the other. The type organizes an archive of data about bodies, arranges that data racially, and offers a means of matching the trace to the body in a scene of transnational mobility.

I have argued throughout this book that race functions as a technology of gathering and sorting in scenes of urban mobility where street-level excess threatens to frustrate the management of the urban network. The management of this network requires an abstract field of shared interaction where a metonymic relationship between part and whole can be imagined and identified. This field opens in the hesitations between street-level legwork and citywide perspectives, between the sublime encounter and the attempt to gather excess into an existing framework. Photography promises the elimination of the sublime encounter altogether; the submission of every object to one standardized format makes everything comparable within the mediated field of photography. Indeed, soon after its invention, photography radically expanded the archive of the street. Although the street persisted as a scene of profuse mobility, photography promised the capture of objects and actors in a field of contiguity. Hence Kracauer defines the photograph as a mode of preserving "the spatial configuration of a moment."[3] Photographs capture catachretic moments of presence, gathering objects and actors into a shared field of contiguities. Although disciplinary surveillance and cinema are two unavoidable reference points for any study of biopolitics, media, and the city, too often in scholarly accounts, surveillance—usually reduced to the panopticon—is understood to lock bodies down, whereas cinema animates them for the first time. But the photographic image promoted an animated imagination of the street before the cinema and in contrast to the confines of the panopticon. As a mode of capturing mobile contiguities and gathering them into a shared field, photography responded to the urban crisis of metonymy.

As images that circulate on a mass scale, contemporary photographs shape public culture by coordinating the visual imaginary.[4] However, despite the widespread availability of photography by the middle of the nineteenth century, the photograph itself could not be reproduced on a mass scale until nearly the turn of the twentieth century. For most of the nineteenth century, the repercussions of photography resonated not in the circulation of any individual photograph but in a visual imaginary coordinated by a layered set of photographic technologies. In this chapter, then, I include hand-drawn lithographs, engravings from daguerreotypes, the wet-plate collodion process, Woodburytypes, and the handheld "detective" camera in the category of photographic technologies capable of coordinating a public photographic imagination. This media archaeological perspective makes it possible to examine the sedimentation and layering of photographic technologies as more and more catachretic "spatial configurations of moments" join the assembly of parts in the metonymic field of contiguities.

I argue that race linked the expanding field of photographically captured and photographically imagined contiguities to the field of management that biopolitics demands. As I will show, in the photographic field, the body appears in and through a technology that also assigns it a race. The key figures and texts of this chapter—Francis Galton's composite photography of racial types, *Punch*'s physiologies of London types, Mayhew's dodgy street photographers, and John Thomson and Adolphe Smith's photographs of London street types, including "Ramo

Samee"—all rely on photographically imagined racial types to recuperate the relationship between part and whole. The type matches the trace to the body (the small footprint to the small-bodied, ugly-faced Adamanese), but the type also organizes bodies in relation to one another (the small footprint is not Hindoo or Mohammedan). Bodies moving on streets are thus apprehended as particular instances of general trends. Photography, therefore, recruits the street to a mediated field that is apprehensible only through the same technologies that make abstraction the condition of managing the particular. As photography disperses the body across a mediated field, the type offers a means of recapture, of arranging dispersed particularities into an apprehensible, abstract, and racialized whole. Photography provided a mediated field for the body's appearance in race. Race, in turn, links the anatamo-politics of the individual body to the biopolitics of the social body and the savage body that underlies it.[5]

I begin with Mayhew's encounter with street photographers, arguing that the "dodges" they used to sell failed photographs relied on the interchangeability of bodies within the mediated field of photography. I then turn to Francis Galton, who developed a media theory and technological practice that rendered the body as a type, which he used as an ideal gauge for measuring bodies, assigning them a location within the racial hierarchy, and thus managing the mediated field of photography. Next, I discuss *Punch*'s satirical take on Galton's ethnological discourse in its illustrated series of London types, which turned the scientific gaze toward the aspiring middle classes making their appearance on London's streets, thus gathering the middle classes into the same racialized field as the savage. I conclude with Mayhew's *London Labour* and Smith and Thomson's *Street Life*. These two texts are tightly linked: Smith's father-in-law, Blanchard Jerrold, was Mayhew's brother-in-law, and Blanchard's father, Douglas Jerrold (Mayhew's father-in-law), was a prominent writer for *Punch* and the author, with the French illustrator Gustave Doré, of *London: A Pilgrimage*, which inspired Smith and Thomson. In the preface to *Street Life*, Smith and Thomson pitched their effort as an update on *London Labour*, and the two texts share the same method: both combine the ethnological and criminological approaches to the body and the archive to track the type on the street by holding it in the same field of vision as the savage. To demonstrate this shared street-to-savage vision at work, I consider the case of "Ramo Samee," the name of an Indian street magician whose death was announced in the periodical press in 1850, but who nevertheless reappeared in Thomson and Smith's 1877 photographs as an Indian street musician. "Ramo Samee" therefore names both historic individuals and the reanimation of the racial type in conditions of mediated urban mobility. The history of "Ramo Samee" thus demonstrates the dispersal of the individual into the type and the inevitable racialization of the body under conditions of urban mobility. First, though, I begin this exploration of the mediated street with a brief discussion on the history of mechanized photographic reproduction. This history offers a media archaeological corrective to claims that photography fundamentally reshaped nineteenth-century visual culture. Materially, much of this reshaping occurred not through photography as such but through lithographic sketches of photographic possibilities, including photographic failures.

PHOTOGRAPHY BEFORE THE AGE OF MECHANICAL REPRODUCTION

By the middle decades of the nineteenth century, individual photographs could not be mass produced, but access to photography was widespread. An 1866 *British Quarterly Review* article surveying the history of photography describes the introduction of *cartes-de-visite*, calling cards containing small portraits of the owner, into the British consumer market at the end of the 1850s, and notes that the "photographic album containing the domestic portrait gallery, soon became the necessary adjunct of every drawing-room table," as collecting portraits of royalty, literary figures, and political leaders became a popular practice.[6] But photography was not confined to domestic spaces. Mayhew—that indefatigable street chronicler—encountered cheap, street-side photography studios, mostly in the poorer districts of London. Although "there may be one or two 'galleries' in the New-road, or in Tottenham-court-road," Mayhew writes, "these supply mostly shilling portraits."[7] The cheaper portraits were to be found "in the eastern and southern districts of London . . . such as in Bermondsey, the New-cut, and the Whitechapel-road," where "one cannot walk fifty yards without passing some photographic establishment, where for six-pence persons can have their portrait taken, and framed and glazed as well."[8] These six-pence portraits were even cheaper than the shilling portraits that caused Lady Eastlake to remark in 1857 that the streets were lined with "legions of petty dabblers" who "display their trays of specimens along every great thoroughfare in London, executing for our lowest servants, for one shilling, that which no money could have commanded for the Rothschild bride of twenty years ago."[9] These street photographers allowed even those who only approached the portrait gallery in the drawing room with a serving tray to join the potentially limitless photographic archive.

By the 1850s, ladies, servants, and the Rothschild bride all had access to photographic technology. Jonathan Crary, Allan Sekula and John Tagg have all argued that the potential limitlessness of the photographic archive inaugurated a new visual culture.[10] Although this archive was, in principle, limitless, it was not always so in practice. The key distinction here is between access to photography, which was widespread, and access to reproductions of individual photographs, which was not. The confusion arises in part because photographic technology improved rapidly throughout the nineteenth century, decreasing exposure times and reducing the size of cameras and the accessory equipment they required. The wet-plate collodion process of 1851—which Mayhew's street photographers used to take quick and cheap portraits—reduced exposure times from fifteen minutes to ten or fifteen seconds. The introduction of readymade dry plates in the 1870s further reduced exposure times and eliminated the cumbrous equipment required for developing wet-plate collodion negatives. The continuous rolling instantaneous gelatin film of the early handheld "detective" cameras of the 1880s made photographing moving objects possible for the first time. And, finally, the flexible celluloid film of the late 1880s provided the basis for the first moving pictures in the cinematographs of the 1890s.

However, for the first half-century of photography's history, the photograph itself—the image fixed by chemical means—still awaited its age of mechanical reproduction. As an 1866 survey of photography's history published in the *British Quarterly Review* put it, "In all the modes of multiplying a photographic image by mechanical printing, it will be seen that the aim has been to make photography conform to the recognized modes of using the printing press."[11] To be sure, in the early decades of photography, photographs circulated widely among consumers, predominantly portraiture in the form of *cartes-de-visite* and through stereoscopes. The London Stereoscopic Company had sold over half a million stereoscopes only two years after its founding in 1854. But no one photograph could be reproduced a half a million times, or even a few thousand times, until late in the century. Successful mass-production of photographic images required a process that was photomechanical, using "permanent, non-fading printer's ink from one matrix"; that eliminated the need for mounting; and, ultimately, that was compatible with moveable type.[12] It was not until the 1880s and the development of relief halftone printing blocks that images produced from photographs could be set alongside type and mass-produced.[13]

All photographic processes aspired to the status of print: The 1839 daguerreotype—which produced one image at a time on a metallic plate—was reproduced through wood engraving, which then allowed for printing. The 1839 talbotype introduced the photographic negative and thus the reproducibility of the photographed image itself. Later efforts sought to combine the negative with existing print technology, usually exposing a chemically treated gelatin plate to light under a photographic negative, such that the gelatin hardens in proportion to the light that strikes it, creating a relief of the photograph that can be inked and rolled onto paper. But the most successful of these processes, the collotype, was still limited to runs of two thousand copies per plate (although some contemporary sources claim that "it is very good work to get 500 impressions" from a collotype), making the process inadequate to the needs of mass circulation.[14] *Punch*, for example, was selling about forty thousand copies per week by the middle of the 1840s, and ninety thousand copies of its yearly almanac.[15]

Although photography had to wait half a century for its age of mechanical reproduction, images still circulated in a visual culture that, as Crary has shown, was fundamentally reshaped by photography, which established a general equivalent by generating a metonymic field of contiguous relations among bodies, technologies, and images. But since the mass circulation of photography through the printing press was not possible until the turn of the century, and since innovations in photography strove toward conformity with the modes of the printing press, studying the contours of the mediated field of photography also requires studying how that field was imagined in the engraving and lithography that circulated in the periodical press. Photography at once offered an advance on these forms and lagged behind them: The photograph, as Kracuaer argued, could capture in its entirety the "spatial configuration of a moment" in a way no artist could, but engraving and the lithograph could reach an audience no one photograph could.[16]

Although the six-pence portrait was affordable even to itinerant laborers, photographic equipment required some outlay. Mr. F—l, the busker-turned-photographer whom Mayhew interviewed, explained that he secured a £3 loan and, "with what I saved, I managed to get together another 5l. 5s. [£5 and 5 shillings], and I went to Gilbert Flemming's, in Oxford-Street, and bought a complete apparatus for taking pictures . . . for 5l. 5s."[17] Mr. F—l was rewarded for his financial risk with a steady queue of portrait seekers, whom he and his former busking partner Jim were more than happy to accommodate in Mr. F—l's studio, which was "built up out of old canvas, and erected on a piece of spare ground in a furniture-broker's yard."[18] But the wet-plate collodion process Mr. F—l used was not automated, and the cocktail of sulphate of iron—"ferri sulp is the word for it"—carbonate of iron, and hyposulphate of soda sometimes produced unexpected reactions.[19] Combine the difficulty of the process with London's uneven supply of sunshine, and a number of blurry, underdeveloped portraits were the inevitable result. Mr. F—l and Jim invented a number of dodges to recover any lost costs from blurry portraits, including charging extra for "chemicalized" treatment from the "Patent American Air-preserver," which sold better than treatment from the "London Air-Preservers," although the device itself never existed.[20] Mr. F—l and Jim convinced their customers of its effects by showing them bits of paper—"old benefit tickets," "brown paper," or "soap wrappings"—that they had collected from the street and "varnished on one side."[21]

But the American Air-Preserver could not enhance portraits that did not come out. For that, as Mr. F—l explained, he and Jim just needed a pin: "If the eyes in the portrait are not seen, and they complain, we take a pin and dot them; and that brings the eye out, and they like it. If the hair, too, is not visible we takes the pin again, and soon puts in a beautiful head of hair. It requires a great deal of nerve to do it; but if they still grumble I say, 'It's a beautiful picture, and worth half-a-crown, at the least'; and in the end they generally go off contented and happy."[22] Mr. F—l and Jim also took a series of "specimens for the window"—successful portraits to display as advertisements. In a material example of Allan Sekula's argument that the photographic archive offers a "vast substitution set,"[23] Mr. F—l explained that these "specimens" doubled as substitutes in case "anybody comes in in a hurry, and won't give us time to do the picture."[24] The strategy then was to mime the photographic process without actually exposing a plate, and then sell the customer one of the specimens from the window, wrapping the portrait in brown paper and ushering them out of the studio while importuning them not to open the package for three days. As Daniel Novak has argued, photography converts subject into "collections of 'abstract' and interchangeable parts."[25] Mr. F—l and Jim well understood that photography standardized subjects, making one image substitutable with another, so long as the paying subject did not scrutinize the intricate details too closely. Mr. F—l and Jim, then, capitalized on the interchangeability of the body captured in photographed form, which gathered particularities into the general equivalent of a technological format, converting subjects into substitutable parts.

Before it was a material media reality, however, this photographic gathering of the details of the world operated in the abstract field of the imaginary. An anecdote Mr. F—l related to Mayhew shows the interchangeability of the photographic subject in action: one woman returned after three days complaining that she had been sold the portrait of someone else. She was a young single woman, but the woman in the portrait was a wearing a widow's cap. Mr. F—l related to Mayhew how Jim insisted that the widow's cap was simply the shadow of the ringlets of her hair, exclaiming "'Oh, miss! why it's a beautiful picture, and a correct likeness,'—and so it was, and no lie," Mr. F—l added, "but it wasn't of her."[26] Eventually the complaining customer was convinced to recognize her likeness in the contours of the photograph she had been sold. Or, more precisely, she was sold the promise of capture in the standardized frame of photography. Far from isolating a likeness, then, the photographic portrait projects a field of equivalence, making any image potentially substitutable with any other.

Thus, even the portrait—the condensation of the fund of self-images—evaporates under the camera lens.[27] The metaphor of the self that is captured in the traditional portrait disperses into the metonymy of moving parts in the photographic field. Photography projects a whole that gathers in each part, binding the general and the particular in a global network, but the cost of this new unity is the borders of the subject: bodies become fungible, replaceable, and interchangeable.[28] As Crary argues, in the nineteenth century, the eye and the camera became "contiguous instruments on the same plane of operation."[29] This "plane of operation"—or mediated field, as I am calling it here—becomes the terrain of the visual. This field functions, as Crary argues, through metonymy: particular elements on the field are contiguous (eye to camera, young single woman to widow, colonial savage to street criminal) and this contiguity under the general equivalent means that particular elements inevitably imply the whole. The young single woman is interchangeable with the widow because they are contiguous under the camera's lens, which gathers particularities in the same mediated field, converting moving parts into metonymic contiguities.

This mediated projection of contiguities explains why Mr. F—l and Jim were able to pull off such dodges as drawing facial features with a pin onto blurry photographs or selling the photograph of an elderly widow as a "correct likeness" of a young single woman. As Mr. F—l explained it to Mayhew, "The fact is, people don't know their own faces. Half of 'em have never looked in a glass half a dozen times in their life, and directly they see a pair of eyes and a nose, they fancy they are their own."[30] Eyes, nose, and mouth are only so many interchangeable parts moving in the mediated field of photography. Under the conditions photography imposes, the portrait does not so much condense an image of the self as combine contiguous parts in a mediated field. The portrait captures not the individual but the type. I turn now to Galton's composite portraiture, showing how the interchangeability of the photographed body promotes the racialization of the face in its attachment to the body.

GAUGING THE BODY: GALTON'S HIEROGLYPHICS OF THE FLESH

In 1887, the Cambridge Scientific Instrument Company advertised scientific instruments "designed under the direction of Mr. Francis Galton" with a pamphlet entitled *A Descriptive List of Anthropometric Apparatus, Consisting of Instruments for Measuring and Testing the Chief Physical Characteristics of the Human Body*; the pamphlet lists instruments for measuring height standing, height sitting, span of arms, breathing capacity, and "standard tints for colours of eyes," among other bodily characteristics and capacities.[31] The advertising copy explicitly linked the anamato-politics of the technologically registered body to the biopolitics of the nation: "The use of periodical measurements is two-fold, personal and statistical. The one shows the progress of the individual; the other, that of portions of the nation, or the nation as a whole."[32] By providing an archive comprised of a "more systematic registration of physical measurements" including "the influences of bodily development of different occupations, residences, schools, races, &c," the advertised anthropometric apparatuses promise to "afford a sufficiently wide basis for general inferences" regarding the "efficiency of the nation as a whole and in its several parts."[33] Rendering the body available to technology thus sustains the biopolitical project of suturing the body (the part) to the social body (the whole) through an archive composed of measurable bodies.

The organizing principle of Galton's method of bodily measurement was the racial type. Galton defined his notion of the type most directly in his book on fingerprints: "By type I understand an ideal form around which the actual forms are grouped, very closely in its immediate neighbourhood, and becoming more rare with increasing rapidity and at an increasing distance from it, just as is the case with shot marks to the right or lift of a line drawn vertically through a bull's eye of a target."[34] The type is thus a recurring feature that captures a general trend. As the analogy to the bull's eye suggests, the notion of the type also presupposes a field within which those trends appear—a target of application. Grouping individuals into types projects those individuals against a shared field.

This field tends toward expansion. Two figures were targeted most frequently in the crosshairs of typification: the street criminal and the savage. Although the savage thrives in distant lands and the street criminal threatens the proximate space of metropolitan public life, the type arranges the two figures contiguously. In an 1877 speech to the Department of Anthropology at the British Association for the Advancement of Science outlining the utility of composite photography, Galton made this link explicit: "The true state of the case appears to be that the criminal population receives steady accessions from classes who, without having strongly marked criminal natures, do nevertheless belong to a type of humanity that is exceedingly ill-suited to play a respectable part in our modern civilization, though they are well suited to flourish under half-savage conditions, being both naturally healthy and prolific."[35] The ideal type was useful not only for identifying criminals but for uncovering potentialities that could be neutralized in advance. The criminal type was thus a potential if not actual criminal. Galton's claim that such types were ill suited for modern civilization resonates with the theories of Kant, Burke, and Mill that I described in the first chapter of this book. The claim is also more specifically an expression of the theory of criminal atavism, the idea that certain bodies retained savage qualities even in advanced civilizations, and that these bodies out of place and time were prone to criminality. The idea is most commonly associated with Cesare Lombroso, but in Havelock Ellis's 1890 synthesis of the fledgling science of criminology, the argument that the "criminal resembles the savage and the prehistoric man" functions as a basic guiding assumption, explaining why criminals and lower races "present a far larger proportion of anatomical abnormalities than our ordinary European population" and why criminals "behave in a way that would be appropriate to savage societies."[36] Criminal atavism is an extension of the theory of savagery itself, outlined succinctly by Darwin in his 1872 *The Expression of the Emotions in Man and Animals*, which charted the surfacing of emotions on the body. As he traces the link between pouting and the protruding lower lip, Darwin noted the frequency of protruding lower lips in apes and lower races, and claimed, "the essence of savagery seems to consist in the retention of a primordial condition, and this occasionally holds good even with bodily peculiarities."[37] This claim offered a point of departure for Galton, Lombroso, and Ellis, and indeed for the theory of the type itself: not only was savagery a surviving anachronism, but this anachronism surfaced in bodily peculiarities. As these peculiarities surfaced, they could be archived in technological media. Such peculiarities—say, a protruding lip—thus formed patterns that could be archived, grouped, classified, and turned into types.

The type always relies on a technology that renders the body available to a field composed of patterns grouped by "ideal forms," in Galton's phrasing. For a body to be typical it must be measured and projected against a field that includes other measurable bodies. The body thus becomes a product of technology and of the typifying practices that technology promotes. Racism is a technology mediated by technologies; producing racial categories requires rendering the body available to technologies that can arrange the body in relation to ideal forms and then gradate those forms hierarchically. To render the body available to technology is to render it available to the measurement of the type.

One such technological practice useful for measuring and tracking bodies in urban and colonial environments was fingerprinting, a practice Galton did not invent but was the first to systematize in print. While acknowledging that fingerprinting was useful for proof of identity while traveling and proof of death for securing life insurance payouts, Galton argued that in "civilised lands in peaceable times, the chief use of a sure means of identification" such as fingerprinting "is to benefit society by detecting rogues," and indeed Galton recommends fingerprinting as a supplement to Alphonse Bertillon's system of street criminal detection.[38] This tool for street criminal detection in civilized lands was developed abroad in the colonies. Fingerprinting was pioneered by Sir William Herschel, magistrate of Hooghly in Bengal, who observed illiterate Bengalis using fingerprints to sign documents and who adapted the process into a method of tracking the colonial subjects under his supervision. As Galton explained, "In India and in many of our colonies the absence of satisfactory means for identifying persons of other races is seriously felt. The natives are mostly unable to sign; their features are not readily distinguishable by Europeans; and in too many cases they are characterised by a strange amount of litigiousness, wiliness, and unveracity."[39] Unable to distinguish the features of the "natives," the Europeans sought to render their bodies available to technology and thus to racial gradations sorted into typical zones of frequency.

Although Galton was ultimately disappointed in his efforts to gradate bodies by race according to fingerprints, it was not for lack of trying. He gathered prints from members of every race he could before finally admitting, "there is no *peculiar* pattern which characterises the persons of any of the above races."[40] Yet this failure to identify a "*peculiar* pattern"—to carve bodies into ideal forms—led Galton to lay bare the tight connection between technology, race, and the body:

The impressions from Negroes betray the general clumsiness of their fingers, but their patterns are not, so far as I could find, different from those of others, they are not simpler as judged either by their contours or by the number of origins, embranchments, islands, and enclosures contained in them. Still, whether it be from pure fancy on my part, or from some real peculiarity, the *general aspect of* the Negro print strikes me as characteristic. The width of the ridges seems more uniform, their intervals more regular, and their courses more parallel than with us. In short, they give an idea of greater simplicity, due to causes that I have not yet succeeded in submitting to the test of measurement.[41]

The "aspect" of the Negro's finger prints struck Galton as "characteristic," but he could not yet identify whether or not it was from "some real peculiarity" because he had not yet submitted the fingerprints to the proper test of measurement. In other words, he had not yet found a means of gauging the shared field that would render the fingerprints comparable and thus the bodies attached to the fingers typical. In seeking to turn the flesh that produced the fingerprints into a racial body, Galton practiced what Hortense Spillers has called "the hieroglyphics of the flesh," which concentrates "'ethnicity'" on the body by confirming the "the human body as a metonymic figure for an entire repertoire of human and social arrangements."[42] As Alexander Weheliye has argued, these "hieroglyphics of the flesh" throw the body "into the vortex of hierarchical indicators" that racialize bodies as "fully humans, not-quite-humans, and nonhumans."[43] Indeed, in his 1869 *Hereditary Genius*, Galton ranked the Negro type as two grades below the Anglo-Saxon type on his scale of civilizational achievement.[44] A century after Kant positioned "black Africans" in what Fanon calls the "zone of nonbeing," Galton similarly ranked the Negro type only above indigenous Americans and Australians and predicted that Negroes would be supplanted by a superior race.[45] What is most significant about the above quotation, then, is the way in which race emerges as the body becomes available to technology. Fingerprinting technology reveals clumsy fingers and simplicity of aspect. Galton lacks the gauge that would make the fingers measurable, but he does not lack the means to project the prints against a shared field, to convert the body into a "metonymic figure of an entire repertoire of human and social arrangements." To secure this conversion, to make it archivable and sortable, Galton required a standardized fingerprinting process—which Galton spent most of his book on fingerprinting describing—and a means of reproducing the prints so that they might be compared. Perhaps not surprisingly, for the latter task Galton recommended photography: "The occupation of finger printing would, however, fall more naturally into the hands of photographers," who possess the manual dexterity to take the prints and the technological means to reproduce them.[46]

Photographic technology promised the capacity to archive the characteristic peculiarities caught in fingerprints and reproduce them in a standardized format.[47] But photographic technology also gathered the savage and the criminal into the same field as every other photographic target—from the bourgeois *cartes-de-visite* collector to the Queen Mother herself, registering the body in a new archive that also offered a new link between part and whole.[48] Thus, as Mr. F—l and Jim discovered, even something as personal as a face becomes substitutable once captured in this technological archive. Faces on film, as Deleuze and Guattari argue, "are not basically individual; they define zones of frequency or probability."[49] Here Deleuze and Guattari describe without naming it the logic of the type, the recurring feature of a general trend that, once captured and categorized, can be charted alongside other general trends to produce a picture of the social field. In defining a zone of frequency—which Galton would call "ideal forms"—the filmed face produces a type. The typical face connects the body to a field. The landscape of this field, Deleuze and Guattari suggest, is composed of zones of frequency—patterned categories composed of recurring trends. Charting these zones allows for the anticipation of typical actions. As Béla Balász suggests in his theory of film, which inspired Deleuze and Guattari, film makes it possible to determine "which type of face is really representative of any nation or race."[50] This is why "a multitude of close-ups can show us the very instant in which the general is transformed into the particular."[51] As Deleuze and Guattari argue, "close-ups animate and invent all of [the face's] correlations."[52] Paradoxically, the close-up foregrounds not the individual but the contiguity of the face to other faces, the face to the body, the face to other bodies, and the face to the media field rendered in film. The close-up reproduces the logic of facial meaning itself, which functions not through metaphor—this face belongs to this individual, and therefore is a representation of this particular subject—but through metonymy—this face exists contiguously to those faces, and therefore is typical of this category. The face as metaphor would collapse the face onto the individual; the face as metonymy disperses bodies through their faces into types arranged in zones of frequency charted across a mediated field. The type projected in a mediated field is thus a technique of biopolitics: It tracks the trend rather than the individual, charting frequencies and probabilities rather than isolated actions.

The primary facial media for Deleuze and Guattari is film, but Galton developed a media theory of the face before motion pictures. His method of composite portraiture used photography to extract the typical face and attach it to a racial landscape.[53] Galton's process of composite portraiture consisted "in throwing faint images of a succession of accurately adjusted prints (or negatives) on the same part of a single sensitized plate, so that the resultant image is an aggregate of all its components, and a pictorial average of them."[54] In an 1885 trip to the Jews' Free School in East London, Galton took a series of composite portraits of Jewish boys and claimed to have successfully photographed the Jewish type with his composite method. In one extended description, Galton explained how he would take a plate that required, for example, sixty seconds of exposure time, and then divide that exposure time by the number of individual portraits out of which he wished to produce a composite. Then, he would mount each individual portrait, using the eyes to center them, and expose each portrait for the same increment of time. This process produced a composite photograph that "will exactly resemble none of its components, but it will have a sort of family likeness to all of them, and it will be an ideal and averaged portrait."[55] The portrait produced, in other words, would be a type: a zone of frequency in Deleuze and Guattari's phrasing, an "ideal form" in Galton's.

Galton's typology required a standardized field. This field would provide the basis for measuring, but in typology the measuring also produces the field. As Galton claimed in the abovementioned address on composite portraiture to the Department of Anthropology at the British Association for the Advancement of Science, "the very foundations of the differences between the mental qualities of man and man admit of being gauged by a scale of inches."[56] A gauge, such as a railway gauge or the gauge of a bullet, is a fixed standard of measurement. By providing a standard, the gauge (like Kant's telescope and microscope) gathers objects into a shared field of comparability, creating the shared field in which objects such as railway tracks crossing vast terrains or bullets shot at bull's eyes can be compared. But a body is more irregular than a bullet. Bodies must be rendered available to technology. Galton's composite photography thus takes advantage of "the great convenience of photographs in conveying those subtle but clearly visible peculiarities of outline which almost elude measurement."[57] In an 1881 article published in *The Photographic Journal*, Galton again referred to gauging, explaining that the use of composite photography "is to form a standard whence deviations towards any particular sub-type may be conveniently gauged."[58] Photography provides the standard format for gauging the body. This standard makes it possible to produce a scale: The body measured in a standard format enables the production of the ideal typical form—the gauge—that in turn provides a basis for compiling and comparing bodily irregularities and peculiarities. The type, then, both collates the individual body and composes the scale; it simultaneously captures the particular and creates the totality within which the particular is captured. The type is thus a mode of measuring that invents its own scale.

The type's mutual production of scale and gauge "projects a virtual whole" that combines bodies, makes them comparable, and as Novak argues, makes them abstract and interchangeable.[59] As Novak suggests, Victorians were keenly aware of the part photography had to play in this virtual projection. Building on the premise that Victorians recognized how "photography effaces rather than records identity," Novak rejects arguments aligning photography with the panoptic police state, concluding "it is unclear how [photography] serves the interest of state surveillance and control."[60] This argument assumes that social control inevitably involves fixing an identity to a body, as in Foucault's disciplinary apparatus.[61] It overlooks the ways in which the effacement of identity is in fact the principle of social control in biopolitics, which tracks not the individual body but the typical body. Where the former tracks the tendencies of the individual, the latter indicates a trend that appears at the level of the population. The technological rendering of the body as type links anatamo-politics to biopolitics. The scale inserts the body into the social body. At the intersection between anatamo- and biopolitics, where Galton works, the body is at once framed as a type and dissolved into parts, located in space and dispersed into a field of equivalence against which all bodies are measured. This mediated field provides the target of application for biopolitical management.

Deleuze and Guattari argue that "Racism operates by the determination of degrees of deviance in relation to the White-Man face."[62] To typify the surface manifestations of savage peculiarities—to measure the frequency of such peculiarities as clumsy fingers, protruding lips, or the Jewish physiognomy, as Galton attempted to do with his composite portraiture—is to measure the degree of deviance from the "White-Man face," but it is also to hold the savage and the "White-Man face" in the same field of vision. Even when Galton focused on producing types in order to identify the savage or the criminal, these types did not function to expel the savage or the criminal from civilization. Indeed, the atavistic theory of savagery and criminality entailed the persistence of both *within* what Galton refers to as "modern civilization." Race as a technique of biopolitics does not "other" so much as it gradates, sorting bodies into typical zones of frequency, collating peculiarities within a metonymic repertoire of hierarchical social statuses, all of them gathered into an expanding mediated field of equivalence. Through the technologically enabled type, racism functions on a principle of inclusion.

However, Galton shared his method of composite photography and fingerprinting with relatively limited audiences. Along with the other leading Darwinians of the Ethnological Society of London, Galton was a member of the "intellectual aristocracy," interested in the free exchange of ideas if not necessarily preoccupied with the democratic dissemination of them.[63] The severe limitations attending to the mass production of photographic images in the 1860s and 1870s, when Galton developed composite portraiture and fingerprinting, were therefore of no real concern to him. Faithful reproduction of photographs—enough to reach an audience of a few hundred learned men—was more important than mass-production for Galton. To be sure, his method resonated in public culture, but it was left to mass circulation periodicals like *Punch* to sketch the contours of the racial type in visual culture. In what follows, I argue that *Punch*, despite never using actual photography, developed a photographic vision of the street before photographic technology itself was adequate to its scale and speed. That *Punch* did so precisely by turning the scientific discourse of men like Galton into a target of satire and by setting that satire on London's streets makes *Punch* a particularly useful site to study the contiguity of the proximate street and the distant savage in the mediated field of photography.

"ANIMATED DAGUERREOTYPES": *PUNCH* AND THE PHOTOGRAPHIC IMAGINATION

In its early years, "*Punch* drew a portion of its initial strength, Antaeus-like, from the London pavements" before shaking "off the association with the street" and consolidating "its respectability in the drawing room" in later years.[64] These early years also coincide with the prolific contributions of Mayhew, who founded the periodical with Mark Lemon and came up with the name,[65] and with *Punch*'s interest in parodying scientific discourse on the body with its physiologies of London types.[66] The vision of the street refined in the parody and graphic art of the early years of *Punch* presents a photographic and filmic vision of the city and the bodies that populate it. As Robert Hariman has argued, parody places a discourse beside itself, putting the conventions of discourse on public display.[67] Parody does not seek to escape the discourse it targets; it enters more fully into it, intensifying its logic in order to subvert it. Kracauer located just such an intensifying potential in photography and film. As Miriam Hansen shows, Kracauer described modernity, like many of his contemporaries, using the image of a distorting hall of mirrors; but instead of seeking out aesthetic forms that would provide an exit from the distorting mirrors, Kracauer turned to popular media—especially photography and film—where he found an "iteration of that distortion" that, "as a kind of double negation, is closer to the truth than any attempt to transcend the state of affairs by traditional aesthetic means."[68] *Punch* reiterates the distortions of scientific discourse both by following the formal structures of that discourse to absurd conclusions and by locating that discourse on the street. *Punch*'s parody immerses itself in scientific discourse and the photographic field at one and the same time, using the street as the scene of intersection. Like Kracauer, *Punch* entered fully into the modern hall of mirrors, following the repercussions of technological change to their logical conclusions and beyond.

Punch functions as what Friedrich Kittler would call a historical a priori to photography, developing a photographic vision before it was technologically possible to circulate actual photographs on the scale of *Punch* and other illustrated periodicals.[69] The combination of image and text is now part of the basic grammar of mass media, but for the first half-century of photography such combinations were impossible. It is in periodicals such as *Punch*, therefore, where this grammar of mass visual culture was first developed. For example, in an 1857 article entitled "The Simple History of a Portrait," *Punch* played with the possibilities of the stereoscope, a device that displayed two different images, one in front of each eye.

When the observer looks at each image simultaneously, the two images combine into one apparently three-dimensional image.[70] Three images accompany "The Simple History of a Portrait," a portrait of "the husband," a portrait of "Old Mrs. Jones," and a third image combining the two (figure 1). This third image mixes the husband's beard with Mrs. Jones's bonnet and curls, adds the husband's coat to Mrs. Jones's dress, and supplements Mrs. Jones's eyes and nose with the husband's smile. Below this image, the caption reads, "This is how the young husband and Old Mrs. Jones would have looked, when, by the unitive effect of stereoscope, their two physiognomies were rolled into one."[71] This innocuous sight gag fully captures a moment in media history: it indexes the centrality of stereoscopy to photographic consumption; highlights the commonplace (and unrigorous) use of terms like physiognomy, which endows portraits of faces with characterological and racial significance; and forecasts what would become the basic grammar of mass visual and photographic media by combining image and text in a way that was technologically impossible with the photograph itself. Most importantly, by rolling two unlike faces into one likeness—which could exist only in the technology of the stereoscope—this sight gag also capitalizes on a photographic archive that projects bodies against a field composed of spatially contiguous parts that can be substituted and combined: a beard moves under a woman's curls, a coat covers a dress, eyes and nose migrate to a new mouth. This hand-drawn image, imagined as a photograph in *Punch*, can only exist under the conditions of a photographic archive. *Punch* imagines the repercussions of a photographic world in a format that remained unavailable to photography itself.

Photography's inadequacies were a recurring theme in *Punch*. In the 1847 article "Photographic Failures," one of its many brief articles mocking photography, *Punch* troped on the fading of daguerreotypes and talbotypes, playing on the dual nature of type as both imprint and recurring instance of a general trend. One of "the advantages or disadvantages, as the case may be, of many photographic portraits," the article began, "is that they fade away by degrees, and thus keep pace with those fleeting impressions or feelings" that accompany "the ordinary run of small affections" between flirting lovers.[72] A reproduced example of one such "portrait" of Mr. Punch follows (figure 2), showing "the state of the portrait through a period of an entire fortnight." Kracauer argues that "it is not the person who appears in the photograph, but the sum of what can be deducted from him or her."[73] As the individuality of Mr. Punch disappears from left to right in this image, "the sum of what can be deducted" from him emerges, and Mr. Punch becomes not an individual but a type. Galton's description of how the type emerges in his composite portraits could double as a description of Mr. Punch's final, most faded image: "Those of its outlines are sharpest and darkest that are common to the largest number of the components; the purely individual peculiarities leave little or no visible trace."[74] In the composite—as in Mr. Punch's fading portrait—what remain

THE HUSBAND.   OLD MRS. JONES.

This is how the young husband and old MRS. JONES would have looked, when, by
the unitive effect of the stereoscope, their two physiognomies were rolled into one :

FIGURE 1. "The Simple History of a Portrait," *Punch, or the London Charivari*, vol. 33,
Punch Publications Ltd: London, 1857, 224. ©British Library Board. All Rights
Reserved / Bridgeman Images.

FIGURE 2. "Photographic Failures," *Punch, or the London Charivari*, vol. 12, Punch Publications Ltd: London,1847, 42. ©British Library Board. All Rights Reserved / Bridgeman Images.

visible are the recurring outlines rather than the individual features. Of course, *Punch* offers a faded portrait of one figure, not a composite of many, but the article does suggest that what appears in the final image is not an individual but an average type. The "pathetic ballad" appended below the image—written from the perspective of the former lover gazing upon Mr. Punch's disappearing visage—tracks this movement from individual to type. The balladeer laments, "Thy hair, thy whiskers, and thine eyes, / Moustachios, manly brow, / Have vanished as affection flies— / Alas! –where is it now?" But then realization sets in as the photograph fades: "But, ah !—thy portrait of thy love, / Is but a type, no doubt, / And serves its fickleness to prove, / For soon 'tis all wiped out."[75] The disappearing portrait thus displays the fleetingness of love. It also shows how the fixity of the person gives way to the mobility of the type: as Mr. Punch's features fade, what begin to appear are the contours of a typical (and typically fleeting) partner in flirtation. Mr. Punch's disappearing individuated visage reveals the contours of his body newly recognizable as a type. The type is submitted to a general economy of emotion rather than an individuated attachment. This sequence of portraits stages the photographic process, which does not reveal Mr. Punch in the original but instead displays what Kracauer calls "the spatial configuration of a moment." He is "but a type, no doubt"—a typically fleeting lover, apprehensible only in his counters, which are in turn apprehensible only in the mediated field of contiguities. In the contours of the photograph, bodies tend toward types.

In typology, each part requires the whole. The type names not only recurring deductible parts but the whole within which those parts operate. The photographable body is both reduced to its parts and expanded to its relationships with all other bodies within an ever-expanding photographable field. This is why Galton could locate the distant savage and the proximate street criminal in the same field of vision: photography renders bodies contiguous against a mediated field. As the contours of the body faded into the spatial contiguities newly apprehensible in photography, assessing the relation between the body and its milieu required a vision that would connect the anatamo-politics of the human body to the biopolitics of the population. Attempts to fulfill this requirement were both tested and satirized in the 1840s in Paris, where a widely popular series of *Physiologies* were published, featuring contributions from Balzac and illustrations from Daumier that sought to typify Parisians.[76] Many of Daumier's illustrations later appeared in *Le Charivari*, from which *Punch* borrowed half of its name.[77] These physiologies divided humans into the types that structured society. Where scientific nomenclature was often applied to track the criminal and the colonized, *Punch*, in a typical maneuver, turned the physiological gaze onto London society, offering a series of physiologies of the London medical student, the London evening party, and the London idler. The physiologies of the London idler focused on such figures as the "Regent-street lounger," "the sole end of whose existence appears to be the accomplishment of a certain number of promenades about the West End thoroughfares, unrecognizing and unrecognized, with the idea that they hold their unheeded station in society by this diurnal labour."[78] As a type, the Regent-street lounger, though "unrecognizing and unrecognized," also attempts, "Antaeus-like," to draw his strength from the London pavements, pursuing social recognition in public space: "Can it be credited, that not a fortnight back we met one of these poor do-nothings on Regent-street, who, not content with the impression his general *contour* had made upon the world, had actually dyed his moustachios, and—we write in pity and disgust—*painted his cheeks!* Should this open page meet his eye, as he listlessly gazes in some shop window, he will not fail to recognise his likeness. Let us be permitted to recommend him immediately to wash his face at the first available accommodation" (emphasis in the original).[79] Though he acts in vain, the Regent-street lounger pursues social recognition by making use of what *Punch*, in an article entitled "Civilisation," calls "the philosophy of the present age," namely, "the philosophy of outsides."[80] *Punch* thus classifies the Regent-street lounger with the racializing optics of physiology. With this classification, *Punch* elaborates this philosophy of outsides in photographic and gendered terms: not satisfied with his "general *contour*"— the same contours that became increasingly visible as Mr. Punch's photographed portrait faded—the Regent-street lounger paints his cheeks, attempting to alter his outward image. By feminizing his own face (or undoing his own gender status), the Regent-street lounger warrants not only *Punch*'s incredulity—he *painted his cheeks!*— but converts himself into a commodity. If he were to gaze in a shop window, though, and see the printed page, "he will not fail to recognise his likeness." The Regent-street lounger thus recognizes himself as a type in the shop window.

As Mayhew's description of the prostitute on Petticoat Lane who makes use of the reflecting shop window to make covert eye contact with window-shopping customers shows, the shop window doubles as display and mirror. In an anticipation and modification of the Lacanian mirror stage, *Punch* suggests the Regent-street lounger will recognize his likeness not only in his reflection—where he might imagine himself as whole—but also in the displayed printed description of a type, which he sees through a window that also reflects his contours as *Punch* describes them: in relation to the contiguous space of the street where he makes his appearance. The idler, then, is ultimately a photographic figure who appears only in a relationship of contiguity to his street surroundings.

This dispersal of bodily contours into the spatial field of the street—a dispersal effected by photography—is the condition of typifying the idler. Put differently, there can be no types without a field through which the body is dispersed. The field is the condition of the type, but the type also conditions the field. In a scene of metonymic contiguities and juxtapositions, the type offers a tracking mechanism that both charts the field and locates bodies (or body parts) within it. In describing this dispersal and developing types to manage it, *Punch* anticipates the function of both instantaneous photography and moving pictures. The camera, Kittler argues, "liquidates the fund of stored self-images," replacing the archive of self-images with the archive of an expanding visual sensorium that includes the continuum of spatial contiguities captured in the photograph.[81] Among cameras, Kittler privileges the movie camera, arguing that cinema "transforms life into a form of trace detection."[82] The key figure in this trace detection is a species of the type: the film doppelgänger. Films in which characters encounter their doppelgängers, Kittler argues, reproduce the experience that all bodies undergo in a filmic media environment. Once the body is liquidated, once "films anatomize the imaginary picture of the body that endows humans . . . with a borrowed I," the dispersed body is made newly contiguous with other traces; film media extend the body over the spatial continuum, where resemblances are discovered in unexpected places.[83] This dispersal of the potential doppelgänger in a scene of mobility explains why in Mach's and Freud's surprise encounters with their doppelgängers, both encounters occur during high-speed travel—the one on the bus and the other on the train.[84] The body that moves through the mediated field is liquidated into traces, and any one body part might recombine in metonymic arrangements of contiguity with any other part.

Contrary to Kittler, though, it is not only the cinematic but also the photographic field that provides the condition for the doppelgänger. This is nowhere clearer than in *Punch*'s description of typical bodies who made their florid appearance on the street but whose actual residence—and associated class status—remained inscrutable.[85] The Gent, one of the subtypes of the London idler, received one of *Punch*'s most bitingly satirical physiologies. The Gent earns *Punch*'s ire as "the most unbearable" of "all the loungers who cross our way in public thorough-fares."[86] The clipped form of "gentleman" indicates the Gent's aspirations and shortcomings. Indeed, the Gent strives to the status of a gentleman's doppelgänger: His "futile apeing of superiority . . . inspires us with feelings of mingled contempt and amusement, when we contemplate his ridiculous pretensions to be considered 'the thing.'"[87] By "apeing" "the thing," the Gent poses the risk of the doppelgänger—the reproduction that threatens the boundaries of the thing itself. Indeed, the Gent's constant visual mimicry creates doubles upon doubles, all of which risk liquidating the stratification that supports the gentlemen's standing, turning stable symbols of status into metonymically substitutable signs. Here is *Punch*'s guide to locating the Gent: "We should say that the finest specimens of the Gent might be seen portrayed in the coloured 'Fashions' with which certain tailors adorn their windows. In these pictorial representations of presumed style, some favourite West-end locality is taken for the back ground, and in front are many Gents, in such attitudes as may display their figures and little boots to the best advantage."[88] The first double is the shop window, where the Gent is both on display and reflected in the visual scene of the reflected street. On display in the shop window, the Gent enters the world of commodities. As Luce Irigaray has argued, "*Commodities, women, are a mirror of value of and for man. . . .* In order to serve as such, they give up their bodies to men as the supporting material of specularization."[89] Like the Regent-street lounger, who recognizes himself as a type in the shop window, the Gent's ungendering (or feminized regendering) promotes his racialization as a type. But where the Regent-street lounger recognizes himself in the display, the Gent is in fact on display.

Not only is the Gent on display, but he is on display as a double: in *Punch*'s description, he is not "the thing" but an element in a pictorial representation. In the image included with the article, the pictured "Gent" stands on a pedestal in front of a tailor's mannequin, as if he had recently been pieced together out of available materials. Indeed, he looks like a cobbled-together imitation: His stare is wide-eyed, his mouth appears to be painted on (another echo of the *painted cheeks!* of the Regent-street lounger), and his fingers are splayed open at his sides as if he were a doll (figure 3). These details imitate clumsy drawing, just as the Gent clum-sily imitates the gentleman. And in this case, "the thing" the image represents—the Gent—is itself an image of the true gentleman. The shop window thus displays and reflects an image of an image. This doubled image stands out against "some favour-ite West-end locality" which "is taken for the background." Thus the image of the Gent—the image of an image—appears in an imaginary spatial continuum, a field of dispersed contiguities, where bodies can display their figures and fashionable boots. Gazing into the shop window, the spectator would see both the reflected street outside the shop and the pictorial representation of a street displayed in the

FIGURE 3. "Physiology of the London
Idler: Chapter VI—Concerning the Gent,"
Punch, or the London Charivari, vol. 3,
Punch Publications Ltd: London, 1842, 60.
©British Library Board. All Rights
Reserved / Bridgeman Images.

shop window. Thus the scene doubles once again, as the "favourite West-end locality" in the pictorial representation of the Gent also appears in the shop window as
display and as part of the mirror image of the street available to the spectator.
Doubles upon doubles, all of them liquidating the borders of "the thing," turning
bodies into a series of contiguous parts and the street into a field composed of
metonymic recombination. The modern "hall of mirrors" thus appears in the form
of shop windows, where bodies on streets are reflected, refracted, and ultimately
recaptured only as types.

But the doubling does not end there. *Punch* catalogs the Gents that might
appear in the pictorial representation, some "arrayed for an evening party,"
some "represented as sportsmen," and some who "are promenade Gents in

frock-coats and corded trousers, bowing to one another with much grace, or leading little Gents by the hand, who look like animated Daguerreotypes of themselves."[90] *Punch* thus animated the doppelgänger a half-century before it was technologically possible. Or perhaps *Punch* recognized in the street the historical a priori of the film doppelgänger and indeed of motion pictures, which *Punch* imagined as animated daguerreotypes. Consider the three portraits of Mr. Punch (figure 2), which fade from left to right. Transferred to celluloid, spooled, and projected, the images would animate Mr. Punch fading from individual to type, the details dissolving into contours. Similarly, typifying the Gent forces *Punch* to imagine animation, comparing Gents to moving daguerreotyped doppelgängers. Kittler claims that "film doppelgängers film filming itself. They demonstrate what happens to people who are in the line of fire of technological media."[91] *Punch* sketched the repercussions of this claim in a media environment dominated by the daguerreotype. Indeed, people were in the line of fire of technological media well before film: the Gent was one of many figures liquidating "the thing" by doubling it in image form. Bodies were becoming "animated Daguerreotypes" in scenes of pictorial representation; individuated bodies were already fading into types. Their spatial milieus were already dispersing into continua of contiguities, extending into fields of endlessly recombining parts. The type provided a framework for capturing and comparing bodies in this field, but also for charting the contours of the field itself. The body that appears in this field thus inevitably appears as a type located on the racial gradation that scores the field.

Photography liquidates the fund of self-images, dispersing the self into a field supported by a media archive. *Punch*'s physiologies reveal that the cost of the new typology is the fund of self-images that sustain the independent I. The innovation of satirizing physiology as a mode of inquiry is to show that it was not only the savage or the street criminal who invited the scientific gaze and whose bodies appeared through race. The London Gents, evening parties, and medical students moved in the same field of contiguities, producing their own zones of frequency that made them traceable as types. These physiologies asked *Punch*'s readers, along with the Regent-street loungers, to discover their likenesses among the mobile images on the street and in the shop window. As media technology archives the type, the street becomes a scene of the self's diffusion. As Sekula argues, photography founds "a shadow archive that encompasses the entire social terrain while positioning individuals within that terrain."[92] This new archive inaugurates what Kracauer calls the "go-for-broke game of the historical process," in which the relation of body to its spatial scene and to technological mediation is radically open to reinscription.[93] The type tracks the body in this radically open field, assuming a dispersed rather than a definable body, a body composed of substitutable parts rather than an isolable individual. I turn now to the changing counters of street-level encounters with these moving, substitutable body parts in the work of Mayhew's *London Labour* and Thomson and Smith's *Street Life in London*.

"TRUE TYPES": RAMO SAMEE AND THE
PHOTOGRAPHIC ARCHIVE

The four volumes of *London Labour and the London Poor* contain seventy-two images, almost all of them of "fair types" of various members of the London poor Mayhew interviewed. Although some of the images are engravings of sketches, most of the images are engravings from daguerreotypes. Although these images are generally set in the street, they were all taken in the photographer Richard Beard's studio, where the subjects were asked to assume characteristic poses (and perhaps don purportedly characteristic clothing) and hold the poses for as long as a few minutes.[94] The engravings from daguerreotypes also include various embellishments. The image the "the Mud-lark," features a teenage boy with rolled-up trousers posing as if he were wading into the Thames in search of scrap metals and textiles (figure 4). The *Punch* illustrator Archibald S. Henning sketched in the Thames itself and the background streetscape. The origins of these images in Beard's studio and the inclusion of sketching has led some to argue that these images would have seemed less alive to audiences.[95] However, at the time of publication the technology to capture street scenes on film was unavailable, so audiences would not have had a livelier media form with which to compare. More importantly, as I have demonstrated in my analysis of *Punch*, the photographic archive began to include the street even before it was technologically possible to do so. Indeed, the use of staged photographs—and in particular of portraits—was precisely the method of obtaining a view of the street. Galton, too, required posed portraits for his composite photographs, which in turn functioned as ideal figures against which to gauge mobile bodies. Typology thus combined street criminals and savage colonial subjects in one mediated archive that offered the key to managing the mobility of embodied encounters.

This combined focus of typology on street criminals and savage colonies is reflected in the career of John Thomson, a photographer who established his reputation by traveling through Thailand, Laos, Cambodia, and China, using the wet-plate collodion process to acquire photographs of landscapes and racial types (a remarkable feat, given the complexities of the wet-plate collodion process in the best of conditions, let alone while traveling). Throughout his travels, "the focus on 'the street' became more and more important."[96] He collected his photographs in a series of books, the most famous of which, the 1874 *Illustrations of China and Its People*, established the pattern Thomson, with his co-author, the journalist Adolphe Smith, would follow in the 1877 *Street Life in London: With Permanent Photographic Illustrations*. In the former text, Thomson included photographs of

THE MUD-LARK.

[From a Photograph.]

FIGURE 4. "The Mud-Lark" from Henry Mayhew, *London Labour and the London Poor: A Cyclopaedia of the Condition and Earnings of Those That Will Work, Those That Cannot Work, and Those That Will Not Work*(London: Charles Griffin and Company, 1864), 505. ©British Library Board. All Rights Reserved / Bridgeman Images.

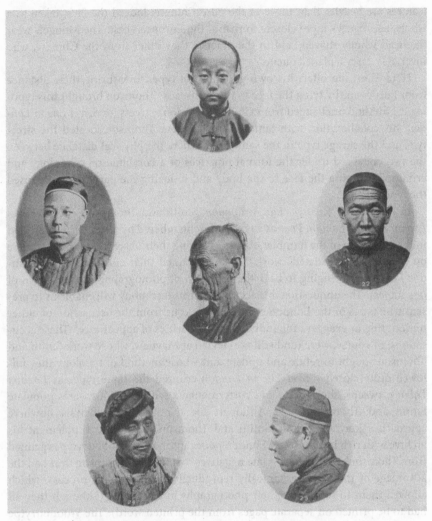

FIGURE 5. "Male Heads, Chinese and Mongolian," from John Thomson, *Illustrations of China and Its People*(London: Sampson Low, Marston, Low, and Searle, 1873), plate IX. Provided by Beinecke Rare Book and Manuscript Library, Yale University.

Chinese landscapes and portraits of Chinese types. Although the frame of these portraits excises the landscapes that other photographs in the book capture, Thomson sought to connect the photographed faces to their landscape, and, through this connection, to establish a racial index to organize the archive he rendered. Describing the photograph entitled "Male Heads, Chinese and Mongolian" (figure 5), Thomson writes: "This type belongs to the north of the empire, and the features are heavier than those of the pure Chinese; indeed the face, taken as a whole, approaches more closely to that of the European cast. The Mongols wear the head wholly shaven, and in the practice they differ from the Chinese, who invariably carry a plaited queue."[97]

Here Thomson offers his own gradation of types, measuring their distance from Europeans by tying the face to the landscape. Thomson brought this typological method unchanged from China to London's streets for *Street Life in London*, his collaboration with Smith. Like Mayhew, Thomson located the street type and the savage type in the same field, where the physical distance between the two collapsed under the formal practices of a combination ethnology and criminology, tying the face to the body and indexing the parts that composed the type.

In the preface to *Street Life in London*, Smith and Thompson cited *London Labour and the London Poor* as a text "still remembered by all who are interested in the condition of the humbler classes," offering their observations as an update on Mayhew's "ante-dated" work.[98] They explained their effort to portray London's poor by "bringing to bear the precision of photography in illustration of our subject. The unquestionable accuracy of this testimony will enable us to present true types of the London poor and shield us from the accusation of either underrating or exaggerating individual peculiarities of appearance." These accusations, of course, were (and still are) levied at Mayhew, whose work Smith and Thomson sought to refine and update, but whose method of typology they followed quite closely. *Street Life in London* covered the same types as *London Labour*: sweeps, shoeblacks, and costermongers selling various wares populate Smith and Thomson's text. Although the depth of the analysis nowhere approaches Mayhew's work, Smith and Thomson did indeed supplement his archive with rich images of the London poor captured in Woodburytypes printed from Thomson's original dry-plate negatives.[99] Smith and Thomson thus had the advantage of the first mechanically reproducible photographic process, which allowed them to reproduce their photographs in rich detail (although they all had to be printed on separate pages from the printed word). The Woodburytype process also allowed the publisher, Sampson Low and Co., to reproduce the photographs in three editions of *Street Life*—one serialized, one single-volume, and one abridged version entitled *Street Incidents*.[100] But, as we have seen, the photograph itself did not exhaust the photographic archive: photography also circulated in engravings, which continued to reach a wider audience than images reproduced with the Woodburytype process, even as the latter process considerably expedited previous processes of photographic reproduction. Thus Smith and Thomson's implication that they improved Mayhew by bringing to bear the precision of photography overlooked the fact that Mayhew was already operating with a photographic archive. This explains why Smith and Thomson replicate Mayhew's method: Mayhew had already established that the search for "true types" presupposed a mediated field of contiguous bodies dispersed into substitutable parts.

Where Beard attempted to hold these parts in place in the studio, the advantage of two decades of decreasing exposure times allowed Thomson to do so on the street. Yet even the "'fast' lenses" Thomson used required a few seconds' exposure time. It would have been difficult for a photographer "with a tripod-based camera, plate boxes, and other equipment" to capture photographs without his subjects being aware of his presence, leading commentators to suggest Thomson must have staged even his street photographs.[101] However, Lynda Nead has argued, there is a stillness to the modern street that narratives of modern mobility too often skip over.[102] The languid walker, the loiterer, and indeed the Regent-street lounger both circulate and stand still, often for long enough that a three-second exposure time could still capture them in action. Thomson did not need to ask all his subjects to pose. "The Old Clothes of St. Giles," for example, shows two women standing and talking in front of a stand of hanging clothes (figure 6). One woman rests her hand on a large pouch attached to her waist while her conversation partner returns her gaze, arms akimbo. Neither woman appears to notice the camera. At the feet of the woman with the pouch stands a small boy whose face is turned toward the camera, but whose features are blurred, as if he noticed the camera in his peripheral vision and turned his head to look directly at it during the crucial conclusion of the exposure. This photograph also has rounded edges, which means it was trimmed, suggesting something else in the frame of the original photograph did not turn out well, most likely because it was also moving.[103] Perhaps Thomson saw the two women, recognized that they had a resting place for their hands and so were unlikely to make sudden movements, and sought to capture a furtive photograph, anticipating the actions of owners of the handheld, or "detective," cameras a decade later.

This stillness of the streets appears again in a photograph entitled "A Convict's Home" (figure 7), which shows a house in Drury Lane that served meals to "hungry convicts or ticket-of-leave men," or parolees.[104] Once again, the window refracts the space of the street encounter, as Thomson positioned himself in front of the window of the convict's home, which advertises "Leg of Beef Soup" for 2d (or two pennies). His camera is angled slightly toward the street in front of him, which continues to the right side of the image and out of the frame. On the left of the image, closer to Thomson, a woman stands in the doorway of the convict's home with her hands on her apron, peering beyond the elbow of a man who stands in front of her, just outside the doorway, one arm on the door frame and the other on his hip, next to a begrimed apron. Between the man in the doorway and the

FIGURE 6. Image of "The Old Clothes of St. Giles," provided by LSE Library, available under CC BY-NC-SA 3.0 athttps://digital.library.lse.ac.uk/objects/lse:gos508mem.

FIGURE 7. Image of "A Convict's Home" provided by LSE Library, available under CC
BY-NC-SA 3.0 at https://digital.library.lse.ac.uk/objects/lse:kej215vep.

man gazing in the window stands an elderly man on the pavement, his gaunt
hands grasping a white cloth held tight to his buttoned-up coat. The man's large
white mustache is just visible on his face, and his head is covered with a scarf atop
of which sits a taqiyah. It seems that the man in the doorway and the elderly man
have been speaking. The photograph's accompanying description explains that the
man in the doorway is Mr. Baylis, who works behind the counter. The elderly man
is not one of the convicts—after all, "the publication of their portraits might have
interfered with their chances of getting employment"—but "Ramo Sammy": "This
characteristic old man, familiar to all Londoners as the tam-tam man, lives nearly
opposite the cook-shop, and often has his meals there. But the old Indian is getting
weak; he does not strike his drum with his wonted energy; and it is to be hoped
that Mr. Baylis, who is officiating behind the counter, will find a tit-bit for him
from time to time, so as to revive his energy."[105] Unlike most of the "characteristic"
street laborers Smith and Thomson described, the authors mentioned Ramo Sammy's name, perhaps because Indians were rare enough in London to warrant individual attention, or perhaps because, as Smith and Thomson suggested, Sammy

was widely known to Londoners. Mayhew, too, named some of the Indians he met on the streets, including Johnny Sepoy, the beggar,[106] and Usef Asman, who, like Ramo Sammy, also played the tom-tom. According to Mayhew, "East Indians playing on the tom-tom have occasionally made their appearance in London's streets."[107] Asman was not, in fact, an East Indian—as he informed Mayhew, he was from Mocha, a port in modern-day Yemen then under Ottoman control.[108] Nevertheless, Mayhew viewed Asman as a typical "East Indian." Asman's and Sammy's shared occupation was peculiar to bodies who appeared as "Indians" in London and thus was typical of them.

But Asman, the tom-tom player Mayhew encountered, also offered his services to painters wishing to paint "true types." As Asman explains, he and his father used to sit before "artists or modelers, to have our likenesses taken. We went to Mr. Armitage, when he was painting a battle in India. If you recollect, I'm leaning down by the rocks, while the others are escaping."[109] Indeed, Edward Armitage did complete a painting of a crowded battle scene in 1843 entitled "The Battle of Meeannee," commemorating the Battle of Miani, which began when British forces attempted to expand into Sindh, in modern-day Pakistan. Thus, even as an individual who aroused the attention of Mayhew, who thought him "as gracefully proportioned, as a bronze image," Asman was nevertheless a type: A tom-tom player and a sitter for artists in need of characteristic Indians.[110] Yet Asman capitalized on his status as type: He recognized that his body appeared against a mediated field, where the typical category within which he fell located him next to an Indian dying on a battlefield, even if he was a Londoner from Mocha.

Thus the "characteristic old man," Ramo Sammy, whom Smith and Thomson described as familiar to all of London, was familiar not as an individual but in his typical status as a street performer and tom-tom player.[111] Indeed, even the name "Ramo Sammy" was less individual than a reader of Smith and Thomson's text alone might think: Mayhew also encountered a version of "Ramo Samee" on the streets of London. Yet this "Ramo Samee" was a juggler and street magician, not a tom-tom player, and was in fact not actually "Ramo Samee" but an English imitator of the "real" Ramo Samee, the famous Indian juggler. As "proof of his talents," this juggler explained to Mayhew "that when Ramo Samee came out," he "not only learned how to do all the Indian's tricks, but also did them so dexterously," that when the two performers took their show on the road, "Samee has often paid him ten shillings not to perform in the same town with him."[112] Ramo Samee, then, was a real historical figure, a magician and juggler from India who inspired imitations, English "Ramo Samees" who mimicked his movements.

It would be fascinating indeed if the Samee Mayhew referred to made his way into the pages of Thomson and Smith, but the "real" Ramo Samee could not be the same Ramo Sammy whom Smith and Thomson photographed for the simple fact that the former died in 1850. The Samee Mayhew mentioned was famous enough that *Bell's Life in London* published an appeal from his widow on August 25, 1850. The widow explained that she had "taken the liberty of conveying to you the first intelligence of the death of my husband, the celebrated Indian juggler, Ramo Samee, with the hope that you will kindly notice it in your widely circulated journal, for the sake of his family."[113] Samee fell ill, his widow explained, after his twenty-three-year-old son died following a sword-swallowing accident, leaving Samee's wife and two daughters in penury. "There are thousands who have witnessed his performances who would now, I am sure, kindly give a trifle to assist in procuring his coffin," the widow hoped.[114] And indeed it seems her hope was merited, as *Bell's Life in London* published a letter from a reader the following week encouraging others to submit a "trifle" to Mrs. Samee, and the editors appended a comment seconding this opinion.[115]

That *Bell's Life in London* published these letters shows that the original Ramo Samee (or at least the Ramo Samee who existed before someone of the same name walked into Thomson's shot) was famous enough that his sudden death and his widow's subsequent penury provoked public mourning that lasted for two issues of a popular weekly periodical in the largest city of the world. Indeed, Samee's stature was such that the English imitator Mayhew interviewed not only mimicked Samee's tricks but also his dress, explaining that he "had an Indian's dress made, with a long horse-hair tail down my back, and white bag-trousers, trimmed with red, like a Turk's, tied right round at the ankles, and a flesh-coloured skull-cap" (an imitation of the taqiyah, which Smith and Thomson's Ramo Sammy wears in his photograph).[116] Outfitted thusly, the juggler explains, "I called myself the Indian Juggler."[117] He was, in other words, a doppelgänger of the "real" Ramo Samee, so alike in dress and gesture that he stole the original's business along with his typical identity. The name for the individual Ramo Samee thus returns us to the logic of the type. Like the gentlemen, Samee spawned his own doppelgänger—the "Indian Juggler"—who borrowed his gesture and copied his dress, piecing together an "Indian costume" just as the Gent pieced together his costume from the tailor's mannequin. Thus when William Hazlitt published his 1821 essay on "The Indian Jugglers," or when William Makepeace Thackeray refers to "Ramo Samee, the Indian juggler" in his 1848 *The Book of Snobs*, they are as likely referring to the historical figure memorialized in *Bell's* as they are to the Indian as racial type.[118]

In the mediated field, individuals disperse into types—bodies are part models, part mannequins, and are partly pieced together from the model and the mannequin. Indeed, Asman, who played the tom-tom (just as Smith and Thomson's Sammy did), served as a model Indian for painters. The type gathers the street into a globalizing mediated field. In India, the Indian was unrecognizable to white men like Herschel, who rendered Indian bodies available to the archive through fingerprinting technology. In London, the Indian body is rendered available to the archive through photographic technology. In both cases, the type gauges the part's location within the whole field and gathers the mediated projection of the field into one vision. This vision attaches body parts to types through the face, assembling these parts somewhere along a racial continuum. The case of Samee and Sammy, the Mochan tom-tom player, and the Indian Juggler—the type, the model, and the mannequin—shows us that when the body appears as a type, it always appears somewhere at a distance on the racial continuum from the "White man's face."

CONCLUSION

In the late 1880s, advances in film technology radically reduced exposure time and the size of the film itself, allowing photographers to capture live street scenes where before popular interest in seeing street people and street laborers had to be satisfied by staged photographs. New, rapid-shutter, handheld cameras acquired the moniker of "detective camera." In his 1893 Hand Camera Manual, Walter D. Welford resisted the "detective camera" moniker, lamenting that "it implies a use of the instrument for purposes to which some of the public emphatically object, viz: —the securing of scenes or incidents, pleasant or otherwise (in their minds generally very much otherwise) which could not be obtained by other means."[119] Yet after extolling the hand camera's ability to produce "quickness of thought and rapid action," Welford found himself seduced by the clandestine contrivances the hand camera promoted: "There are many little wiles and tricks—in fact, the up-to-date hand camera man should be a deceiver of the deepest dye—such as lighting a pipe or cigar, buttoning a coat, taking off the hat to wipe the forehead, blowing the nose, looking into a shop window, &c. &c. Anything and everything in fact to cheat the public, to deceive them as to his purpose" of photographing of street scenes.[120]

In the 1890s, the freelance photographer Paul Martin began using the detective camera the Facile, adopting some of the tricks Welford recommended in order to secure photographs of street scenes populated by working-class types without his subjects' knowing. Inspired by lanternslides of statues in which all but the statue was blackened out, Martin began using India ink to blacken out everything in the photograph but the people and the ground they stood on, giving them the appearance of statues on a pedestal. Describing these working-class types surrounded in ambient blackness, Nead argues, "the search for a means of representing urban life had finally led Martin to a method of pictorial embalming rather than animation."[121] Similarly, Nancy Armstrong claims that this "effort to monumentalize" the working classes in fact "detached" them "from the symbolic economy in which they once had human purpose and labor value."[122] To be sure, Martin's types appear extracted from the street, and they thus become abstractions rather than individuals situated in a particular location. As I have argued here, though, animation implies abstraction. Under conditions of animation—imagined as early as the daguerreotype—bodies are dispersed into parts under the line of fire of technological media. Scattered across this mediated field, bodies can be recaptured only as types. To typify the body is to arrange the body along a racial gradation. It is also to establish a principle for tracing the contours of the body in an animated scene of mobility. Martin's statuesque types are, therefore, fully consonant with Galton's ideal types, *Punch*'s playful physiologies, Bertillon's indexical body parts, and Mayhew and Smith and Thomson's "characteristic" types: they reveal that abstraction is a necessary approach to the particularities that proliferate in the archive of the street. Under the conditions of a mediated field extending itself from the street to the savage world, the body cannot appear without race, and the street—the structuring principle of the urban network and the site most recalcitrant to the network's completion—is apprehensible only through the same technologies that make abstraction the condition of managing the particular.

Epilogue

Catachresis, Cliché, and the Legacy of Race

This book has traced a counter-history of race as a technology of gathering, assembling, and networking the modern city. I have argued that race offered a technological solution to a problem of local governance in nineteenth-century London. In a scene of overwhelming excess, race responded to a crisis in metonymy; as the relationship between part and whole broke down, race supplied resources for the canon of arrangement. Functioning as a technology rather than an ideology, race responded to the demand to gather the teeming particularities of street life and street culture into one manageable framework. Race as a technology gathers, sorts, and assembles particularities into manageable networks.

The genealogy of modern racism began with Mayhew's monumental, mid-nineteenth-century account of London's streets. Although Mayhew achieved some measure of fame during his *Morning Chronicle* reporting and *London Labour* publishing, his reputation eventually succumbed to his chronic cash-flow problems; he died with little money and less public notice. In this sense, Mayhew was a typical Grub Street hack—a character who would perhaps be at home in George Gissing's 1891 novel of literary London life, *New Grub Street*. Indeed, this novel offers a means of returning to the opening questions of this book: How does a moment of catachresis—a novel response to a scene of excess—harden into cliché? And how does this career from catachresis to cliché sustain a cyclical history of the city, such that race as a technology becomes sedimented and layered into modes of governance?

In *New Grub Street*, London streets act as reservoirs of time, as topical storehouses of historical presence. The novel begins in the fictional countryside town of Finden as the bells chime to mark 8:00 a.m., causing Jasper Milvain, enterprising

Grub Street journalist and "alarmingly modern young man" on holiday with his mother and sisters, to remark, "There's a man being hanged in London at this moment."[1] Noting the hanging simply reminds Jasper of the distance between his life and that of the condemned man, but, as the novel proceeds, we discover that many of his colleagues and comrades carving out an existence on Grub Street find themselves similarly condemned—not by the state, but by a cruelly competitive society—to a death slower than the hanged man's, but a death nonetheless. The failed novelist Edward Reardon succumbs to a fever exacerbated by poverty, Harold Biffen poisons himself after his visionary form of new hyperrealism—purged of Dickensian melodrama—is coolly ignored by the public, and Alfred Yule, relic of a bygone age of sober criticism struggling on the crass new Grub Street, falls victim to blinding cataracts that issue the decisive death sentence to his limping literary career. Henry Mayhew, victim of arcane lawsuits, constant cash-flow shortages, strained relationships with editors, and an even more strained relationship with a wealthy and influential father-in-law, would be at home among the promising failures populating New Grub Street.

Jasper Milvain, though, simply refuses to fail. Unlike Reardon, Biffen, Yule, or Mayhew, Jasper has no pretensions to aesthetic or intellectual achievement; he wants only to produce profitable literature, whatever will sell: "I am the literary man of 1882," Jasper proudly announces, displaying keen awareness of the relationship between the type and the historical situation I explored in chapter 2.[2] Where an artist working on "Sam Johnson's Grub Street" could consider artistic merit, "our Grub Street of to-day is quite a different place: it is supplied with telegraphic communication, it knows what literary fare is in demand in every part of the world, its inhabitants are men of business, however seedy."[3] The Grub Street of 1882 is networked to a global market, and Jasper means to meet that market's demands, whatever they may be. If, as I suggested in chapter 1, Mayhew approached London's position in a globalizing network through the category of the sublime, Jasper does so through the category of the banal: London, in 1882, was global, but one mustn't make a fuss about it—just keep calm and carry on writing profitably.

In New Grub Street, the London network runs from the city to the country and back. While holidaying in Finden, Jasper meets Alfred Yule's daughter and amanuensis-cum-ghostwriter, Marian, her close-cropped hair marking her as an avatar of the New Woman. During his daily holiday walk, Jasper happens upon Marian seated on a bench upon a hill overlooking the countryside and invites her to continue walking with him. When they come to a bridge over a line of the Great Western Railway, Jasper checks his watch and asks Marian if she wouldn't mind waiting to watch the London Express—due in five minutes—race by. She agrees, they pause briefly, and soon find themselves rewarded with "a blinding rush" as the train approaches with its "great volley of sunlit steam" only to disappear within seconds, leaving the "leafy branches" that grew over the line swaying "violently backwards and forwards in the perturbed air."[4] The sight and sound of the passing train signals the pull of the city even in the country. Jasper declares himself "eager to go back and plunge into the fight again," while Marian laments that the train has only reminded her of the endless drudgery of Grub Street.[5]

Even in the *New Grub Street* countryside, space is thoroughly linked to an urban network that communicates symbolically and materially: Express trains crosshatch the countryside; cabs, omnibuses, and the Metropolitan Rail (forerunner of the tube) cover transport for London; the post (delivered multiple times daily) keeps characters in communication; and telegrams deliver information instantaneously across vast distances. Indeed, when the failed novelist Edward Reardon, idling in his garret in Islington, receives a telegram from Brighton from his estranged wife informing him that their son has fallen gravely ill, he has only to catch a cab to London Bridge and then a train to Brighton before arriving at that seaside town that same evening. All in all, he is only in transit for about two hours—or about the same amount of time it would take today. The same globally linked communicative network that sustains a market uninterested in Reardon's psychological fiction supports his rapid movement between Islington and Brighton.

The key link in this network—as the novel's title suggests, and as I have argued in this book—is the street. It signals both an abstraction—a node in a global public sphere—and a material reality—a phenomenal scene of interaction. Unlike in a novel like Dickens's 1852 *Bleak House*, where streets "swarm with misery," the material street in *New Grub Street* is entirely functional, and street walking is entirely banal: Where Lady Dedlock of *Bleak House* only enters the street bodily, without carriage or escort, after donning a disguise—first as a servant and second as a brickmaker's wife—Marian of *New Grub Street*, a most respectable young woman, albeit not a Lady, walks the streets alone as part of her daily routine.[6] Indeed, Jasper and Marian's courtship occurs primarily in the street, as they walk together after leaving the British Museum Reading-Room, or as they depart together after visiting Jasper's sisters in London. In one such scene, the London fog strains their talk, "making their eyes water and getting into their throats. By when they reached Tottenham Court Road they were both thoroughly uncomfortable. The 'bus had to be waited for, and in the meantime they talked scrappily, coughily. In the vehicle things were little better, but here one could not converse with freedom."[7] Although the smoky pollution stymied conversation, the street itself did not. Indeed, the public space of the street freed them to talk; whenever they were on the street, they were, as Jasper repeatedly says to Marian, punning on the title of Reardon's one successful novel, "on neutral ground," free from Marian's disapproving father or the eavesdropping of omnibus passengers. Jasper and Marian make frequent use of this freedom during their courtship, with Jasper often accompanying Marian halfway to her destination before turning to his own. It is significant that Jasper never walks Marian all the way to wherever she is going, and that she never requests that he do so. Marian seems to have no need to perform the dressage of respectability Eliza Lynn Linton recommends in her 1862 article "Out Walking." Unlike the walkers I describe in chapter 3, she does not fear the glance of passersby or the chance association with the prostitute.

How to explain this difference in the street in the course of three decades, from the 1852 *Bleak House*, to the 1862 "Out Walking," to the *New Grub Street* scenes set in 1882? Of course, *Bleak House* was published in the same year that Mayhew lamented that "about 200 miles [of London sewers] are still, in the year 1852, *open sewers!*"[8] London was now a city where "the literary man of 1882"—and the literary woman who was more than his intellectual match—made their way upon streets charted by Mayhew, renovated by Bazalgette, and reshaped by Pennethorne. Between 1852 and 1882, the street had become a very different place.

Or had it? In *Bleak House*, when the impoverished street sweeper Jo, who "don't know nothink," eats his morning crust of bread, he pauses to do so on the front steps of the "Society for the Propagation of the Gospel in Foreign Parts," an ironic tableaux that gestures toward the common critique of imperialism abroad amid ignorance and suffering at home.[9] As I indicate in chapter 1, Mayhew articulated this critique in 1852 when he wrote that "the moral and religious state" of many street workers and street people "is a foul disgrace to us, laughing to scorn our zeal for the 'propagation of the gospel in *foreign* parts,' and making our many societies for the civilization of savages on the other side of the globe appear like a 'delusion, a mockery, and a snare,' when we have so many people sunk in the lowest depths of barbarism round about our very homes."[10] These issues do not seem to trouble Gissing in *New Grub Street*, but Jack London would use precisely the same critique as Mayhew a half-century later in the 1902 *The People of the Abyss*, which opens by comparing the streets of the East End to darkest Africa.[11] Before *The People of the Abyss*, the 1883 pamphlet *The Bitter Cry of Outcast London* describes streets where the sun rarely shines, the sewage routinely reeks, the refuse is often "flowing beneath your feet," and where "thousands are crowded together amid horrors which call to mind what we have heard of the middle passage of the slave ship."[12] In 1890, the Salvation Army "General" William Booth published his reform program in book form under the title *In Darkest England*, a direct echo of Henry Morton Stanley's *In Darkest Africa*.[13] Even the sober-minded social statistician Charles Booth, in his 1889 *Life and Labour of the People in London*, described his "Class A" as a "savage semi-criminal class of people" who "degrade whatever they touch."[14] Indeed, the street sweeper Jo would count as member of Booth's racially tinged Class A, which perhaps explains why, after Jo shows her the location of her dead lover's body on the "black, dilapidated street" named Tom-all-Alone's, Lady Dedlock pays him by dropping "a piece of money in his hand without touching it, and shuddering as their hands approach."[15] Like the purportedly objective statistician in 1889, Lady Dedlock recognized that Jo's touch was degrading.

Of course, Charles Booth would have bristled at comparison with Dickens. As he explained in the *Journal of the Royal Statistical Society*, "The material for sensational stories lies plentifully in every book of our notes; but even if I had the skill to use my material in this way—that gift of the imagination which is called 'realistic'—I should not wish to use it here."[16] Despite his wish to distance himself from realism, an imaginary endeavor he distinguishes from his empiricist efforts, Booth's justification of his project aligns neatly with Lukács's description of the realist novel. Where Booth claimed that "Without . . . general knowledge we cannot tell whether the example given is truly typical or in what respects it diverges from a true type,"[17] Lukács claimed that the goal of the novel was to arrive at that "peculiar synthesis which organically binds together the general and the particular" through the type.[18] The sober-minded statistician and the sensationalistic novelist both attempt to gather the particularities into a totality, an abstract field of shared interaction that relies on the racial logic of the type—which surfaces in Booth's Class A and the degrading touch of Jo—and which in turn allows the particular to be identified, measured, and collated within an archive—whether the synthetic world of *Bleak House* or Booth's street-by-street, statistically informed poverty map of London. Both the realist and the sociologist succumb to the paradox I describe in chapter 4: Abstraction is the condition of apprehending the particular. And both rely on the same racial technology to resolve the paradox: The racial type figures the body in a mediated field of contiguities, where bodily traces can be captured, measured according to a common gauge, and collated in a standardized format.

Indeed, Booth took the principle of standardized measurement to its logical conclusion, refusing to include anything in his inquiry that could not be measured and rendered as a statistic. Booth is now seen as the first to perfect the method of urban sociology that the Chicago School would later institutionalize. Mayhew, in contrast, is seen as a mere dilettante dabbler. To be sure, Mayhew's inquiry lacks the methodological rigor of Booth's, but Booth, by his own admission, lacks the imagination of Mayhew. This does not mean, as some have implied, that Mayhew was a mere sensationalist whose data are not to be trusted. As I have argued in this book, rather than dismissing Mayhew for his contradictions and inconsistencies—which a more rigorous and evenly applied methodology like Booth's would perhaps have eradicated—we should read Mayhew's mistakes as symptoms of his minor status. He was a figure hesitating between sensation and sociology, the periodical press account and the parliamentary inquiry, the realist novel and the empirical report. These discursive hesitations issue from the materiality of the street itself. Recall Mayhew's encounter with the costermongers and crossing sweeps on the fish-spine side-bone street that I relate in chapter 1. There he discovered a complex scene of social interaction and described the scene with enough detail to pass muster for a rigorous ethnographic account and a realist novel alike.

But he also discovered the circulation of sensation—the affective charge that could summon an unruly crowd—and shifted in only a few columns of prose from detailed description to the sensationalism that his reading public demanded. If Jasper Milvain was the literary man of 1882, Mayhew was the literary man of 1852, attempting to grapple with a rapidly changing metropolitan scene, to invent a catachretic form capable of gathering its particularities into a manageable totality, all the while remaining subject to the demands attendant to finding remuneration on Grub Street.

But Mayhew's text also shows how 1852 survives in 1882 and beyond. His account contains the seeds of Booth's rigorous inquiry alongside the sensationalistic account of the savage street world that would survive as a cliché for another half-century. Indeed, even Booth failed to purge the figure of the savage from his account of the street. He claimed the savage Class A was "hereditary to a considerable extent."[19] The class "kept strictly apart . . . from civilisation," marking them as "the true outcasts, a term which evoked the untouchables of the Pearl of the Empire."[20] Class A, in Booth's account, issued from the street itself: Class A was composed of "the battered figures who slouch through the streets," the excess that resisted the regular London labor market.[21] The members of Booth's Class A—the wandering tribes of street people—were the subject of Mayhew's entire enquiry. The inflection of class categories into racial ones—or the extent to which race is classed—is a familiar topic. As I have argued in this book, though, it is important to consider as well how class is often raced. Just as Mayhew's class-based *Morning Chronicle* categories turned racial when he turned to the street, so Booth's street class—Class A—was overlaid with racial description. As I have argued in this book, race functions as a technology for gathering forms of excess into an expanding field of the totality.

Indeed, the particularities appearing on the street seem to be in a constant state of expansion, as new technologies, new commodities, and new bodies make their entry into the city. It is sometimes argued that women were rarely on the streets in the mid-nineteenth century. Yet accounts of the rise of the Victorian New Woman in the late nineteenth century—embodied in *New Grub Street* by Marian Yule— ought not occasion a forgetting of the Victorian street woman. The angel of the household may have been a middle-class ideal, but women still moved through and worked upon public streets. Mayhew refers to women and girls working on the streets as fruit sellers, cats-meat gatherers, pure finders, and sundry other occupations. Although such mentions far outnumber his reference to prostitutes in London, prostitution was nevertheless the specter haunting women who wished to walk the streets, as Deborah Nord has made clear.[22] In Volume 4 of *London Labour*, Mayhew and Bracebridge Hemyng undertook a voluminous survey of the status of prostitution in civilizations and tribes around the world. The survey takes the form of a synthesis of other writings. Methodologically, it is utterly out of place with the writings on London's streets that comprise volumes 1–3, but it is prompted by the same impulse to situate London's streets in a global imaginary: As a type, the prostitute was seen as a link to savage habits and customs, thus occasioning Hemyng and Mayhew's global prostitution review, which ultimately answers to a local London problem. As Linton's "Out Walking" suggests, to walk the streets was—at least in some cases—to risk being mistaken for a prostitute. Women, then, were everywhere on the nineteenth-century streets, but they made their appearance in conditions mediated by racial technologies. For Lady Dedlock to appear in Tom-all-Alone's, she had to costume herself in the garb of a worker, just as Jack London donned secondhand clothes to blend into the East End. As I have argued in this book, to appear in the position of a street person is to face the totality in the garb of excess, and thus to be subject to the racial technologies that assemble the social into a manageable totality. The street is the scene of this excess and the basic structure of the urban totality, the communicative network sustaining city life. Within this immanent scene of circulating affects, racial technologies recalibrate the categories sustaining the manageable totality. Race thus recalibrates class along with gender.

The racial inflection of class and gender categories is not static. Instead, race is a persistently deployed yet remarkably plastic response to changing conditions, a technology for assembling the expanding scene of particularities into an equally expanding totality. Assembling this totality requires that the imagination Booth derided accompany the empirical investigation he developed. We can see these two tendencies merging in the novel I briefly analyze in chapter 3, Israel Zangwill's *Children of the Ghetto: A Study of a Peculiar People*, the first novel of the immigrant East End written from the position of the immigrant insider rather than the outside investigator. Yet even this insider position is vexed: Zangwill describes the novel in sociological and ethnological terms, as "a study, through typical figures, of a race whose persistence is the most remarkable fact in the history of the world."[23] The language echoes Booth's description of his project and Lukács's definition of the novel. Zangwill's opening description of his novel also indicates a subject that would not be out of place at a meeting of the Royal Anthropological Institute, where Francis Galton elaborated the method of composite photography I describe in chapter 4, or where Joseph Jacobs, using Galton's composite photographs of young pupils at an East End Jewish boys school as evidence, sought to distinguish between the primary and secondary racial qualities of the Jewish type.[24] Indeed, Zangwill's theme is, as he suggests, the location of the racial type within an expanding totality in the street scenes of late-nineteenth-century Petticoat Lane, the market street in the heart of an increasingly immigrant East End.

Zangwill captures these tensions between type and totality in the character of Esther Ansell, an individual straining against her position as type. Like Ramo

Samee, who makes his appearance in text and Woodburytype photograph in chapter 4, her name is not her own; it belongs both to the ghetto and to the abstract visions that reshape ghetto streets, including Pennethorne's slum- and market-clearing Commercial Street—an ironic name from the perspective of the street sellers it was meant to clear out. Near the end of the novel, Esther returns to the ghetto after living for years as an adopted member of a wealthy West End Jewish family—a form of exile from her original exile. Back in the neighborhood around Petticoat Lane, she observes Yom Kippur at her childhood synagogue. Upon leaving the service, Esther is returned bodily to the street: "The crowd bore Esther downstairs and into the blank indifferent street. But the long exhausting fast, the fetid atmosphere, the strain upon her emotions, had overtaxed her beyond endurance. Up to now the frenzy of the service had sustained her, but as she stepped across the threshold on to the pavement she staggered and fell."[25] This scene echoes the opening scene of the novel, when Esther trips as she runs up the stairs of her family's garret and spills the soup in the family pitcher that "an individualistic instinct of cleanliness" made her prefer over the tin cans supplied by the charitable "Institution in Fashion Street" that distributed dinners to the needy who gathered in a "jostling crowd" outside its doors.[26] With her first trip, she breaks the pitcher and spills the precious dinner, her individualistic instinct punished. With her second trip, her individualistic instinct is again thwarted, but this time the thwarting comes through her self-selected return to Petticoat Lane, the peculiar home to a peculiar people. She rejoins the crowd as a type rather than an individual and submits herself again to the streets and pavements that sustain ghetto life. She loses her individuality within the excess of the streets, where she becomes again a "human paradox," a type whose inclusion into the totality at once expands the totality's reach and threatens its boundaries. Zangwill thus probes the same problem of the type and its location within the totality that troubled Mayhew.

Mayhew's text thus exists in a genealogy of street discourse gathered in an expanding street archive; the expansion of this archive opens new channels for further expansion. Indeed, projects like *London Labour and the London Poor* established an archive that made novels like *New Grub Street* and *The Children of the Ghetto* possible. Like waste through Bazalgette's sewers, discourse flows through established channels, but the channels also respond to the flows. In Mayhew's text we can discover a transition from the sensationalistic account of the street as excess to the account of the street as the scene of social life—the same transition that surfaces from Dickens to Zangwill and Gissing. Yet if Mayhew's innovations augur change, his hesitations forecast the return of what was repressed. This is why the sensationalistic *The People of the Abyss* can still follow Zangwill's *Study of a Peculiar People*. It is also why Mayhew contradicts his own careful account of the fish-spine side-bone street with a sensationalistic description of a gathering crowd in the space of only a few columns. In a minor text like Mayhew's, we can find future modalities of street investigation anticipated alongside contemporary clichés.

These anticipatory moments surface in Mayhew's attempts to account for the everyday life of the streets through close description. Although the sensationalism that follows Mayhew's opening description of the side-bone street draws on a set of clichés that preceded Mayhew and survived long after him, the first few columns describing the social life of the slum street anticipates by a half-century "A Street," the opening chapter of Arthur Morrison's 1894 *Mean Streets*, in which Morrison describes the surprising banality of the East End street. In Morrison's account, we find careful description of a street sustaining a complex social organization. Just as Mayhew emphasized to his readers (through the voice of two young street sweepers) that the street he entered was "very civil," so Morrison cautions against contemporary misconceptions of the East End, writing, "Many and misty are people's notions of the East End; and each is commonly but the distorted shadow of a minor feature. Foul slums there are in the East End, of course, as there are in the West. . . . But they are not often spectacular in kind."[27] Morrison proceeds to describe the life of this anonymous street in a fashion that anticipates, in its own way, Jane Jacobs's canonical account of the "street ballet" performed daily on Hudson Street in Manhattan.[28] Morrison describes a baker's, a chandler's, and a beer-shop; workers who commute to the gasworks and the docks; young lodgers and families; night-watchmen and police officers—in short, all of the components of mixed-use, mixed-income urban living that Jacobs would celebrate as a model of urban planning a half-century later. Jacobs's description of city life—in all its echoes of Mayhew on the side-bone street and Morrison in the banal East End—did more to change urban planning than any other text in the twentieth century. It also established a blueprint for a form of gentrification that has retrenched the very urban inequalities and forms of segregation Jacobs sought to combat. Expanding the archive that would capture the particularities of the street cannot eliminate outmoded archival entries and their attendant ways of approaching the street. Nor can those who seek to expand the archive anticipate what developments—progressive or regressive—their expansions might stimulate. Every contribution to the street archive carves channels through which new discourses can flow, but the repressed can return through the same channels that were carved to supersede it.

The street archive is thus subject to the paradox of the street. As I have argued throughout this book, the street is the scene of a paradox, the basic structure of the urban network and the site most recalcitrant to its completion. Pennethorne's abstract plan for the city could never fully succeed, precisely because abstraction is not an imposition onto the particular but a technique for gathering the particularities. Yet these street-level particularities always slip out of the grasp of the gatherer. In Jacobs's model—which the texts of Mayhew and Morrison prefigure, in their own ways—the particularities are gathered in a different mode, one that attempts immersion in the immanence of the street rather than abstract distance from it. Inevitably, though, the phenomenal world of the street finds new ways to overflow the courses and channels that street models would chart for it. And this excess, of course, only prompts those models to expansion. And so the paradox of the street unfolds.

. . .

Today, despite ongoing technological change—where Jasper Milvain's streets were supplied with "telegraphic communication," ours are supplied with so-called smart technologies capable of gathering data on an unprecedented scale—the street persists as the basic structure of the urban network and the site most recalcitrant to that network's completion. Indeed, the paradox persists on one of the streets this book describes: Petticoat Lane. That street survives as a market in a rapidly gentrifying East End still home to a large immigrant population. Bangladeshis, Pakistanis, and Indians have replaced Eastern European Jews, but the conditions of their apprehension in an expanding field of governmentality are remarkably similar. They are apprehended as the contemporary wandering tribes, migrants who exist in transnational networks that make their appearance on the London streets. Here I return to one of the racist clichés with which I opened this book: In 2009, the Salvation Army "Captain" Nick Coke—taking his inspiration from "General" William Booth's 1890 writings—summoned the clichés of the nineteenth century to describe the scene on Mile End Road, which intersects with both Petticoat Lane and Commercial Street:

> On the occasions when I walk down Mile End Road towards Whitechapel, I sense their presence among the people milling around the busy street and market. Look closer and I observe them living in the shadows: innocent men, women, and children terrified of the authorities—a hard-working mother exploited by unscrupulous business people and resigned to accept low wages so she can feed and clothe her children. An honest father forced into dealing on the black market because years of waiting in limbo has stripped him of the power to make any other kind of choice. . . . As much as this sounds like something from early Salvation Army history, it is not 1865—this is Whitechapel in 2009. Those of us who live in London's East End are only too aware that "darkest England" is still well and truly with us. The "shadow people" are irregular migrants living in the UK.[29]

Yet another social investigator risks a walk to the East End, where his uniquely attuned senses alert him to the shadowy figures populating "darkest England." 1852, 1862, 1882, 1902, and 2009—the clichés keep surfacing, barely recycled. Of course, there aren't really any shadows on Mile End Road—it is a broad, bright, busy thoroughfare. When Coke refers to the shadows, he adopts a metaphor to speak of street-level *excess*. Mile End Road structures a network and stages the excess that overwhelms that same network. Coke—as so many before him have done—turns to race as a technology to resolve the paradox. Race gathers the shadowy excess into the field of the totality, the target of application for modern governmentality. Functioning on a principle of inclusion, race charts the abstract field that conditions the phenomenal world. The excesses of that world continue to revitalize race as a technological approach to managing an expanding totality. The recalcitrance of the street—and the continued recourse to race as a technology to manage that recalcitrance—reanimates a technological repertoire that sustains a cyclical history.

INTRODUCTION

1. Paul Ricoeur, *Freud and Philosophy: An Essay on Interpretation* (New Haven, CT: Yale University Press, 1970).

2. Salvation Army "Captain" Nick Coke, quoted in "Strangers into Citizens Briefing Paper No. 4" (Strangers into Citizens Campaign, London, 2009), 12.

3. On stowaways and historiography as a rhetoric of presence, see Eelco Runia, "Presence," *History and Theory* 45 (2006): 1–29.

4. Rita Felski, "'Context Stinks!,'" *New Literary History* 42, no. 4 (2011): 573–91.

5. For an excellent polemic addressing this issue in Victorian studies, see Felski, "Context Stinks!" For a less austere exploration of these themes, see Lauren M. E. Goodlad and Andrew Sartori, "The Ends of History: Introduction," *Victorian Studies* 55, no. 14 (2013): 591–614. For a reminder that the suspicion of the previous generation's model of critique is a perennial theme, see Catherine Gallagher, "The Ends of History: Afterword," *Victorian Studies* 55, no. 4 (2013): 683–91. Examples of scholars' rhetoric searching for a theoretical model not based solely on ideology and suspicion include Debra Hawhee, "Rhetoric's Sensorium," *Quarterly Journal of Speech* 101, no. 1 (2015): 2–17; Thomas Rickert, *Ambient Rhetoric: The Attunements of Rhetorical Being* (Pittsburgh: University of Pittsburgh Press, 2013); and Nathan Stormer, "Rhetoric: A Working Paper on Rhetoric and Mnesis," *Quarterly Journal of Speech* 99, no. 1 (2013): 27–50. For an increasingly canonical intervention against critiques of ideology and representation, see Nigel Thrift, *Non-Representational Theory: Space, Politics, Affect* (New York: Routledge, 2007). For an argument about how affect theory can revitalize approaches to how history catches up with and impinges upon experience, see Lauren Berlant, *Cruel Optimism* (Durham, NC: Duke University Press, 2011). Finally, for another polemic against ideology critique, see Bruno Latour, "Why Has Critique Run Out of Steam? From Matters of Fact to Matters of Concern," *Critical Inquiry* 30 (2004): 225–48.

6. Frantz Fanon describes this casting of subjects as racialized objects through the notion of a "zone of nonbeing." See Fanon, *Black Skins, White Masks*, translated by Charles Lam Markmann (London: Pluto Press, 2008).

7. For a critique of recent efforts to unseat the category of the human, see Alexander G. Weheliye, *Habeas Viscus: Racializing Assemblages, Biopolitics, and Black Feminist Theories of the Human* (Durham, NC: Duke University Press, 2014), 9–12.

8. Critical feminist approaches have raised similar concerns about new materialism, arguing that new materialist scholars too often presume that feminists have rejected materiality and biology, ignoring in the process a long history of feminist inquiries into the ways in which biological and material questions structure gender. For more on this argument, see Sara Ahmed, "Some Preliminary Remarks on the Founding Gestures of 'New Materialism,'" *European Journal of Women's Studies* 15, no. 1 (2008): 23–39. For an extended critique of the failure of feminist new materialist thinkers to engage with feminist postcolonial approaches, see Angela Willey, "A World of Materialisms: Postcolonial Feminist Science Studies and the New Natural," *Science, Technology, and Human Values* 41, no. 6 (2016): 991–1014.

9. Nathan Stormer, "Rhetoric's Diverse Materiality: Polythetic Ontology and Genealogy," *Review of Communication* 16, no. 4 (2016): 299–316.

10. Diane Davis, "Addressing Alterity: Rhetoric, Hermeneutics, and the Nonappropriative Relation," *Philosophy and Rhetoric* 38, no. 3 (2005): 191.

11. See Diane Davis, *Inessential Solidarity: Rhetoric and Foreigner Relations* (Pittsburgh: University of Pittsburgh Press, 2010); Rickert, *Ambient Rhetoric*; Nathan Stormer, "Articulation: A Working Paper on Rhetoric and *Taxis*," *Quarterly Journal of Speech* 90, no. 3 (2004): 257–84; Debra Hawhee, *Rhetoric in Tooth and Claw: Animals, Language, Sensation* (Chicago: University of Chicago Press, 2016); Debra Hawhee, "Bestiaries, Past and Future," *Rhetoric Society Quarterly* 47, no. 3 (2017): 285–91. On animal rhetorics, see also George Kennedy, "A Hoot in the Dark: The Evolution of General Rhetoric," *Philosophy and Rhetoric* 25, no. 1 (1992): 1–21.

12. Prominent object-oriented ontologist Graham Harman suggests that recognizing the futility of human thought in the face of this recalcitrance is the first step toward breaking the spell of "correlationism," or the Kantian notion that being can only be accessed through thinking, or that objects are epistemologically and ontologically significant only insofar as they are significant to human ontology and epistemology. For an overview, see Graham Harman, *Prince of Networks: Bruno Latour and Metaphysics* (Melbourne: re.press, 2009), 122–34.

13. See Christopher N. Gamble, "Figures of Entanglement: A Special Issue Introduction," *Review of Communication* 16, no. 4 (2016): 265–80; Jane Bennett, *Vibrant Matter: A Political Ecology of Things* (Durham, NC: Duke University Press, 2010), 13.

14. Jussi Parikka, *What Is Media Archaeology?* (Cambridge, UK: Polity, 2012), 3.

15. Bruno Latour, *Reassembling the Social: An Introduction to Actor-Network-Theory* (Oxford: Oxford University Press, 2007).

16. Fanon, *Black Skins, White Masks*, 4.

17. David Marriott, "Inventions of Existence: Sylvia Wynter, Frantz Fanon, Sociegeny, and 'the Damned,'" *CR: The Centennial Review* 11, no. 3 (2011): 57.

18. Sylvia Wynter, "Unsettling the Coloniality of Being/Power/Truth/Freedom: Toward the Human, After Man, Its Overrepresentation—An Argument," *CR: The New Centennial Review* 3, no. 3 (2003): 264.

19. Katherine McKittrick, *Demonic Grounds: Black Women and the Cartographies of Struggle* (Minneapolis: University of Minnesota Press, 2006), 3.

20. Fanon, *Black Skins, White Masks*, 85.

21. Ibid., 83.

22. Ibid., 83.

23. Ann Laura Stoler, *Carnal Knowledge and Imperial Power: Race and the Intimate in Colonial Rule* (Berkeley: University of California Press, 2002): 83.

24. Ann McClintock, *Imperial Leather: Race, Gender, and Sexuality in the Colonial Context* (New York: Routledge, 1995), 270.

25. Cedric J. Robinson, *Black Marxism: The Making of the Black Radical Tradition* (Chapel Hill: University of North Carolina Press, 2000), 2.

26. Ibid.

27. This project's focus on the racial dynamics of circulation takes its cue from recent studies of "cultures of circulation." See Benjamin Lee and Edward LiPuma, "Cultures of Circulation: The Imaginations of Modernity," *Public Culture* 14, no. 1 (2002): 191–213; Dilip Parameshwar Gaonkar and Elizabeth A. Povinelli, "Technologies of Public Form: Circulation, Transfiguration, Recognition," *Public Culture* 15, no. 3 (2003): 385–97; and Brian T. Edwards, "Logics and Contexts of Circulation," in *A Companion to Comparative Literature*, ed. Ali Behdad and Dominic Thomas (Malden, MA: Blackwell Publishing, 2011).

28. Ruth Wilson Gilmore, "Race and Globalization," in *Geographies of Global Change: Remapping the World*, ed. R. J. Johnston, Peter J. Taylor, and Michael J. Watts (New York: Blackwell Publishing, 2002), 261.

29. Here I draw on Jodi Melamed, "Racial Capitalism," *Critical Ethnic Studies* 1, no. 1 (2015): 76–85. See especially pp. 77–80 on the ways in which racial capitalism enforces separation in order to structure new forms of interrelation that benefit capital.

30. Kyla Schuller, *The Biopolitics of Feeling: Race, Sex and Science in the Nineteenth Century* (Durham, NC: Duke University Press, 2018), 26.

31. Ibid., 26.

32. Edward Burnett Tylor, *Primitive Culture* (London: John Murray, 1877), 1.

33. Elizabeth Caitlin McCabe, "How the Past Remains: George Eliot, Thomas Hardy, and the Victorian Anthropological Doctrine of Survivals" (PhD diss., Northwestern University, 2013), 84.

34. For more on the notion of a "flat ontology," see Levi R. Bryant, *The Democracy of Objects* (Ann Arbor, MI: Open Humanities Press, 2011).

35. Achille Mbembe, *Critique of Black Reason*, translated by Laurent Dubois (Durham, NC: Duke University Press, 2017). See especially pp. 4–6.

36. See Mbembe, *Critique of Black Reason*; Schuller, *The Biopolitics of Feeling*; Charles Mills, *The Racial Contract* (Ithaca, NY: Cornell University Press, 1997); Ann Laura Stoler, *Race and the Education of Desire: Foucault's History of Sexuality and the Colonial Order of Things* (Durham, NC: Duke University Press, 1995); and David Theo Goldberg, *Racial State* (Malden, MA: John Wiley & Sons, 2001).

37. This is a play on Michael Omi and Howard Winant's famous "racial formations" phrase, which I view as too stagnant a metaphor to capture the transnational forms of circulation that sustain global imperialism. Michael Omi and Howard Winant, *Racial Formation in the United States: From the 1960s to the 1990s*, 2nd ed. (New York: Routledge, 1994).

38. Wendy Hui Kyong Chun, "Race and/as Technology; or How to Do Things to Race," *Camera Obscura* 70, 24, no 1 (2009): 7–35.

39. Hortense Spillers, "Mama's Baby, Papa's Maybe: An American Grammar Book," in *Black, White, and in Color: Essays on American Literature and Culture* (Chicago: University of Chicago Press, 2003): 203–29.

40. Eric King Watts, "Postracial Fantasies, Blackness, and Zombies," *Communication and Critical/Cultural Studies* 14, no. 4 (2017): 317–33.

41. Darrel Wanzer-Serrano (as Darrel Allan Wanzer), "Delinking Rhetoric, or Revisiting McGee's Fragmentation Thesis through Decoloniality," *Rhetoric and Public Affairs* 15, no. 4 (2012): 647–57.

42. Lisa Flores, "Between Abundance and Marginalization: The Imperative of Racial Rhetorical Criticism," *Review of Communication* 16, no. 1 (2016): 4–24.

43. Kirt H. Wilson, *The Reconstruction Desegregation Debate: The Policies of Equality and the Rhetoric of Place, 1870–1875* (East Lansing: Michigan State University Press, 2002); Josue David Cisneros, *The Border Crossed Us: Rhetorics of Borders, Citizenship, and Latina/o Identity* (Tuscaloosa: University of Alabama Press, 2014); Darrel Wanzer-Serrano, *The New York Young Lords and the Struggle for Liberation* (Philadelphia: Temple University Press, 2015); Bryan J. McCann, *The Mark of Criminality: Rhetoric, Race, and Gangsta Rap in the War-on-Crime Era* (Tuscaloosa: University of Alabama Press, 2017).

44. See Michel Foucault, *The History of Sexuality Vol. 1*, trans. Robert Hurley (New York: Vintage Books, 1978); Michel Foucault, "Governmentality," in *The Foucault Effect*, ed. Graham Burchell, Colin Gordon, and Peter Miller, trans. Pasquale Pasquino (London: Harvester Wheatsheaf, 1991); Michel Foucault, *"Society Must Be Defended": Lectures at the Collège de France, 1975–1976*, trans. David Macey (New York: Picador, 1997); Michel Foucault, *Security, Territory, Population: Lectures at the Collège de France 1977–1978*, trans. Graham Burchell (New York: Picador, 2009).

45. A partial list of work on the Victorian city includes H. J. Dyos, "The Slums of Victorian London," *Victorian Studies* 11, no. 1 (1967): 5–40; Alain Corbin, *The Foul and the Fragrant: Odor and the French Social Imagination* (Cambridge, MA: Harvard University Press, 1986); Herbert, "Rat Worship and Taboo in Mayhew's London," *Representations* 23 (1988): 1–24; Judith R. Walkowitz, *City of Dreadful Delight: Narratives of Sexual Danger in Late-Victorian London* (Chicago: University of Chicago Press, 1992); James H. Winter, *London's Teeming Streets: 1830–1914* (London: Routledge, 1993); Lynda Nead, *Victorian Babylon: People, Streets and Images in Nineteenth-Century London* (New Haven, CT: Yale University Press, 2000); Michelle Allen, "From Cesspool to Sewer: Sanitary Reform and the Rhetoric of Resistance, 1848–1880," *Victorian Literature & Culture* 30, no. 2 (2002): 383–402; David L. Pike, *Subterranean Cities: The World beneath Paris and London, 1800–1945* (Ithaca, NY: Cornell University Press, 2005); Seth Koven, *Slumming: Sexual and Social Politics in Late Victorian England* (Princeton, NJ: Princeton University Press, 2006); Jonathan H. Grossman, *Charles Dickens's Networks: Public Transport and the Novel*, 2013.

46. Metropolitan Sanitary Association, *Memorials on Sanitary Reform, and on the Economical and Administrative Principles of Water-Supply for the Metropolis: Addressed to the Right Hon. Lord John Russell and the Right Hon. Sir George Grey: Including Correspondence between John Stuart Mill, Esq. . . . and the Metropolitan Sanitary Association: On the Proper*

Agency for Regulating the Water-Supply for the Metropolis, as a Question of Economical and Administrative Principle (London, 1851), 21.

47. William Rendle, *Fever in London: Social and Sanitary Lessons* (London: Metropolitan Sanitary Association, 1866), 3.

48. Metropolitan Board of Works: Report of the Streets Committee on the Plans of Railways, propose to be proceed with in the present session of parliament, approved by the board 12 February 1864, 3.

49. In a famous essay, James W. Carey argues that the telegraph "permitted for the first time the separation of communication from transportation," separating message from movement. See Carey, "Technology and Ideology: The Case of the Telegraph," in *Communication as Culture: Essays on Media and Society* (New York: Routledge, 1989), 201–30. This book begins before the telegraph and concludes after its invention and initial implementation, but the simultaneously symbolic and material meaning of communication persisted beyond the first decades of the telegraph. Residual meanings, uses, and practices tend to survive seemingly watershed moments in technological history.

50. William Haywood, "Report to the Honourable Commissioners of Sewers and the City of London on the Accidents to Horses on Carriageway Pavements," 1873, 18.

51. Ato Quayson, "Signs of the Times: Discourse Ecologies and Street Life on Oxford St., Accra," *City & Society* 22, no. 1 (2010): 72, 73. For another approach to the street as an archive, see Suzanne Hall, *City, Street and Citizen: The Measure of the Ordinary* (London: Routledge, 2012).

52. Brian Massumi, "The Autonomy of Affect," *Cultural Critique* 31 (1995): 94.

53. Quayson, "Signs of the Times," 73.

54. For accounts of Parisian modernity, see Paul Rabinow, *French Modern: Norms and Forms of the Social Environment* (Chicago: University Of Chicago Press, 1995), and David Harvey, *The Condition of Postmodernity: An Enquiry into the Origins of Cultural Change* (Cambridge, MA: Blackwell Publishing, 1990).

55. The *Economist* disapprovingly remarked upon Mayhew's public comments. See "Distressed Populations," *Economist*, November 16, 1850.

56. Anne Humpherys, *Travels into the Poor Man's Country: The Work of Henry Mayhew* (Athens: University of Georgia Press, 1977), 24.

57. Ibid., 106.

58. Ibid., 108, 28.

CHAPTER 1

1. John Stuart Mill, *Essays on Economics and Society* (Toronto: University of Toronto Press, 1967), 432.

2. Ibid., 433.

3. Ibid., 434.

4. Ibid.

5. Metropolitan Sanitary Association, *Memorials on Sanitary Reform, and on the Economical and Administrative Principles of Water-Supply for the Metropolis: Addressed to the Right Hon. Lord John Russell and the Right Hon. Sir George Grey: Including Correspondence between John Stuart Mill, Esq. . . . and the Metropolitan Sanitary Association: On the Proper*

Agency for Regulating the Water-Supply for the Metropolis, as a Question of Economical and Administrative Principle, 1851, 21.

6. Ibid., 25.

7. Henry Mayhew, "A View from St. Paul's," in *The Unknown Mayhew: Selections from the Morning Chronicle, 1849–50*, ed. E. P. Thompson and Eileen Yeo (Harmondsworth, UK: Penguin Classics, 1973), 114.

8. Rosalind Williams's canonical treatment of the sublime focuses on this confrontation between technology and nature. See Rosalind Williams, *Notes on the Underground: An Essay on Technology, Society, and the Imagination*, 2nd edition (Cambridge, MA: MIT Press, 2008).

9. Henry Mayhew, *London Labour and the London Poor* (London: Dover Publications, 1968), vol. 1, xvi. Hereafter, citations will take the form *LL* 1:xvi.

10. Although I am not interested in assessing the claim that Mayhew held racist views in this chapter, the evidence to refute it outweighs the evidence to support it. Whichever way one pursues this claim, though, it inevitably leads into the black box of racism understood as an ideology, something that exists in the minds of humans, making them close-minded and discriminatory in thought, words, and action. Analyses seeking to judge Mayhew's racism will have no way to parse passages from *London Labour* such as his contradictory assessment of anti-Semitism, which would seem to support the claim that Mayhew was at once racist and antiracist: "That there was too much foundation for many of these accusations [against the Jews], and still *is*, no reasonable Jew can now deny; that the wholesale prejudice against them was absurd, is equally indisputable" (*LL* 2:117).

11. Eelco Runia, "Presence," *History and Theory*, 1. See also Runia, "Inventing the New from the Old: From White's 'Tropics' to Vico's 'Topics,'" *Rethinking History* 14, no. 2 (2010): 229–41.

12. See Eelco Runia, "Presence," *History and Theory* 45 (2006): 13.

13. Jacques Derrida, *Margins of Philosophy*, translated by Alan Bass (Brighton, UK: Harvester Press, 1982).

14. Ernesto Laclau, *On Populist Reason* (London: Verso Books, 2005), 72, 71.

15. Hortense J. Spillers, "Introduction—Peter's Pans: Eating in the Diaspora," in *Black, White, and in Color: Essays on American Literature and Culture* (Chicago: University of Chicago Press, 2003): 20.

16. Here I am influenced by Nathan Stormer's notion of *taxis* as rhetorical figure of materialist "ordonnance" or arrangement, and thus a figure describing a "specific articulation of bodies and languages." See Stormer, "Articulation: A Working Paper on Rhetoric and *Taxis*," *Quarterly Journal of Speech* 90, no. 3 (2004): 261.

17. Gertrude Himmelfarb, "Mayhew's Poor: A Problem of Identity," *Victorian Studies* 14 (1971): 314.

18. *LL* 2:162.

19. Henry Mayhew, "The Task: Letter I—19 October 1849," in *The Unknown Mayhew: Selections from the Morning Chronicle, 1849–50*, ed. E. P. Thompson and Eileen Yeo (Harmondsworth, UK: Penguin Classics, 1973), 120.

20. *LL* 1:1.

21. Mayhew, "The Task: Letter I—19 October 1849," 120.

22. *LL* 1:320.

23. Ibid.

24. Ibid.

25. *LL* 1:175.

26. Falguni A. Sheth, "The Technology of Race: Enframing, Violence, and Taming the Unruly," *Radical Philosophy Review* 7, no. 1 (2004): 81.

27. See Friedrich A. Kittler, "Towards an Ontology of Media," *Theory, Culture & Society* 26, nos. 2–3 (2009): 23–31.

28. Bruno Latour, "Morality and Technology: The End of the Means," trans. Couze Venn, *Theory, Culture & Society* 19, nos. 5–6 (2002): 248–49.

29. Ibid., 250.

30. For more on *taxis* and arrangement, see Stormer, "Articulation: A Working Paper on Taxis," 260–61.

31. *LL* 2:499.

32. *LL* 2:504.

33. Ibid. See Edward W. Said, *Orientalism* (London: Penguin Books, 2003).

34. Ibid.

35. Ibid.

36. For an account of Mayhew applying an emphasis on savage desire to his account of the London rat, see Herbert, "Rat Worship and Taboo in Mayhew's London," *Representations* 23 (1988):15–16.

37. On Prichard's argument that variation in man "was stimulated by civilization," see George Stocking, "From Chronology to Ethnology: James Cowles Prichard and British Anthropology, 1800–1850," in James Cowles Prichard, *Researches into the Physical History of Man*, ed. George W. Stocking Jr. (Chicago: University of Chicago Press, 1973), iii.

38. For an account of how the Darwinians—some of whom, including Thomas Huxley, recognized the value of certain strains of polygenism—aligned with the staunchly monogenist Christian ethnologists against the polygenists advocating the fixity of racial type, see Mayhew, "A View from St. Paul's," 113–21. For an account of how Prichard shifted his views in response to pressures from polygenists arguing for the fixity of hereditarian traits, see Stocking, "From Chronology to Ethnology," xxx. For an overview of mid-to-late-nineteenth century theory, see Elizabeth Caitlin McCabe, "How the Past Remains: George Eliot, Thomas Hardy, and the Victorian Anthropological Doctrine of Survivals" (PhD diss., Northwestern University, 2013), 20–30.

39. *LL* 2:504.

40. Ibid.

41. Ibid.

42. Ibid.

43. Ibid.

44. Ibid.

45. Ibid.

46. Ibid.

47. Adam Phillips, "Introduction," in *A Philosophical Enquiry into the Origin of Our Ideas of the Sublime and Beautiful*, by Edmund Burke (Oxford: Oxford University Press, 1990), xxii.

48. The view that savages were entirely subject to the whims of passion was a cliché in nineteenth-century thought, but the position underwent a reversal in the late-nineteenth century. As critiques of the "machinery of police" became widespread, "it became a natural

operation now to discover" that same machinery in savage societies subject no longer to fleeting passion but to the static forces of custom, which were said to exert almost total control over savage life (Herbert 66). Kant and Burke tend to describe savages as captive to passion, but in either case the savage would be disqualified for the sublime: Subject to passion, they are unable to introduce the reasoned distinctions that would mitigate sublime terror; tied to custom, they are unable to expand the scope of their reason and thus satisfy the sublime demand. See Christopher Herbert, *Culture and Anomie: Ethnographic Imagination in the Nineteenth Century* (Chicago: University of Chicago Press, 1991), 60–68.

49. Mayhew, "A View From St. Paul's," 114.

50. For Wordsworth, the sublime functions to unite humans to a nature that far surpasses human actions that occur "'mid the din of towns and cities," and, through this surpassing, simultaneously compels and connects thought and action: "And I have felt / A presence that disturbs me with the joy / Of elevated thoughts; a sense sublime / Of something far more deeply interfused, / Whose dwelling is the light of setting suns, / And the round ocean and the living air, / And the blue sky, and in the mind of man; / A motion and a spirit, that impels / All thinking things, all objects of all thought, / And rolls through all things." From William Wordsworth, "Lines Composed a Few Miles above Tintern Abbey on Revisiting the Banks of the Wye During a Tour," in *The Complete Poetical Works* (London: MacMillan and Co, 1888) (see Bartleby.com, https://www.bartleby.com/41/376.html).

51. See *LL* 2:247 and 2:293–94.

52. Immanuel Kant, *Critique of Judgement*, trans. James Creed Meredith (Oxford: Oxford University Press, 2008), 81.

53. Paul De Man, "Phenomenality and Materiality in Kant," in *Hermeneutics: Questions and Prospects*, ed. Gary Shapiro and Alan Sica (Amherst: University of Massachusetts Press, 1984), 127. Postmodern approaches to the sublime typically emphasize this connection between the sublime and the unrepresentable. This is Jean-François Lyotard's approach in his *Lessons on the Analytic of the Sublime*, translated by Elizabeth Rottenberg (Stanford, CA: Stanford University Press, 1994). Frederic Jameson also associates the sublime with the postmodern encounter with the inability to represent globalized capital. See Jameson, *Postmodernism, or the Cultural Logic of Late Capitalism* (Durham, NC: Duke University Press, 1991).

54. Longinus theorizes the sublime as a mode of aesthetic, and therefore civilizational, elevation. For an extended treatment of Longinus and "aesthetic elevation," see Robert Doran, *The Theory of Sublime from Longinus to Kant* (Cambridge: Cambridge University Press, 2015).

55. Stormer suggests that the sublime recruits the subject to a space of appearance by invoking an addressee that cannot be adequately represented, and that therefore exists beyond the representational. The sublime therefore encourages attention not only to human agents but to the relationships between humans and nonhuman entities. See Stormer, "Addressing the Sublime: Space, Mass Representation, and the Unrepresentable," *Critical Studies in Media Communication* 21, no. 3 (2004): 212–40.

56. For a full account of Kant's views on race, see Emmanuel Chukwudi Eze, "The Colour of Reason: The Idea of 'Race' in Kant's Anthropology," in *Postcolonial African Philosophy: A Critical Reader*, ed. Emmanuel Chukwudi Eze (Cambridge, MA: Blackwell, 1997), 103–31.

57. For a debate over the significance of Kant's opposition to the slave trade, see Pauline Kleingeld, "Kant's Second Thoughts on Race," *Philosophical Quarterly* 57, no. 229 (2007):

573–92, and Robert Bernasconi, "Kant's Third Thoughts on Race," in *Reading Kant's Geography*, edited by Stuart Elden and Eduardo Mendieta (Albany: State University of New York Press, 2011), 291–318.

58. See Bernasconi, "Kant's Third Thoughts on Race," 302.

59. Kleingeld argues that this opposition to the slave trade reveals that Kant revised his thinking on race. See Kleingeld, "Kant's Second Thoughts on Race." For a response to this argument, see Bernasconi, "Kant's Third Thoughts on Race." For further discussion of Kant's published and unpublished statements on race, see Mark Larrimore, "Sublime Waste: Kant on the Destiny of the 'Races,'" *Canadian Journal of Philosophy* 29, no. 1 (1999): 99–125.

60. Quoted in Larrimore, "Sublime Waste," 114. As Larrimore documents, Kant included this statement in a fragment in the *Reflexionen* entitled "On the Character of the Races," which was presumably written at some point in 1770s or 1780s. See Larrimore, 113–16.

61. Frantz Fanon, *Black Skins, White Masks*. Translated by Charles Lam Markmann (London: Pluto Press, 2008), 2, 143.

62. John Stuart Mill, "Considerations on Representative Government," in *On Liberty and Other Essays* (Oxford: Oxford University Press, 2008), 218.

63. Ibid., 231.

64. Ibid., 290.

65. Ibid., 209.

66. Ibid., 232.

67. Ibid., 208.

68. LL 1:101.

69. Ibid.

70. LL 1:320.

71. LL 2:504.

72. Ibid.

73. Ibid.

74. Edmund Burke, *A Philosophical Enquiry into the Origin of Our Ideas of the Sublime and Beautiful*, ed. Adam Phillips (Oxford: Oxford University Press, 1990), 160.

75. Ibid., 75–76.

76. LL 3:373.

77. LL 3:504.

78. LL 3:504.

79. Burke, *Philosophical Enquiry*, 159.

80. As Dilip Gaonkar, argues, "Within the liberal imaginary, the individual is the bedrock of social ontology, moral responsibility, and economic calculation and the crowd jeopardizes all those invaluable assets. Every crowd is a potential mob and susceptible to rioting." See Gaonkar, "After the Fictions: Notes Towards a Phenomenology of the Multitude," *E-Flux Journal* 58 (2014), http://www.e-flux.com/journal/after-the-fictions-notes-towards-a-phenomenology-of-the-multitude/.

81. Kant, *Critique of Judgement*, 103.

82. Ibid., 104.

83. LL 1:2.

84. LL 2:364.

85. LL 1:44.

86. Ibid.
87. *LL* 3:368.
88. *LL* 3:301.
89. *LL* 3:302.
90. Ibid.
91. *LL* 3:301.
92. Ibid.
93. *LL* 3:305.
94. *LL* 3:303.
95. Ibid.
96. *LL* 3:309.
97. Gaonkar, "After the Fictions".
98. *LL* 1:101.
99. Ibid.
100. Michel Foucault, *"Society Must Be Defended": Lectures at the Collège de France, 1975–1976*, translated by David Macey (New York: Picador, 1997), 254.

CHAPTER 2

1. Kenneth Burke, *The Philosophy of Literary Form*, 3rd edition (Berkeley: University of California Press, 1974), 23.
2. Dominique Laporte, *History of Shit*, trans. Nadia Benabid and Rodolphe el Khoury (Cambridge, MA: MIT Press, 2002), 13.
3. *The Sanitary Condition of the City of London from the City Remembrancer on the Statements of the Sub-Committee of the Health of Towns Association; with the Sub-Committee's Reply and Lord Ashley's Letter* (London: Health of Towns Association, 1848), 8.
4. Ibid., 9.
5. Ibid.
6. Ibid., 6.
7. Christopher Herbert, "The Doctrine of Survivals, the Great Mutiny, and Lady Audley's Secret," *Novel: A Forum on Fiction* 42, no. 3 (2009): 431–36.
8. Ibid., 37.
9. Ibid.
10. Sigmund Freud, *Civilization and Its Discontents*, trans. James Strachey (New York: W. W. Norton, 1962), 44.
11. Sir Joseph William Bazalgette, *On the Main Drainage of London, and the Interception of the Sewage from the River Thames* (London, 1865), 9.
12. *LL* 2:389
13. *LL* 2:160. The claims are difficult to evaluate because they cannot be crosschecked, as Mayhew is often the only source for the figures he cites.
14. Mayhew *LL* 2:215, *LL* 2:166, *LL* 2:196,
15. *LL* 2:166
16. David L. Pike, *Subterranean Cities: The World beneath Paris and London, 1800–1945* (Ithaca, NY: Cornell University Press, 2005); David L. Pike, *Metropolis on the Styx: The Underworlds of Modern Urban Culture, 1800–2001* (Ithaca, NY: Cornell University Press,

2007); Rosalind Williams, *Notes on the Underground: An Essay on Technology, Society, and the Imagination* (Cambridge, MA: MIT Press, 2008); Paul Dobraszczyk, "Sewers, Wood Engraving, and the Sublime: Picturing London's Main Drainage System in the *'Illustrated London News*,' 1859–1862," *Victorian Periodicals Review* 38, no. 4 (2005): 349–78.

17. Pike, *Subterranean Cities.*

18. *LL* 2:407.

19. *LL* 2:394.

20. In this sense, the dirt in London was more than matter "out of place," as Mary Douglas has argued, but matter that challenged the foundations of place itself. See Mary Douglas, *Purity and Danger: An Analysis of Concepts of Pollution and Taboo* (London : Routledge, 2002).

21. See Jeff Rice, *Digital Detroit: Rhetoric and Space in the Age of the Network* (Carbondale: Southern Illinois University Press, 2012), 30.

22. Vijay Prashad, "Native Dirt/Imperial Ordure: The Cholera of 1832 and the Morbid Resolutions of Modernity," *Journal of Historical Sociology* 7, no. 3 (1994): 247.

23. Christopher Herbert, "Rat Worship and Taboo in Mayhew's London," *Representations* 23 (1988):8.

24. Hamlin, "Providence and Putrefaction: Victorian Sanitarians and the Natural Theology of Health and Disease," *Victorian Studies* 28, no. 3 (1985): 389.

25. Douglas, *Purity and Danger.*

26. *LL* 2:471.

27. *LL* 2:475.

28. *LL* 2:262.

29. *LL* 2:144.

30. *LL* 2:430.

31. *LL* 2:385

32. Such a question hints at a fear of savagery surfacing in civilization. After all, as Stephen Greenblatt has argued, "proper control of" the "body's products: urine, feces, mucus, saliva, and wind . . . distinguishes . . . the civilized from the savage" (2). See Greenblatt, "Filthy Rites," *Daedalus* 111, no. 3 (1982): 1–16.

33. Mid-nineteenth-century Londoners would have required little encouragement to heed Rickert's call for attunement with the human and nonhuman environments he names with his notion of "ambience." See Thomas Rickert, *Ambient Rhetoric: Attunements of Rhetorical Being* (Pittsburgh: University of Pittsburgh Press, 2013).

34. Bazalgette, *On the Main Drainage of London*, 2.

35. Ibid.

36. John Stuart Mill opens his *Consideration on Representative Government* with a similar survey of governance beginning with savage and moving toward increasingly civilized nations.

37. Bazalgette, *On the Main Drainage of London*, 6.

38. Ibid.

39. Edmund Cooper, "Report to the Metropolitan Commission of Sewers on the House-Drainage of St. James, Westminster, during the Recent Cholera Outbreak," Metropolitan Commission of Sewers, September 22, 1854.

40. Bazalgette, *On the Main Drainage of London*, 6.

41. *LL* 2:386.

42. Bruno Latour, "Where Are the Missing Masses? The Sociology of a Few Mundane Artifacts," in *Technology and Society: Building Our Sociotechnical Future* (Cambridge, MA: MIT Press, 2008), 174.

43. Cooper, "Report to the Metropolitan Commission of Sewers."

44. Georg Lukács, *Studies in European Realism*. Translated by John Mander and Ecke Mander. London: Merlin, 1963.

45. Ian Baucom, *Specters of the Atlantic: Finance Capital, Slavery, and the Philosophy of History* (Durham, NC: Duke University Press, 2005).

46. Geoffrey Clark, *Betting on Lives: The Culture of Life Insurance in England, 1695–1775* (Manchester: Manchester University Press, 1999).

47. As James Chandler has argued, the case form forwards a particular instance as evidence of a general trend or historical situation. See James Chandler, *England in 1819: The Politics of Literary Culture and the Case of Romantic Historicism* (Chicago: University of Chicago Press, 1999), 207–12.

48. Edwin Chadwick, *An Essay on the Means of Insurance against the Casualties of Sickness, Decrepitude, and Mortality*, Comprising an Article Reprinted from the *Westminster Review* (No. XVIIII), for April 1828, with Additional Notes and Corrections (London: Charles Knight, 1836), 2.

49. Ibid., 45–46.

50. Ibid., 61.

51. Ibid., 47.

52. *LL* 1:171

53. *LL* 1:108

54. *LL* 1:48

55. *LL* 2:365.

56. *LL* 2:495.

57. This is not to suggest, of course, that problems having to do with social imaginaries are any less real than problems having to do with material space. Indeed, recent turns in Victorian studies to actor-network theory, theories of technologies, and theories of globalization share an interest in how new ways of materially connecting distant spaces both make possible and pose problems to social and cultural imaginaries. See, for example, Richard Menke, *Telegraphic Realism: Victorian Fiction and Other Information Systems* (Stanford, CA: Stanford University Press, 2007); Lauren M. E. Goodlad, "Trollopian 'Foreign Policy': Rootedness and Cosmopolitanism in the Mid-Victorian Global Imaginary," *PMLA* 124, no. 2 (2009): 437–54; and Jonathan H. Grossman, *Charles Dickens's Networks: Public Transport and the Novel* (Oxford: Oxford University Press, 2013). For an overview of these trends, see Lauren M. E. Goodlad and Andrew Sartori, "The Ends of History: Introduction," *Victorian Studies* 55, no. 14 (2013): 591–614.

58. For Mayhew's description of the transnational seashell, fish, bird, and dog trade, see *LL* 2:92, 2:78, 2:61, and 2:51 respectively.

59. *LL* 2:148.

60. *LL* 2:262.

61. Cesspools were outlawed in 1847, and Mayhew did not begin the research and reporting that would first appear in the *Morning Chronicle* and later in *London Labour and*

the London Poor until 1849. This suggests that, like so many things in Victorian London, the laws outlawing cesspools were unevenly enforced.

62. One could marshal countless other examples of Mayhew's type-building efforts, all of which tend to follow similar patterns, although with slight differences that generate differing analyses from Mayhew.

63. *LL* 2:151.

64. *LL* 2:428.

65. *LL* 2:452.

66. *LL* 2:451.

67. *LL* 2:152.

68. *LL* 2:448.

69. *LL* 2:448.

70. Chandler, *England in 1819*, 208.

71. *LL* 2:448.

72. Chadwick, *An Essay on the Means of Insurance*, 2.

73. Ibid., 5.

74. Ibid., 6.

75. Ibid., 7.

76. Ibid., 6–7.

77. *LL* 2:179

78. *LL* 2:238

79. *LL* 2:217.

80. *LL* 2:389

81. *LL* 2:393

82. *LL* 2:393, 2:400

83. *LL* 2:403

84. *LL* 2:392–93

85. *LL* 2:392

86. *LL* 2:400

87. Chandler, *England in 1819*, 209.

88. Ibid., 206.

89. Ibid., 228.

90. *LL* 2:390.

91. Chandler, *England in 1819*, 206.

92. See Lynda Walsh, et al., "Forum: Bruno Latour on Rhetoric," *Rhetoric Society Quarterly* 47, no. 5 (2017), 456, 457.

CHAPTER 3

1. *LL* 2:11.

2. *Second Report from Select Committee on Metropolis Improvements* (London: House of Commons, August 2, 1838), 102.

3. Ibid., x.

4. I have chosen these two dates because they reflect the earliest and latest dates of sources specifically describing Petticoat Lane that I use in this chapter.

5. In rhetorical studies, Roxanne Mountford's adaptation of Lefebvre to theorize gender, rhetoric, and space has been particularly influential in launching the spatial turn in rhetoric. See Roxanne Mountford, "On Gender and Rhetorical Space," *Rhetoric Society Quarterly* 31, no. 1 (2001): 41–71. Other key texts in the spatial turn in rhetoric include Carole Blair, "Contemporary U.S. Memorial Sites as Exemplars of Rhetoric's Materiality," in *Rhetorical Bodies*, edited by Jack Selzer and Sharon Crowley (Madison: University of Wisconsin Press, 1999): 16–57; Greg Dickinson, "Joe's Rhetoric: Finding Authenticity at Starbucks," *Rhetoric Society Quarterly* 32, no. 4 (2002): 5–27; and Richard Marback, "The Rhetorical Space of Robben Island," *Rhetoric Society Quarterly* 34, no.2 (2004): 7–27.

6. Henri Lefebvre, *The Production of Space*, trans. Donald Nicholson-Smith (Malden, MA: Blackwell Publishing, 1991), 50–51.

7. Michel de Certeau, *The Practice of Everyday Life*, trans. Steven Rendall (Berkeley: University of California Press, 1984). See especially "Walking in the City," 91–110. For a study of the rhetoric of walking, see Robert Topinka, "Resisting the Fixity of Suburban Space: The Walker as Rhetorician," *Rhetoric Society Quarterly* 42, no. 1 (2012): 65–84.

8. Mary Poovey, *Making a Social Body: British Cultural Formation, 1830–1864* (Chicago: University of Chicago Press, 1995), 29.

9. Bruno Latour, *Reassembling the Social: An Introduction to Actor-Network-Theory*. Oxford: Oxford University Press, 2007, 85.

10. Ibid., 31. On circulation and rhetorical ecologies, see Jenny Edbauer Rice, "Unframing Models of Public Distribution: From Rhetorical Situation to Rhetorical Ecologies," *Rhetoric Society Quarterly* 35, no. 4 (2005): 5–24.

11. Richard Sennett, *Flesh and Stone: The Body and the City in Western Civilization* (London: Faber & Faber, 1994), 264, 324.

12. Gilles Deleuze and Felix Guattari, *A Thousand Plateaus: Capitalism and Schizophrenia*, trans. Brian Massumi (Minneapolis: University of Minnesota Press, 1987), 371.

13. Ibid., 494.

14. Ibid., 371.

15. In another formulation of this point, Deleuze and Guattari describe smooth space as if smooth space is the space of "smallest deviation" (ibid., 371). To striate smooth space is to make one point deviate from the other.

16. Deleuze and Guattari, *A Thousand Plateaus*, 371.

17. *Reports on the Volume and Effects of Recent Immigration from Eastern Europe into the United Kingdom: Presented to Both Houses of Parliament by Command of Her Majesty* (United Kingdom: Parliament, 1894), 36. As the reports state, "Within these districts whole streets and areas are nearly monopolised by the foreign Jewish colony, and the attraction of these 'congested districts' on such Russian and Polish immigrants as arrive for settlement in London appears to have undergone no diminution" (36).

18. *Second Report from Select Committee on Metropolis Improvements*, 104.

19. A. W. Bennett, *The Sin of Great Cities; or, The Great Social Evil: A National Sin* (London: Charles Cull, Harberdashers' Street, Hoxton, 1859), 24.

20. *LL* 1:139.

21. Count E. Armfelt, "Oriental London," in *Living London*, vol. 1 (London: Cassell and Company, Limited, 1902), 81.

22. *LL* 1:11.

23. *Fourth Report of the Commissioners Appointed by Her Majesty to Inquire into and Consider the Most Effectual Means of Improving the Metropolis and of Providing Increased Facilities of Communication within the Same* (United Kingdom: Parliament, 1845), 3.

24. *First Report from the Select Committee on Metropolis Improvement* (London: House of Commons, June 25, 1840), iii.

25. Ibid., 8.

26. Ibid.

27. Ibid.

28. Ibid.

29. F. H. W. Sheppard, ed., *Survey of London: Volume 27, Spitalfields and Mile End New Town* (London: London County Council, 1957), v–vi, http://www.british-history.ac.uk/survey-london/vol27/v-vi.

30. Ibid.

31. Ibid.

32. Ibid.

33. Ibid.

34. Percy J. Edwards, *History of London Street Improvements, 1855–1897* (London: London County Council, P. S. King & Son, 1898), 49.

35. Ibid.

36. *First Report from the Select Committee on Metropolis Improvement*, 21.

37. *Second Report from Select Committee on Metropolis Improvements*, 102.

38. Reverend William Denton, *Observations on the Displacement of the Poor by Metropolitan Railways and by Other Public Improvements* (London: Bell and Daldy, 1864), 5.

39. LL 1:196.

40. LL 1:298.

41. LL 2:297.

42. "Penny Satirist," *Penny Satirist*, June 1, 1839, Issue 111, 2.

43. Ibid.

44. Ibid.

45. William Rendle, *Fever in London: Its Social and Sanitary Lessons* (London: Metropolitan Sanitary Association, 1866), 4.

46. Denton, *Observations on the Displacement of the Poor*, 16.

47. "Penny Satirist," 2.

48. There was a rash of alarmist reporting on Petticoat Lane in the summer of 1858. The *Daily News* also reported on a meeting held by the inhabitants of Petticoat Lane to combat charges made against them in the *City Press*, the *Standard*, the *Daily Telegraph*, the *Morning Post*, and the *Jewish Chronicle*, which claimed that "the stolen property at the fair is immense" and referred to the "almost impregnable mass" of people congregating on Petticoat Lane. See "Indignation Meeting in Petticoat-Lane," *Daily News*, August 17, 1858, Issue 3824.

49. "The Petticoat-Lane Marts," *Daily News*, August 3, 1858, Issue 3812; "The Petticoat-Lane Marts," *Morning Post*, August 3, 1858, Issue 26394, 3.

50. "The Petticoat-Lane Marts," *Morning Chronicle*, August 3, 1858, Issue 28564.

51. "The Police and the Sunday Fair in Petticoat-Lane," *Daily News*, August 2, 1858, Issue 3811.

52. Ibid.

53. Ibid.

54. "The Petticoat-Lane Marts," *Morning Chronicle*, August 3, 1858.

55. *Report from the Select Committee of the House of Lords Appointed to Consider the Bill, Intituled "An Act to Prevent Unnecessary Trading on Sunday in the Metropolis"; and to Report Thereon to the House* (London: House of Commons, June 1, 1850), 167.

56. Ibid., 14.

57. Mayhew discusses at length the problem associated with paying workers on Saturday nights, often at pubs. See, for example, *LL* 3:283–85. This was a common practice for paying dockworkers in particular. It is also a key theme of the *Report . . . to Consider the Bill, Intituled, "An Act to Prevent Unnecessary Trading."* The *Morning Chronicle* references this issue when praising the cooperation between the Metropolitan and City police, who with "with great good sense . . . decided to treat the matter as one simply of obstruction, without regard to the Sunday question, and that Petticoat-lane should be made as free for general traffic during the week as the other streets of the City." See "The Petticoat-Lane Marts," *Morning Chronicle* August 3, 1858.

58. Brian Harrison, "The Sunday Trading Riots of 1855," *Historical Journal* 8, no. 2 (1965): 221.

59. Ibid., 222–23.

60. Ibid., 224.

61. *Report . . . to Consider the Bill, Inituled, "An Act to Prevent Unnecessary Trading,"* 133.

62. The crowd as a conduit of emotion is a key them in Gustave Le Bon's crowd theory. See Gustave Le Bon, *The Crowd: A Study of the Popular Mind*, trans. Robert Nye (Mineola, NY: Dover Publications, Inc, 2002).

63. *Report . . . to Consider the Bill, Intituled "An Act to Prevent Unnecessary Trading on Sunday in the Metropolis,"* 152.

64. Ibid., 156.

65. Ibid., 160.

66. Ibid., 126.

67. Ibid., 119.

68. Ibid., 125.

69. *First Report from the Select Committee on Metropolis Improvement*, vi.

70. Ibid. Emphasis added.

71. *Fourth Report of the Commissioners*, 3. Emphasis added.

72. Pike, *Subterranean Cities*, 90.

73. *Fourth Report of the Commissioners*, 10.

74. Denton, *Observations on the Displacement of the Poor*, 10.

75. James H. Winter, *London's Teeming Streets: 1830–1914* (London: Routledge, 1993).

76. This is also a theme in Le Bon, *The Crowd*.

77. Max Schlesinger and Otto von Wenckstern, *Saunterings in and about London* (London: N. Cooke, 1853), 155–56, http://archive.org/details/saunteringsinaboooschluoft.

78. *LL* 1:248. Wentworth Street, which combined with Middlesex Street to form Petticoat Lane, is specifically mentioned as a site of crowded lodging houses hosting promiscuous sexual exchange in both the *Second Report from Select Committee on Metropolis Improvements*, 104, and the *Report . . . to consider of The Bill intituled "An Act to prevent Unnecessary Trading on Sunday in the Metropolis,"* 183.

79. Charles Dickens, "On Duty with Inspector Field," in *Reprinted Pieces*, ed. Jim Manis (Hazleton, PA: Electronic Classics Series, 1999), 143, 145.

80. Ibid., 151.

81. Ibid., 143.

82. Ibid., 144.

83. Eliza Lynn Linton, "Out Walking," *Temple Bar*, July 1, 1862, 132–39.

84. Lynda Nead, *Victorian Babylon: People, Streets and Images in Nineteenth-Century London* (New Haven, CT: Yale University Press, 2007), 63.

85. Linton, "Out Walking," 132.

86. Ibid.

87. Ibid.

88. Nead, *Victorian Babylon*, 66.

89. Linton, "Out Walking," 134.

90. Ibid., 133.

91. Ibid.

92. Schlesinger and Wenckstern, *Saunterings in and about London*, 17.

93. Linton, "Out Walking," 135.

94. LL 1:258.

95. LL 1:i.

96. LL 1:375.

97. Bruce Robbins, *Secular Vocations: Intellectuals, Professionalism, Culture* (London: Verso, 1983), 181; Bruce Robbins, "Cosmopolitanism: New and Newer," *Boundary* 2 34, no. 3 (2007): 51.

98. Amanda Anderson, *The Powers of Distance: Cosmopolitanism and the Cultivation of Detachment* (Princeton, NJ: Princeton University Press, 2001), 15.

99. Robbins, "Cosmopolitanism: New and Newer," 51.

100. Georg Simmel, "The Metropolis and Mental Life," in *The Sociology of Georg Simmel*, trans. Kurt Wolff (New York: Free Press, 1950), 409–24.

101. LL 2:10.

102. LL 2:11.

103. LL 2:39.

104. Israel Zangwill, *Children of the Ghetto: A Study of a Peculiar People*, 3rd ed. (London: Project Gutenberg, 1914), http://www.gutenberg.org/ebooks/12680.

105. Ibid.

106. Zygmunt Bauman, *Modernity and Ambivalence* (Cambridge: Polity Press, 1991), 169.

107. Karl Marx, "On the Jewish Question," *Marxists.org*, 1844, https://www.marxists.org/archive/marx/works/1844/jewish-question/.

108. Anderson, *The Powers of Distance*, 131.

109. George Elliot, *Daniel Deronda* (Oxford: Oxford University Press, 2014).

110. Zangwill, *Children of the Ghetto*.

111. LL 1:348.

112. LL 2:37.

113. LL 2:118.

114. LL 2:63.

115. *LL* 2:70.

116. Ibid.

117. Ibid.

118. *LL* 2:71.

119. *LL* 2:80.

120. *LL* 2:30.

121. *LL* 2:28.

122. *LL* 2:154, 139.

123. *LL* 2:30.

124. *LL* 2:39.

CHAPTER 4

1. Arthur Conan Doyle, *The Sign of the Four* (1890; Project Gutenberg EBook, 2008).

2. Ibid.

3. Siegfried Kracauer, "Photography," trans. Thomas Y. Levin, *Critical Inquiry* 19, no. 3 (1993): 431.

4. This argument has been made most effectively in Robert Hariman and John Lucaites, *No Caption Needed: Iconic Photographs, Public Culture, and Liberal Democracy* (Chicago: University of Chicago Press, 2007).

5. The significance of this linkage—which I explored earlier in the connection among worker's bodies, sewer technology, and insurance discourses—is argued for in Ian Hacking, "Biopolitics and the Avalanche of Printed Numbers," *Humanities in Society* 5, nos. 3–4 (1982): 279–95.

6. "Photography: Its History and Application," *British Quarterly Review* 44, no. 87 (1866): 372.

7. *LL* 3:204.

8. Ibid.

9. Lady Elizabeth Eastlake, "Photography," *The London Quarterly Review* 101 (1857): 442.

10. See Allan Sekula, "The Body and the Archive," *October* 39 (1986): 3, doi:10.2307/778312; Jonathan Crary, *Techniques of the Observer: On Vision and Modernity in the Nineteenth Century* (Cambridge: MIT Press, 1990); John Tagg, "The Archiving Machine; or, the Camera and the Filing Cabinet," *Grey Room* 47 (2012): 24–37; and John Tagg, *Burden of Representation: Essays on Photographies and Histories* (Minneapolis: University of Minnesota Press, 1993).

11. "Photography: Its History and Application," 369.

12. Helena E. Wright, "Photography in the Printing Press: The Photomechanical Revolution," *Presenting Pictures* 4 (2004): 22.

13. Ibid., 34.

14. H. Trueman Wood, from his 1887 book *Method of Illustrating Books*, quoted in Denis Defibaugh, *The Collotype: History, Process, and Photographic Documentation* (master's thesis, Rochester Institute of Technology, 1997), 12.

15. "History of Punch," *Punch*, www.punch.co.uk/about, accessed January 8, 2019.

16. Kracauer, "Photography," 431.

17. *LL* 3:206.

18. *LL* 3:204.

19. *LL* 3:206.

20. *LL* 3:207.

21. Ibid.

22. *LL* 3:206.

23. Sekula, "The Body and the Archive," 17.

24. *LL* 3:208.

25. Daniel Novak, *Realism, Photography and Nineteenth-Century Fiction* (Cambridge: Cambridge University Press, 2008), 8.

26. *LL* 3:208.

27. Siegfried Kracauer describes the portrait as a metaphoric condensation of the fund of self-images in "Photography," 421–36.

28. Building on Crary, as I do below, Novak makes a similar argument using synecdoche rather than metonymy. Novak writes, "Rather than scattering the body's parts, synecdoche projects a virtual whole to which these parts refer. In other words, synecdoche functions as a defense against the fragmentation that it is usually taken to produce." Metonymy and synecdoche both name the whole by referring to one of its parts, but synecdoche tends to imply that the referenced part is literally on or of the whole, as in the classic example of "hands" to refer to workers. Metonymy, on the other hand, refers to a part that is *associated* with the whole. Metonymy thus assembles associations, and this assembling is what "projects the virtual whole" Novak references. Association also implies the relationships of contiguity that make parts interchangeable and substitutable. Synecdoche forecloses association and interchange. For Novak's argument on synecdoche, see *Realism, Photography and Nineteenth-Century Fiction*, 32.

29. Crary, *Techniques of the Observer*, 31.

30. *LL* 3:209.

31. Francis Galton, *A Descriptive List of Anthropometric Apparatus, Consisting of Instruments for Measuring and Testing the Chief Physical Characteristics of the Human Body* (Cambridge: Cambridge Scientific Instrument Company, 1887), 4.

32. Ibid., 3.

33. Ibid., 3.

34. Francis Galton, *Finger Prints* (London: Macmillan and Co, 1892), 198.

35. Francis Galton, "Address to the Department of Anthropology," *Report of the British Association for the Advancement of Science*, 1877, 99.

36. Havelock Ellis, *The Criminal* (New York: Scribner and Welford, 1890), 64, 208.

37. Charles Darwin, *The Expression of the Emotions in Man and Animals* (London: John Murray, Albermarle Street, 1872), 235.

38. Galton, *Finger Prints*, 149. Alphonse Bertillon, "The Bertillon System of Identification." *Forum*, May 1891, 330–42. For Galton on Bertillonage, see Francis Galton, "The Bertillon System of Identification," *Nature* 1407, no. 54 (1896): 569–70.

39. Galton, *Finger Prints*, 149.

40. Ibid., 192–93.

41. Ibid., 196.

42. Hortense J. Spillers, "Mama's Baby, Papa's Maybe," in *Black, White, and in Color: Essays on American Literature and Culture*, (Chicago: University of Chicago Press, 2003), 205.

43. Alexander G. Weheliye, *Habeas Viscus: Racializing Assemblages, Biopolitics, and Black Feminist Theories of the Human* (Durham, NC: Duke University Press, 2014), 39, 3.

44. Francis Galton, *Hereditary Genius: An Inquiry into Its Laws and Consequences* (London: Macmillan and Co, 1869), 339.

45. In *Hereditary Genius* (1869), Galton writes, "it may prove that the Negroes, one and all, will fail as completely under the new conditions as they have failed under the old ones, to submit to the needs of a civilization superior to their own; in this case their races, numerous and prolific as they are, will in course of time be supplanted and replaced by their betters" (xxvi). Galton also writes of the "savage man" in "the North American continent, in the West Indian Islands, in the Cape of Good Hope, in Australia, New Zealand, Van Diemen's Land," claiming that "the human denizens of vast regions have been entirely swept away in the short space of three centuries less by the pressure of a stronger race than through the influence of a civilization they were incapable of supporting" (345).

46. Galton, *Finger Prints*, 147.

47. In striving for standardization and reproducibility, the racial type is certainly analogous to the stereotype, which came in to use in printing in the early nineteenth century and was used in order to standardize and reproduce a frame of set type. The stereotype involved taking a papier-mâché or plaster cast of set type in order to reprint a frame of type, obviating the need to reset individual type later. "Stereotype" came to mean "something continued or constantly repeated without change" by 1850, but did not acquire its contemporary connotation of a "preconceived and oversimplified idea of the characteristics which typify a person, situation, etc." until the twentieth century. See "stereotype, n. and adj.," *OED Online*, December 2014, Oxford University Press, http://www.oed.com.turing.library.northwestern.edu/view/Entry/189956?rskey=n16SMC&result=1&isAdvanced=false (accessed January 7, 2019).

48. For Queen Victoria's role in the history of photography, see Anne M. Lyden, *A Royal Passion: Queen Victoria and Photography* (Los Angeles: Getty Publications, 2014).

49. Gilles Deleuze and Felix Guattari, *A Thousand Plateaus: Capitalism and Schizophrenia*. Translated by Brian Massumi (Minneapolis: University of Minnesota Press, 1987), 168.

50. Béla Balázs, *Theory of the Film*, trans. Edith Bone (London: Dennis Dobson LTD, 1951), 81, https://archive.org/details/theoryofthefilm000665mbp.

51. Ibid., 55.

52. Deleuze and Guattari, *A Thousand Plateaus*, 172.

53. Galton considered his most successful composite portraits to be that of the Jew. The Jewish social statistician Joseph Jacobs helped Galton find Jews from the Jews' Free School and the Jewish Working Men's Club to photograph for his portraits. For Jacobs's description of the results, see Joseph Jacobs, "Of the Racial Characteristics of Modern Jews," *Journal of the Anthropological Institute of Great Britain and Ireland* 15 (1886): 23–62. For more on Galton, Jacobs, and the Jewish type, see Sekula, "The Body and the Archive," 52, and Novak, *Realism, Photography and Nineteenth-Century Fiction*, 90–118.

54. Francis Galton, "Photographic Composites," *Photographic News* 17 (1885): 243.

55. Francis Galton, "Composite Portraiture," *The Photographic Journal* 24 (1881): 140.

56. Galton, "Address to the Department of Anthropology," 95. In this passage Galton refers to the experiments of Gustav Theodor Fechner, who developed a scale for measuring mental response to physical stimuli.

57. Galton, "Address to the Department of Anthropology," 97.

58. Galton, "Composite Portraiture," 144.

59. Novak, *Realism, Photography and Nineteenth-Century Fiction*, 32.

60. Ibid., 48.

61. Michel Foucault, *Discipline and Punish: The Birth of the Prison*, trans. Alan Sheridan, 2nd edition (New York: Vintage Books, 1995).

62. Novak, *Realism, Photography and Nineteenth-Century Fiction*, 48.

63. Stocking, "What's in a Name? The Origins of the Royal Anthropological Institute (1837–1871)," *Man* 6, no. 3 (1971): 381. See Stocking's essay for a rich account of the tensions between the ethnological and anthropological societies of London. Although the work of Darwinists such as Galton was more in line with anthropology than ethnology, many Darwinists joined the Ethnological Institute of London in order to distance themselves from the brash populism of upstart anthropologists. Eventually the disputes were settled and the Royal Anthropological Institute formed.

64. Robert Altick, *Punch: The Lively Youth of a British Institution, 1841–1851* (Columbus: Ohio State University Press, 1997), 509.

65. The naming story, which is perhaps apocryphal, is that the men sitting around the famous *Punch* table—before it was called the *Punch* table—agreed that the magazine should be like a good Punch mixture, which is nothing without a bit of (Mark) Lemon. Mayhew then shouted, "A capital idea! Let us call the paper Punch!" (see www.punch.co.uk/about). Mayhew, though, drifted away from *Punch* after the first few years of its existence (Ibid., 44).

66. Other examples that I lack the space to cover here include *Punch*'s series "The Natural History of Courtship," which ran concurrently with the physiologies; a February 12, 1842, issue dedicated entirely to London types; an article entitled "A Nigger Professor of Cramanology" (January 29, 1842); an article entitled "The Zoology and Architecture of Lawyers' Clerks," *Punch*, vol. 3 (London, Bradbury and Evans, 1842), 182; and an announcement from the "British Association for the Advancement of Everything in General, and Nothing in Particular," which included this report: "Section F.—Statistics.—This section came out, as usual, particularly strong. A paper was read on the average number of Congreves in each box sold in the streets, and some very interesting calculations were gone into of the amount of cherry-stones picked up between Clerkenwell Green, and Clapham Common, on the 15th of last August" (*Punch* vol. 3, 1842, 6–7).

67. Robert Hariman, "Political Parody and Public Culture," *Quarterly Journal of Speech* 94, no. 3 (2008): 251.

68. Miriam Bratu Hansen, *Cinema and Experience: Siegfried Kracauer, Walter Benjamin, and Theodor W. Adorno* (Berkeley: University of California Press, 2011), 8. Kracauer argued, "Genuine film drama has the task of rendering ironic the phantomlike quality of our life by exaggerating its unreality and thus to point toward true reality" (quoted in Hansen, 12).

69. See Friedrich A. Kittler, *Gramophone, Film, Typewriter*, trans. Geoffrey Winthrop-Young, Michael Wutz, and Geoffrey Winthrop Young (Stanford, CA: Stanford University Press, 1999).

70. The stereoscope is fundamental to Jonathan Crary's argument, because the stereoscope produces an image that does not exist in reality, shattering any notion of a stable space of representation that exists outside the body.

71. "The Simple History of a Portrait," *Punch, or the London Charivari*, vol. 33, November 28, 1857, Punch Publications Ltd: London, 1857, 224.

72. "Photographic Failures," *Punch, or the London Charivari*, vol. 12, April 3, 1847, Punch Publications Ltd: London, 1847, 42.

73. Kracauer, "Photography," 431.

74. "Photographic Failures."

75. Ibid.

76. As Altick demonstrates, illustrated types were a popular form with a long history, appearing in contemporary publications such as *Bell's Life in London* and Dickens's *Sketches by Boz*, but also in Francis Wheatley's 1804 "The Itinerant Traders of London," Rowlandson's 1820 "Characteristic Sketches of the Lower Orders," George and Robert Cruikshank's 1827–29 etchings of London characters, and Kenny Meadows's 1840 *Heads of the People: or, Portraits of the English with Original Essays by Distinguished Writers*. See Altick, *Punch*, 496–499.

77. Ibid., 499.

78. "Physiology of the London Idler: Chapter V—Concerning Exhibition Loungers," *Punch, or the London Charivari*, vol. 3 (Bradbury and Evans: London, 1842), 37.

79. Ibid.

80. "Civilisation," *Punch, or the London Charivari*, July 31, 1841.

81. Kittler, *Gramophone, Film, Typewriter*, 150.

82. Ibid., 149.

83. Ibid., 150.

84. Ibid., 152.

85. Here, for example, is *Punch* on the homes of the Regent-street loungers: "We believe it has never yet been ascertained for a certainty where the Regent-street loungers live when they are at home. They affect the neighbourhood of the West-end generally, and sometimes give their day address at a club; but beyond this we can give no clue to their domiciles, for some of these gay loiterers reside in localities only known to tax-collectors, election canvassers, water-rate men, and people who engrave maps of London." See "The Physiology of the London Idler: Chapter II—The Regent-Street Lounger," *Punch, or the London Charivari*, vol. 3, 13.

86. "Physiology of the London Idler: Chapter VI—Concerning the Gent," *Punch, or the London Charivari*, vol. 3, 60.

87. Ibid.

88. Ibid.

89. Luce Irigaray, *This Sex Which Is Not One* (Ithaca, NY: Cornell University Press, 1985), 177.

90. "Physiology of the London Idler: Chapter VI—Concerning the Gent."

91. Kittler, *Gramophone, Film, Typewriter*, 149.

92. Kracauer, "Photography," 435.

93. For more in Kracauer's "Photography" essay, see Hansen, *Cinema and Experience*, 27–39.

94. Staging studio pictures to produce "characteristic" was a common and controversial practices. See, for example, Seth Koven, "Dr. Barnardo's 'Artistic Fictions': Photography, Sexuality, and the Ragged Child in Victorian London," *Radical History Review* 69 (1997): 6–45.

95. Nead suggests that the city could not be animated in media until the advent of cinema. See Lynda Nead, *The Haunted Gallery: Painting, Photography, Film C.1900* (New Haven, CT: Yale University Presss, 2007). Elizabeth Kathryn Morgan suggest that Beards daguerreotypes appeared "static." See Morgan, *Street Life in London: Context and Commentary* (Edinburgh: Museums Etc, 2014). These arguments are emblematic of a widely shared assumption that mobility is best rendered in cinema. This assumption ignores the long tradition of imaging mobility in pre-cinematic media.

96. Richard Ovenden, *John Thomson (1837–1921): Photographer* (Edinburgh: Stationery Office, 1997), 78.

97. Quoted in Allen Hockley, "John Thomson's China," *MIT: Visualizing Cultures*, 2010, http://ocw.mit.edu/ans7870/21f/21f.027/john_thomson_china_01/ct_essay04.html.

98. John Thomson and Adolphe Smith, *Victorian London Street Life in Historic Photographs* [Reprint of *Street Life in London*] (New York: Dover Publications, Inc, 1994), preface.

99. Ovenden, *John Thomson (1837–1921)*, 83.

100. For more on the publication history of *Street Life in London*, see Morgan, *Street Life in London*, 2014.

101. Ovenden, *John Thomson (1837–1921)*, 84.

102. Nead, *The Haunted Gallery*, 110.

103. As Morgan argues, trimmed edges likely reflect "flaws in the negative" (180).

104. Thomson and Smith, *Victorian London Street Life in Historic Photographs*, 58.

105. Ibid., 62.

106. See LL 4:425.

107. LL 3:185.

108. Mayhew used terms like Indian, Hindoo, and East Indian loosely and interchangeably. This was relatively common at the time, as "even at the height of British colonial conquest across India, relatively few Britons in Britain had knowledge of how to identify an actual person from India," as Herschel's recourse to fingerprinting technology makes clear. See Michael H. Fisher, "Excluding and Including 'Natives of India': Early-Nineteenth-Century British-Indian Race Relations in Britain," *Comparative Studies of Asia, Africa and the Middle East* 27, no. 2 (2007): 305.

109. LL 3:185.

110. LL 3:185.

111. Although the "Indian Juggler" or street performer was a well-recognized type, Indians in Britain—who were arriving at the rate of several thousand per year by the 1850s—were also Lascars, "diplomats, scholars, soldiers, officials, tourists, businessmen, and students and wives and children of Britons." See Fisher, "Excluding and Including 'Natives of India'," 304.

112. LL 3:104.

113. "Death of Ramo Samee: Appeal of the Widow," *Bell's Life in London*, August 25, 1850.

114. Ibid.

115. "The Late Ramo Samee and His Widow: To the Editor of Bell's Life in London," *Bell's Life in London*, September 1, 1850.

116. LL 3:105.

117. LL 3:105.

118. William Hazlitt, "The Indian Jugglers," in *Table Talk: Essays on Men and Manners* (Project Gutenberg EBook, 2017 [1821]) William Makepeace Thackeray, *The Book of Snobs* (Project Gutenberg EBook, 2018 [1848]). In *Sea of Poppies*, Amitav Ghosh's 2008 novel, the second of a triology set during the Opium Wars, the English first mate Jack Crowle refers to all non-white sailors not by names but as types: all the Lascars were either "Bub-dool" or "Rammer-Sammy." Ghosh thus satirizes the dispersal of the individual name into type. See Ghosh, *Sea of Poppies* (Farrar, Straus and Giroux, 2008), 237.

119. Walter D. Welford, *The Hand Camera Manual: A Beginner's Guide to Photography in Its Connection with the Hand Camera* (London: L. Upcott Gill, 1893), 7.

120. Ibid., 68, 75.

121. Nead, *The Haunted Gallery*, 7.

122. Nancy Armstrong, *Fiction in the Age of Photography: The Legacy of British Realism*, new edition. Cambridge, MA: Harvard University Press, 2002, 102.

EPILOGUE

1. George Gissing, *New Grub Street* (Oxford: Oxford World Classics, 2008), 5.

2. Ibid., 9.

3. Ibid.

4. Ibid., 32, 33.

5. Ibid., 33.

6. Charles Dickens, *Bleak House*, Project Gutenberg E-Book (Project Gutenberg, 1997), http://www.gutenberg.org/ebooks/1023?msg=welcome_stranger#c59.

7. Gissing, *New Grub Street*, 110.

8. LL 2:400

9. Dickens, *Bleak House*.

10. LL 1:101.

11. Jack London, *The People of the Abyss* (Project Gutenberg, 2005), http://www.gutenberg .org/files/1688/1688-h/1688-h.htm.

12. W. C. Preston, "The Bitter Cry of Outcast London : An Inquiry into the Condition of the Abject Poor," *Internet Archive*, 1883, 4, https://archive.org/details/bittercryofoutcaoopres.

13. William Booth, *In Darkest England and the Way Out*, 2 vols. (London: International Headquarters of the Salvation Army, 1890). I was reminded of this connection by Christian Topalov, "The City as Terra Incognita: Charles Booth's Poverty Survey and the People of London, 1886–1891," *Planning Perspectives* 8, no. 4 (1993), 411.

14. Charles Booth, *Life and Labour of the People in London*, vol. 1, East London (London: Williams and Norgate, 1889), 594, 38.

15. Dickens, *Bleak House*.

16. Charles Booth, "The Condition of the People of East London and Hackney, 1887," *Journal of the Royal Statistical Society* 51 (1888): 277–78.

17. Charles Booth, "Life and Labour of the People in London: First Results of an Inquiry Based on the 1891 Census. Opening Address of Charles Booth, Esq., President of the Royal Statistical Society, Session 1893–93," *Journal of the Royal Statistical Society* 56 (1893): 591.

18. Georg Lukács, *Studies in European Realism*, trans. John Mander and Ecke Mander (London: Merlin, 1963), 6.

19. Booth, *Labour and Life of the People*, vol. 1, East London, 38.

20. Topalov, "The City as Terra Incognita," 404.

21. Booth, *Labour and Life of the People*, Volume 1, East London, 60.

22. Deborah Epstein Nord, *Walking the Victorian Streets: Women, Representation, and the City* (Ithaca, NY: Cornell University Press, 1995).

23. Israel Zangwill, *Children of the Ghetto: A Study of a Peculiar People*, 3rd ed. (London: Project Gutenberg, 1914), http://www.gutenberg.org/ebooks/12680.

24. See Joseph Jacobs, "Of the Racial Characteristics of Modern Jews," *The Journal of the Anthropological Institute of Great Britain and Ireland* 15 (1886): 23–62.

25. Zangwill, *Children of the Ghetto*.

26. Ibid. For further discussion of this passage, see Meri-Jane Rochelson, "Language, Gender, and Ethnic Anxiety in Zangwill's *Children of the Ghetto*," *English Literature in Transition, 1880–1920* 31, no. 4 (1988): 403.

27. Arthur Morrison, *Tales of Mean Streets*, Project Gutenberg E-Book (Project Gutenberg, 2012), http://www.gutenberg.org/ebooks/40569.

28. Jane Jacobs, *The Death and Life of Great American Cities* (New York: Vintage Books, 1994).

29. Salvation Army "Captain" Nick Coke, quoted in "Strangers into Citizens Briefing Paper No. 4" (Strangers into Citizens Campaign, London, 2009), 12.

BIBLIOGRAPHY

Ahmed, Sara. "Some Preliminary Remarks on the Founding Gestures of 'New Material-ism." *European Journal of Women's Studies* 15, no. 1 (2008): 23–39.

Allen, Michelle. "From Cesspool to Sewer: Sanitary Reform and the Rhetoric of Resistance, 1848–1880." *Victorian Literature & Culture* 30, no. 2 (2002): 383–402.

Altick, Robert. *Punch: The Lively Youth of a British Institution, 1841–1851*. Columbus: Ohio State University Press, 1997.

Anderson, Amanda. *The Powers of Distance: Cosmopolitanism and the Cultivation of Detachment*. Princeton, NJ: Princeton University Press, 2001.

Armfelt, Count E. "Oriental London." In *Living London*, 1:81–86. London: Cassell and Company, Limited, 1902.

Armstrong, Nancy. *Fiction in the Age of Photography: The Legacy of British Realism*. New edition. Cambridge, MA: Harvard University Press, 2002.

Balázs, Béla. *Theory of the Film*. Translated by Edith Bone. London: Dennis Dobson LTD, 1951. https://archive.org/details/theoryofthefilm000665mbp.

Baucom, Ian. *Specters of the Atlantic: Finance Capital, Slavery, and the Philosophy of History*. Durham, NC: Duke University Press, 2005.

Bauman, Zygmunt. *Modernity and Ambivalence*. Cambridge, UK: Polity Press, 1991.

Bazalgette, Sir Joseph William. *On the Main Drainage of London, and the Interception of the Sewage from the River Thames*. London, 1865.

Benjamin, Walter. *The Arcades Project*. Translated by Howard Eiland and Kevin McLaughlin. Cambridge, MA: The Belknap Press of Harvard University Press, 1999.

———. "The Work of Art in the Age of Mechanical Reproduction." In *Illuminations: Essays and Reflections*, translated by Harry Zohn, 217–52. New York: Schocken Books, 1969.

Bennett, A. W. *The Sin of Great Cities; or, The Great Social Evil: A National Sin*. London: Charles Cull, Harberdashers' Street, Hoxton, 1859.

Bennett, Jane. *Vibrant Matter: A Political Ecology of Things*. Durham, NC: Duke University Press, 2010.

Berlant, Lauren. *Cruel Optimism*. Durham, NC: Duke University Press, 2011.

Bernasconi, Robert. "Kant's Third Thoughts on Race." In *Reading Kant's Geography*, edited by Stuart Elden and Eduardo Mendieta, 291–318. Albany: State University of New York Press, 2011.

Bertillon, Alphonse. "The Bertillon System of Identification." *Forum*, May 1891, 330–42.

Blair, Carole. "Contemporary U.S. Memorial Sites as Exemplars of Rhetoric's Materiality." In *Rhetorical Bodies*, edited by Jack Selzer and Sharon Crowley, 16–57. Madison: University of Wisconsin Press, 1999.

Booth, Charles. "The Condition of the People of East London and Hackney, 1887." *Journal of the Royal Statistical Society* 51 (1888): 277–78.

———. *Life and Labour of the People in London*. Volume 1, East London. London: Williams and Norgate, 1889.

———. "Life and Labour of the People in London: First Results of an Inquiry Based on the 1891 Census. Opening Address of Charles Booth, Esq., President of the Royal Statistical Society, Session 1893–93." *Journal of the Royal Statistical Society* 56 (1893): 591.

Booth, William. *In Darkest England and the Way Out*. 2 vols. London: International Headquarters of the Salvation Army, 1890.

Bryant, Levi R. *The Democracy of Objects*. Ann Arbor, MI: Open Humanities Press, 2011.

Burke, Edmund. *A Philosophical Enquiry into the Origin of Our Ideas of the Sublime and Beautiful*. Edited by Adam Phillips. Oxford: Oxford University Press, 1990.

Burke, Kenneth. *The Philosophy of Literary Form*. 3rd edition. Berkeley: University of California Press, 1974.

Carey, James W. "Technology and Ideology: The Case of the Telegraph." In *Communication as Culture: Essays on Media and Society*, 201–30. New York: Routledge, 1989

Carey, John. *The Intellectuals and the Masses: Pride and Prejudice among the Literary Intelligentsia, 1880–1939*. New edition. London: Faber & Faber, 1992.

Chadwick, Edwin. *An Essay on the Means of Insurance against the Casualties of Sickness, Decrepitude, and Mortality*. Comprising an Article Reprinted from the *Westminster Review* (No. XVIIII), for April 1828, with Additional Notes and Corrections. London: Charles Knight, 1836.

Chandler, James. *England in 1819: The Politics of Literary Culture and the Case of Romantic Historicism*. Chicago: University of Chicago Press, 1999.

Chun, Wendy Hui Kyong. "Race and/as Technology; or, How to Do Things to Race." *Camera Obscura* 70, 24, no. 1 (2009): 7–35.

Cisneros, Josue David. *The Border Crossed Us: Rhetorics of Borders, Citizenship, and Latina/o Identity*. Tuscaloosa: University of Alabama Press, 2014.

Clark, Geoffrey. *Betting On Lives: The Culture of Life Insurance in England, 1695–1775*. Manchester: Manchester University Press, 1999.

Cooper, Edmund. "Report to the Metropolitan Commission of Sewers on the House-Drainage of St. James, Westminster, during the Recent Cholera Outbreak." Metropolitan Commission of Sewers, September 22, 1854.

Corbin, Alain. *The Foul and the Fragrant: Odor and the French Social Imagination*. Cambridge, MA: Harvard University Press, 1986.

Crary, Jonathan. *Techniques of the Observer: On Vision and Modernity in the Nineteenth Century.* Cambridge, MA: MIT Press, 1990.

Darwin, Charles. *The Expression of the Emotions in Man and Animals.* London: John Murray, Albermarle Street, 1872.

Davis, Diane. "Addressing Alterity: Rhetoric, Hermeneutics, and the Nonappropriative Relation," *Philosophy and Rhetoric* 38, no. 3 (2005): 191–212.

———. *Inessential Solidarity: Rhetoric and Foreigner Relations.* Pittsburgh: University of Pittsburgh Press, 2010.

"Death of Ramo Samee: Appeal of the Widow." *Bell's Life in London.* August 25, 1850.

de Certeau, Michel. *The Practice of Everyday Life.* Translated by Steven Rendall. Berkeley: University of California Press, 1984.

Defibaugh, Denis. *The Collotype: History, Process, and Photographic Documentation.* Rochester, NY: Rochester Institute of Technology, 1997.

Deleuze, Gilles. *Kant's Critical Philosophy: The Doctrine of the Faculties.* Edited by Hugh Tomlinson. Minneapolis: University of Minnesota Press, 1985.

Deleuze, Gilles, and Felix Guattari. *A Thousand Plateaus: Capitalism and Schizophrenia.* Translated by Brian Massumi. Minneapolis: University of Minnesota Press, 1987.

De Man, Paul. "Phenomenality and Materiality in Kant." In *Hermeneutics: Questions and Prospects,* edited by Gary Shapiro and Alan Sica. Amherst: University of Massachusetts Press, 1984.

Denton, Reverend William. *Observations on the Displacement of the Poor by Metropolitan Railways and by Other Public Improvements.* London: Bell and Daldy, 1864.

Derrida, Jacques. *Margins of Philosophy.* Translated by Alan Bass. Brighton, UK: Harvester Press, 1982.

Dickens, Charles. *Bleak House.* Project Gutenberg E-Book. Project Gutenberg, 1997. http://www.gutenberg.org/ebooks/1023?msg=welcome_stranger#c59.

———. "On Duty with Inspector Field." In *Reprinted Pieces,* edited by Jim Manis, 139–51. Hazleton, PA: Electronic Classics Series, 1999.

———. *Our Mutual Friend.* Oxford: Oxford University Press, 2008.

Dickinson, Greg. "Joe's Rhetoric: Finding Authenticity at Starbucks." *Rhetoric Society Quarterly* 32, no. 4 (2002): 5–27

"Distressed Populations." *Economist,* November 16, 1850.

Dobraszczyk, Paul. "Sewers, Wood Engraving, and the Sublime: Picturing London's Main Drainage System in the 'Illustrated London News,' 1859–1862." *Victorian Periodicals Review* 38, no. 4 (Winter 2005): 349–78.

Doran, Robert. *The Theory of Sublime from Longinus to Kant.* Cambridge: Cambridge University Press, 2015.

Douglas, Mary. *Purity and Danger: An Analysis of Concepts of Pollution and Taboo.* London: Routledge, 2002.

Doyle, Arthur Conan. *The Sign of the Four.* 1890; Project Gutenberg EBook, 2008.

Dyos, H. J. "The Slums of Victorian London." *Victorian Studies* 11, no. 1 (1967): 5–40.

Eastlake, Lady Elizabeth. "Photography." *The London Quarterly Review* 101 (1857): 442–68.

Edwards, Brian T. "Logics and Contexts of Circulation." In *A Companion to Comparative Literature.* Edited by Ali Behdad and Dominic Thomas. Malden, MA: Blackwell Publishing, 2011.

Edwards, Elizabeth. "Photographic 'Types': The Pursuit of Method." *Visual Anthropology* 3, nos. 2–3 (1990): 235–58.

Edwards, Percy J. *History of London Street Improvements, 1855–1897.* London: London County Council, P. S. King & Son, 1898.

Eliot, George. *Daniel Deronda.* Oxford: Oxford University Press, 2014.

Ellis, Havelock. *The Criminal.* New York: Scribner and Welford, 1890.

Eze, Emmanuel Chukwudi. "The Colour of Reason: The Idea of 'Race' in Kant's Anthropology." In *Postcolonial African Philosophy: A Critical Reader,* edited by Emmanuel Chukwudi Eze, 103–31. Cambridge, MA: Blackwell, 1997.

Fanon, Frantz. *Black Skins, White Masks.* Translated by Charles Lam Markmann. London: Pluto Press, 2008.

Felski, Rita. "Context Stinks!" *New Literary History* 42, no. 4 (2011): 573–91.

First Report from the Select Committee on Metropolis Improvement. United Kingdom: House of Commons, June 25, 1840.

Fisher, Michael H. "Excluding and Including 'Natives of India': Early-Nineteenth-Century British-Indian Race Relations in Britain." *Comparative Studies of Asia, Africa and the Middle East* 27, no. 2 (2007): 303–14.

Flores, Lisa. "Between Abundance and Marginalization: The Imperative of Racial Rhetorical Criticism." *Review of Communication* 16, no. 1 (2016): 4–24.

Foucault, Michel. *Discipline and Punish: The Birth of the Prison.* Translated by Alan Sheridan. 2nd edition. New York: Vintage Books, 1995.

———. "Governmentality." In *The Foucault Effect,* edited by Graham Burchell, Colin Gordon, and Peter Miller, translated by Pasquale Pasquino. London: Harvester Wheatsheaf, 1991.

———. *The History of Sexuality Vol. 1.* Translated by Robert Hurley. New York: Vintage Books, 1978.

———. *Security, Territory, Population: Lectures at the Collège de France 1977–1978.* Translated by Graham Burchell. New York: Picador, 2009.

———. *"Society Must Be Defended": Lectures at the Collège de France, 1975–1976.* Translated by David Macey. New York: Picador, 1997.

Fourth Report of the Commissioners Appointed by Her Majesty to Inquire into and Consider the Most Effectual Means of Improving the Metropolis and of Providing Increased Facilities of Communication within the Same. United Kingdom: Parliament, 1845.

Freud, Sigmund. *Civilization and Its Discontents.* Translated by James Strachey. New York: W. W. Norton, 1962.

Gallagher, Catherine. "The Ends of History: Afterword." *Victorian Studies* 55, no. 4 (2013): 683–91.

Galton, Francis. "Address to the Department of Anthropology." *Report of the British Association for the Advancement of Science,* 1877, 94–100.

———. "The Bertillon System of Identification." *Nature* 1407, no. 54 (1896): 569–70.

———. "Composite Portraiture." *Photographic Journal* 24 (1881): 140–46.

———. *A Descriptive List of Anthropometric Apparatus, Consisting of Instruments for Measuring and Testing the Chief Physical Characteristics of the Human Body.* Cambridge: Cambridge Scientific Instrument Company, 1887.

———. *Finger Prints.* London: Macmillan and Co, 1892.

————. *Hereditary Genius: An Inquiry into Its Laws and Consequences*. London: Macmillan and Co, 1869.

————. "Photographic Composites." *The Photographic News* 17 (1885): 243–45.

Gamble, Christopher N. "Figures of Entanglement: A Special Issue Introduction." *Review of Communication* 16, no. 4 (2016): 265–80.

Gaonkar, Dilip Parameshwar. "After the Fictions: Notes Towards a Phenomenology of the Multitude." *E-Flux Journal* 58 (2014). http://www.e-flux.com/journal/after-the-fictions-notes-towards-a-phenomenology-of-the-multitude/.

Gaonkar, Dilip Parameshwar, and Elizabeth A. Povinelli. "Technologies of Public Form: Circulation, Transfiguration, Recognition." *Public Culture* 15, no. 3 (2003): 385–97.

Ghosh, Amitav. *Sea of Poppies*. Farrar, Straus and Giroux, 2008.

Gissing, George. *New Grub Street*. Oxford: Oxford World Classics, 2008.

Gilmore, Ruth Wilson. "Race and Globalization." In *Geographies of Global Change: Remapping the World*, edited by R. J. Johnston, Peter J. Taylor, and Michael J. Watts, 261–74. New York: Blackwell Publishing, 2002.

Goldberg, David Theo. *Racial State*. Malden, MA: John Wiley & Sons, 2001.

Goodlad, Lauren M. E. "Trollopian 'Foreign Policy': Rootedness and Cosmopolitanism in the Mid-Victorian Global Imaginary." *PMLA* 124, no. 2 (2009): 437–54.

Goodlad, Lauren M. E., and Andrew Sartori. "The Ends of History: Introduction." *Victorian Studies* 55, no. 14 (2013): 591–614.

Greenblatt, Stephen. "Filthy Rites." *Daedalus* 111, no. 3 (1982): 1–16.

Grossman, Jonathan H. *Charles Dickens's Networks: Public Transport and the Novel*. Oxford: Oxford University Press, 2013.

Hacking, Ian. "Biopolitics and the Avalanche of Printed Numbers." *Humanities in Society* 5, nos. 3–4 (1982): 279–95.

Haley, James L. *Wolf: The Lives of Jack London*. New York: Basic Books, 2011.

Hall, Suzanne. *City, Street and Citizen: The Measure of the Ordinary*. London: Routledge, 2012.

Hamlin, Christopher. "Providence and Putrefaction: Victorian Sanitarians and the Natural Theology of Health and Disease." *Victorian Studies* 28, no. 3 (1985): 381–411.

Hansen, Miriam Bratu. *Cinema and Experience: Siegfried Kracauer, Walter Benjamin, and Theodor W. Adorno*. Berkeley: University of California Press, 2011.

Hariman, Robert. "Political Parody and Public Culture." *Quarterly Journal of Speech* 94, no. 3 (2008): 247–72.

Hariman, Robert, and John Lucaites. *No Caption Needed: Iconic Photographs, Public Culture, and Liberal Democracy*. Chicago: University of Chicago Press, 2007.

Harman, Graham. *Prince of Networks: Bruno Latour and Metaphysics*. Melbourne: re.press, 2009.

Harrison, Brian. "The Sunday Trading Riots of 1855." *The Historical Journal* 8, no. 2 (1965): 219–45.

Harvey, David. *The Condition of Postmodernity: An Enquiry into the Origins of Cultural Change*. Cambridge, MA: Blackwell Publishing, 1990.

Hawhee, Debra. "Bestiaries, Past and Future." *Rhetoric Society Quarterly* 47, no. 3 (2017): 285–91.

————. *Rhetoric in Tooth and Claw: Animals, Language, Sensation*. Chicago: University of Chicago Press, 2016.

———. "Rhetoric's Sensorium." *Quarterly Journal of Speech* 101, no. 1 (2015): 2–17.

Haywood, William. "Report to the Honourable Commissioners of Sewers and the City of London on the Accidents to Horses on Carriageway Pavements." London, 1873.

Hazlitt, William. "The Indian Jugglers." In *Table Talk: Essays on Men and Manners*. Project Gutenberg EBook, 2017 [1821].

Herbert, Christopher. *Culture and Anomie: Ethnographic Imagination in the Nineteenth Century*. Chicago: University of Chicago Press, 1991.

———. "Rat Worship and Taboo in Mayhew's London." *Representations* 23 (1988): 1–24.

———. "The Doctrine of Survivals, the Great Mutiny, and Lady Audley's Secret." *Novel: A Forum on Fiction* 42, no. 3 (2009): 431–36.

Hesse, Barnor. "Racialized Modernity: An Analytics of White Mythologies." *Ethnic and Racial Studies* 30, no. 4 (2007): 643–63.

Himmelfarb, Gertrude. "Mayhew's Poor: A Problem of Identity." *Victorian Studies* 14 (1971): 307–20.

Hockley, Allen. "John Thomson's China." *MIT: Visualizing Cultures*, 2010. http://ocw.mit .edu/ans7870/21f/21f.027/john_thomson_china_01/ct_essay04.html.

Humpherys, Anne. *Travels into the Poor Man's Country: The Work of Henry Mayhew*. Athens: University of Georgia Press, 1977.

"Indignation Meeting in Petticoat-Lane." *Daily News*, August 17, 1858, Issue 3824.

Irigaray, Luce. *This Sex Which Is Not One*. Ithaca, NY: Cornell University Press, 1985.

Jacobs, Jane. *The Death and Life of Great American Cities*. New York: Vintage Books, 1994.

Jacobs, Joseph. "Of the Racial Characteristics of Modern Jews." *Journal of the Anthropological Institute of Great Britain and Ireland* 15 (1886): 23–62.

Jameson, Frederic. *Postmodernism, or the Cultural Logic of Late Capitalism*. Durham, NC: Duke University Press, 1991.

Kant, Immanuel. *Critique of Judgement*. Translated by James Creed Meredith. Oxford: Oxford University Press, 2008.

Kennedy, George. "A Hoot in the Dark: The Evolution of General Rhetoric." *Philosophy and Rhetoric* 25, no. 1 (1992): 1–21.

Kittler, Friedrich A. *Gramophone, Film, Typewriter*. Translated by Geoffrey Winthrop-Young, Michael Wutz, and Geoffrey Winthrop Young. Stanford, CA: Stanford University Press, 1999.

———. "Towards an Ontology of Media." *Theory, Culture & Society* 26, nos. 2–3 (2009): 23–31.

Kleingeld, Pauline. "Kant's Second Thoughts on Race." *Philosophical Quarterly* 57, no. 229 (2007): 573–92.

Koven, Seth. "Dr. Barnardo's 'Artistic Fictions': Photography, Sexuality, and the Ragged Child in Victorian London." *Radical History Review* 69 (1997): 6–45.

———. *Slumming: Sexual and Social Politics in Late Victorian England*. Princeton, NJ: Princeton University Press, 2006.

Kracauer, Siegfried. "Photography." Translated by Thomas Y. Levin. *Critical Inquiry* 19, no. 3 (1993): 421–36.

Lacan, Jacques. *The Seminar of Jacques Lacan: The Four Fundamental Concepts of Psychoanalysis (Vol. XI)*. Edited by Jacques-Alain Miller. Translated by Alan Sheridan. New York: W. W. Norton & Company, 1998.

Laclau, Ernesto. *On Populist Reason*. London: Verso Books, 2005.

Laporte, Dominique. *History of Shit*. Translated by Nadia Benabid and Rodolphe el Khoury. Cambridge, MA: MIT Press, 2002.

Larrimore, Mark. "Sublime Waste: Kant on the Destiny of the 'Races.'" *Canadian Journal of Philosophy* 29, no. 1 (1999): 99–125.

"The Late Ramo Samee and His Widow: To the Editor of Bell's Life in London." *Bell's Life in London*. September 1, 1850.

Latour, Bruno. "Morality and Technology: The End of the Means." Translated by Couze Venn. *Theory, Culture & Society* 19, nos. 5–6 (2002): 247–60.

———. *Reassembling the Social: An Introduction to Actor-Network-Theory*. Oxford: Oxford University Press, 2007.

———. "Where Are the Missing Masses? The Sociology of a Few Mundane Artifacts." In *Technology and Society: Building Our Sociotechnical Future*, 151–80. Cambridge, MA: MIT Press, 2008.

———. "Why Has Critique Run Out of Steam? From Matters of Fact to Matters of Concern." *Critical Inquiry* 30 (2004): 225–48.

Le Bon, Gustave. *The Crowd: A Study of the Popular Mind*. Translated by Robert Nye. Mineola, NY: Dover Publications, Inc, 2002.

Lee, Benjamin, and Edward LiPuma. "Cultures of Circulation: The Imaginations of Modernity." *Public Culture* 14, no. 1 (2002): 191–213.

Lefebvre, Henri. *The Production of Space*. Translated by Donald Nicholson-Smith. Malden, MA: Blackwell Publishing, 1991.

Linton, Eliza Lynn. "Out Walking." *Temple Bar*. July 1, 1862.

London, Jack. *The People of the Abyss*. Project Gutenberg, 2005. http://www.gutenberg.org /files/1688/1688-h/1688-h.htm.

Lukács, Georg. *Studies in European Realism*. Translated by John Mander and Ecke Mander. London: Merlin, 1963.

Lyden, Anne M. *A Royal Passion: Queen Victoria and Photography*. Los Angeles: Getty Publications, 2014.

Lyotard, Jean-François. *Lessons on the Analytic of the Sublime*, translated by Elizabeth Rottenberg. Stanford, CA: Stanford University Press, 1994.

Marback, Richard. "The Rhetorical Space of Robben Island." *Rhetoric Society Quarterly* 34, no. 2 (2004): 7–27.

Marriott, David. "Inventions of Existence: Sylvia Wynter, Frantz Fanon, Sociegeny, and 'the Damned.'" *CR: The Centennial Review* 11, no. 3 (2011): 45–89.

Marx, Karl. "On the Jewish Question." *Marxists.org*, 1844. https://www.marxists.org /archive/marx/works/1844/jewish-question/.

Massumi, Brian. "The Autonomy of Affect." *Cultural Critique* 31 (1995): 83–109.

Mayhew, Henry. *London Labour and the London Poor*. Volumes 1–4. London: Dover Publications, 1968.

———. *London Labour and the London Poor: A Cyclopaedia of the Condition and Earnings of Those That Will Work, Those That Cannot Work, and Those That Will Not Work*. Charles Griffin and Company, London: 1864,

———. "The Task: Letter I—19 October 1849." In *The Unknown Mayhew: Selections from the Morning Chronicle, 1849–50*, edited by E. P. Thompson and Eileen Yeo, 120–21. Harmondsworth, UK: Penguin Classics, 1973.

———. "A View from St. Paul's." In *The Unknown Mayhew: Selections from the Morning Chronicle, 1849–50*, edited by E. P. Thompson and Eileen Yeo, 113–21. Harmondsworth, UK: Penguin Classics, 1973.

Mbembe, Achille. *Critique of Black Reason*. Translated by Laurent Dubois. Durham, NC: Duke University Press, 2017.

McCabe, Elizabeth Caitlin. "How the Past Remains: George Eliot, Thomas Hardy, and the Victorian Anthropological Doctrine of Survivals." PhD diss., Northwestern University, 2013.

McCann, Bryan J. *The Mark of Criminality: Rhetoric, Race, and Gangsta Rap in the War-on-Crime Era*. Tuscaloosa: University of Alabama Press, 2017.

McClintock, Ann. *Imperial Leather: Race, Gender, and Sexuality in the Colonial Contest*. New York: Routledge, 1995.

McKittrick, Katherine. *Demonic Grounds: Black Women and the Cartographies of Struggle*. Minneapolis: University of Minnesota Press, 2006.

Melamed, Jodi. "Racial Capitalism." *Critical Ethnic Studies* 1, no. 1 (2015): 76–85.

Menke, Richard. *Telegraphic Realism: Victorian Fiction and Other Information Systems*. Stanford, CA: Stanford University Press, 2007.

Metropolitan Sanitary Association. *Memorials on Sanitary Reform, and on the Economical and Administrative Principles of Water-Supply for the Metropolis: Addressed to the Right Hon. Lord John Russell and the Right Hon. Sir George Grey: Including Correspondence between John Stuart Mill, Esq. . . . and the Metropolitan Sanitary Association: On the Proper Agency for Regulating the Water-Supply for the Metropolis, as a Question of Economical and Administrative Principle*. London, 1851.

Mill, John Stuart. *Considerations on Representative Government*. In *On Liberty and Other Essays*, 205–470. Oxford: Oxford University Press, 2008.

———. *Essays on Economics and Society*. Toronto: University of Toronto Press, 1967.

———. *On Liberty*. In *On Liberty and Other Essays*, 5–130. Oxford: Oxford University Press, 2008.

Mills, Charles. *The Racial Contract*. Ithaca, NY: Cornell University Press, 1997.

Morgan, Elizabeth Kathryn. *Street Life in London: Context and Commentary*. Edinburgh: Museums Etc, 2014.

Morrison, Arthur. *Tales of Mean Streets*. Project Gutenberg E-Book. Project Gutenberg, 2012. http://www.gutenberg.org/ebooks/40569.

Mountford, Roxanne. "On Gender and Rhetorical Space." *Rhetoric Society Quarterly* 31, no. 1 (2001): 41–71.

Nead, Lynda. *The Haunted Gallery: Painting, Photography, Film c. 1900*. New Haven, CT: Yale University Press, 2007.

———. *Victorian Babylon: People, Streets and Images in Nineteenth-Century London*. New Haven, CT: Yale University Press, 2000.

Nord, Deborah Epstein. *Walking the Victorian Streets: Women, Representation, and the City*. Ithaca, NY: Cornell University Press, 1995.

Novak, Daniel A. *Realism, Photography and Nineteenth-Century Fiction*. Cambridge: Cambridge University Press, 2008.

Omi, Michael, and Howard Winant. *Racial Formation in the United States: From the 1960s to the 1990s*. 2nd ed. New York: Routledge, 1994.

Otter, Chris. *The Victorian Eye: A Political History of Light and Vision in Britain, 1800–1910*. Chicago: University of Chicago Press, 2008.

Ovenden, Richard. *John Thomson (1837–1921): Photographer*. Edinburgh: Stationery Office, 1997.

Parikka, Jussi. *What Is Media Archaeology?* Cambridge, UK: Polity, 2012.

Parsons, Deborah L. *Streetwalking the Metropolis: Women, the City, and Modernity*. Oxford: Oxford University Press, 2000.

"Penny Satirist." *Penny Satirist*, June 1, 1839, Issue 111.

"The Petticoat-Lane Marts." *Daily News*, August 3, 1858, Issue 3812 edition.

"The Petticoat-Lane Marts." *Morning Post*, August 3, 1858, Issue 26394 edition.

"The Petticoat-Lane Marts." *Morning Chronicle*, August 3, 1858, Issue 28564 edition.

Phillips, Adam. "Introduction." In Edmund Burke, *A Philosophical Enquiry into the Origin of Our Ideas of the Sublime and Beautiful*, ix–xxiii. Oxford: Oxford University Press, 1990.

"Photography: Its History and Application." *British Quarterly Review* 44, no. 87 (1866): 346–90.

Pike, David L. *Metropolis on the Styx: The Underworlds of Modern Urban Culture, 1800–2001*. Ithaca, NY: Cornell University Press, 2007.

———. *Subterranean Cities: The World beneath Paris and London, 1800–1945*. Ithaca, NY: Cornell University Press, 2005.

"The Police and the Sunday Fair in Petticoat-Lane." *Daily News*, August 2, 1858, Issue 3811 edition.

Poovey, Mary. *A History of the Modern Fact: Problems of Knowledge in the Sciences of Wealth and Society*. Chicago: University of Chicago Press, 1998.

———. *Making a Social Body: British Cultural Formation, 1830–1864*. Chicago: University of Chicago Press, 1995.

Porter, George Richardson. *The Progress of the Nation*. C. Knight & Co., 1836. http://archive.org/details/progressnation03portgoog.

Prashad, Vijay. "Native Dirt/Imperial Ordure: The Cholera of 1832 and the Morbid Resolutions of Modernity." *Journal of Historical Sociology* 7, no. 3 (1994): 243–60.

Preston, W. C. "The Bitter Cry of Outcast London : An Inquiry into the Condition of the Abject Poor." *Internet Archive*, 1883. https://archive.org/details/bittercryofoutcaoopres.

Prichard, James Cowles. *Researches into the Physical History of Man*. Edited by George W. Stocking. Chicago: University of Chicago Press, 1973.

Punch. "British Association for the Advancement of Everything in General, and Nothing in Particular." *Punch, or the London Charivari*. Vol. 3. Punch Publications Ltd: London, 1842.

———. "Civilisation." *Punch, or the London Charivari*. July 31, 1841.

———. "The Natural History of Courtship." *Punch, or the London Charivari*. February 12, 1842.

———. "A Nigger Professor of Cramanology." *Punch, or the London Charivari*. January 29, 1842.

———. "Photographic Failures." *Punch, or the London Charivari*. Vol. 12. Punch Publications Ltd: London, 1847, 42.

———. "The Physiology of the London Idler: Chapter II—The Regent-Street Lounger." *Punch, or the London Charivari*. Vol. 3, January 1842

———. "Physiology of the London Idler: Chapter V—Concerning Exhibition Loungers." *Punch, or the London Charivari*. Vol. 3, January 1842.

———. "Physiology of the London Idler: Chapter VI—Concerning the Gent." *Punch, or the London Charivari*. Vol. 3. Punch Publications Ltd: London, 1842, 60.

———. "The Simple History of a Portrait." *Punch, or the London Charivari*. Vol. 33. Punch Publications Ltd: London, 1857, 224.

———. "The Zoology and Architecture of Lawyers' Clerks." *Punch, or the London Charivari*. Vol. 3. Punch Publications Ltd: London, 1842.

Quayson, Ato. "Signs of the Times: Discourse Ecologies and Street Life on Oxford St., Accra." *City & Society* 22, no. 1 (2010): 72–96.

Rabinow, Paul. *French Modern: Norms and Forms of the Social Environment*. Chicago: University Of Chicago Press, 1995.

Rendle, William. *Fever in London: Its Social and Sanitary Lessons*. London: Metropolitan Sanitary Association, 1866.

Report from the Select Committee of the House of Lords Appointed to Consider the Bill, Intituled "An Act to Prevent Unnecessary Trading on Sunday in the Metropolis"; and to Report Thereon to the House. United Kingdom: House of Commons, June 1, 1850.

Reports on the Volume and Effects of Recent Immigration from Eastern Europe into the United Kingdom: Presented to Both Houses of Parliament by Command of Her Majesty. United Kingdom: Parliament, 1894.

Rice, Jeff. *Digital Detroit: Rhetoric and Space in the Age of the Network*. Carbondale: Southern Illinois University Press, 2012.

Rice, Jenny Edbauer. "Unframing Models of Public Distribution: From Rhetorical Situation to Rhetorical Ecologies." *Rhetoric Society Quarterly* 35, no. 4 (2005): 5–24.

Rickert, Thomas. *Ambient Rhetoric: The Attunements of Rhetorical Being*. Pittsburgh: University of Pittsburgh Press, 2013.

Ricoeur, Paul. *Freud and Philosophy: An Essay on Interpretation*. New Haven, CT: Yale University Press, 1970.

Robbins, Bruce. "Cosmopolitanism: New and Newer." *Boundary 2* 34, no. 3 (2007): 47–60.

———. *Secular Vocations: Intellectuals, Professionalism, Culture*. London: Verso, 1983.

Robinson, Cedric J. *Black Marxism: The Making of the Black Radical Tradition*. Chapel Hill: University of North Carolina Press, 2000.

Rochelson, Meri-Jane. "Language, Gender, and Ethnic Anxiety in Zangwill's Children of the Ghetto." *English Literature in Transition, 1880–1920* 31, no. 4 (1988): 399–412.

Ryan, James R. *Picturing Empire: Photography and the Visualization of the British Empire*. Chicago: University of Chicago Press, 1998.

Runia, Eelco. "Inventing the New from the Old: From White's 'Tropics' to Vico's 'Topics.'" *Rethinking History* 14, no. 2 (2010): 229–41.

———. "Presence." *History and Theory* 45 (2006): 1–29.

Said, Edward W. *Orientalism*. London: Penguin Books, 2003.

The Sanitary Condition of the City of London from the City Remembrancer on the Statements of the Sub-Committee of the Health of Towns Association; with the Sub-Committee's Reply and Lord Ashley's Letter. London: Health of Towns Association, 1848.

Schlesinger, Max, and Otto von Wenckstern. *Saunterings in and about London*. London: N. Cooke, 1853. http://archive.org/details/saunteringsinaboooschluoft.

Schuller, Kyla. *The Biopolitics of Feeling: Race, Sex and Science in the Nineteenth Century.* Durham, NC: Duke University Press, 2018.

Second Report from Select Committee on Metropolis Improvements. London: House of Commons, August 2, 1838.

Sekula, Allan. "The Body and the Archive." *October* 39 (1986): 3. doi:10.2307/778312.

Sennett, Richard. *Flesh and Stone: The Body and the City in Western Civilization.* London: Faber & Faber, 1994.

Shannon, Mary L. *Dickens, Reynolds, and Mayhew on Wellington Street: The Print Culture of a Victorian Street.* Burlington, VA: Ashgate, 2015.

Sheppard, F. H. W., ed. *Survey of London: Volume 27, Spitalfields and Mile End New Town.* London: London County Council, 1957. http://www.british-history.ac.uk/survey-london /vol27/v-vi.

Sheth, Falguni A. "The Technology of Race: Enframing, Violence, and Taming the Unruly." *Radical Philosophy Review* 7, no. 1 (2004): 77–98.

Shih, Shu-Mei, and Francoise Lionnet. "Thinking through the Minor, Transnationally." In *Minor Transnationalisms,* edited by Shu-Mei Shih and Francoise Lionnet, 1–27. Durham, NC: Duke University Press, 2005.

Simmel, Georg. "The Metropolis and Mental Life." In *The Sociology of Georg Simmel,* translated by Kurt Wolff, 409–24. New York: Free Press, 1950.

Spillers, Hortense J. "Introduction—Peter's Pans: Eating in the Diaspora." In *Black, White, and in Color: Essays on American Literature and Culture,* 1–64. Chicago: University of Chicago Press, 2003.

———. "Mama's Baby, Papa's Maybe: An American Grammar Book." In *Black, White, and in Color: Essays on American Literature and Culture.* Chicago: University of Chicago Press, 2003. 203–29.

Stallybrass, Peter. *The Politics and Poetics of Transgression.* Ithaca, NY: Cornell University Press, 1986.

Stocking, George. "From Chronology to Ethnology: James Cowles Prichard and British Anthropology, 1800–1850." In James Cowles Prichard, *Researches into the Physical History of Man,* edited by George W. Stocking, ix–cx. Chicago: University of Chicago Press, 1973.

———. "What's in a Name? The Origins of the Royal Anthropological Institute (1837–1871)." *Man* 6, no. 3 (1971): 369–90.

Stoler, Ann Laura. *Carnal Knowledge and Imperial Power: Race and the Intimate in Colonial Rule.* Berkeley: University of California Press, 2002.

———. *Race and the Education of Desire: Foucault's History of Sexuality and the Colonial Order of Things.* Durham, NC: Duke University Press, 1995.

Stormer, Nathan. "Addressing the Sublime: Space, Mass Representation, and the Unrepresentable," *Critical Studies in Media Communication* 21, no. 3 (2004): 212–40.

———. "Articulation: A Working Paper on Rhetoric and *Taxis,*" *Quarterly Journal of Speech* 90, no. 3 (2004): 257–84.

———. "Rhetoric: A Working Paper on Rhetoric and Mnesis." *Quarterly Journal of Speech* 99, no. 1 (2013): 27–50.

———. "Rhetoric's Diverse Materiality: Polythetic Ontology and Genealogy," *Review of Communication* 16, no. 4 (2016): 299–316

"Strangers into Citizens Briefing Paper No. 4." Strangers into Citizens Campaign, London, 2009.

Tagg, John. *Burden of Representation: Essays on Photographies and Histories*. Minneapolis: University of Minnesota Press, 1993.

———. "The Archiving Machine; or, the Camera and the Filing Cabinet." *Grey Room* 47 (2012): 24–37.

Talbot, William Henry Fox. *The Pencil of Nature*. London: Longman, Brown, Green and Longmans, 1844.

Thackeray, William Makepeace. *The Book of Snobs*. Project Gutenberg EBook, 2018 [1848].

Thomas, Ronald R. *Detective Fiction and the Rise of Forensic Science*. Cambridge England; New York: Cambridge University Press, 2000.

Thompson, E. P., and Eileen Yeo, eds. *The Unknown Mayhew: Selections from the Morning Chronicle, 1849–50*. Harmondsworth, UK: Penguin Classics, 1973.

Thomson, John. *Illustrations of China and Its People*. London: Sampson Low, Marston, Low, and Searle,1873.

Thomson, John, and Adolphe Smith. *Victorian London Street Life in Historic Photographs*. New York: Dover Publications, Inc, 1994.

Thrift, Nigel. *Non-Representational Theory: Space, Politics, Affect*. New York: Routledge, 2007.

Topalov, Christian. "The City as Terra Incognita: Charles Booth's Poverty Survey and the People of London, 1886–1891." *Planning Perspectives* 8, no. 4 (1993): 395–425.

Topinka, Robert. "Resisting the Fixity of Suburban Space: The Walker as Rhetorician," *Rhetoric Society Quarterly* 42, no. 1 (2012): 65–84.

Tylor, Edward Burnett. *Primitive Culture*. 2 vols. London: John Murray, 1871.

Walkowitz, Judith R. *City of Dreadful Delight: Narratives of Sexual Danger in Late-Victorian London*. Chicago: University of Chicago Press, 1992.

Walsh, Lynda, Nathaniel A. Rivers, Jenny Rice, Laurie E. Gries, Jennifer L. Bay, Thomas Rickert, and Carolyn Miller. "Forum: Bruno Latour on Rhetoric." *Rhetoric Society Quarterly* 47, no. 5 (2017): 403–62.

Watts, Eric King. "Postracial Fantasies, Blackness, and Zombies." *Communication and Critical/Cultural Studies* 14, no. 4 (2017): 317–33.

Wanzer-Serrano, Darrel (as Darrel Allan Wanzer). "Delinking Rhetoric, or Revisiting McGee's Fragmentation Thesis through Decoloniality." *Rhetoric and Public Affairs* 15, no. 4 (2012): 647–57.

———. *The New York Young Lords and the Struggle for Liberation*. Philadelphia: Temple University Press, 2015.

Weheliye, Alexander G. *Habeas Viscus: Racializing Assemblages, Biopolitics, and Black Feminist Theories of the Human*. Durham, NC: Duke University Press, 2014.

Welford, Walter D. *The Hand Camera Manual: A Beginner's Guide to Photography in Its Connection with the Hand Camera*. London: L. Upcott Gill, 1893.

Willey, Angela. "A World of Materialisms: Postcolonial Feminist Science Studies and the New Natural." *Science, Technology, and Human Values* 41, no. 6 (2016): 991–1014.

Williams, Rosalind. *Notes on the Underground: An Essay on Technology, Society, and the Imagination*. 2nd edition. Cambridge, MA: MIT Press, 2008.

Wilson, Kirt H. *The Reconstruction Desegregation Debate: The Policies of Equality and the Rhetoric of Place, 1870–1875*. East Lansing: Michigan State University Press, 2002.

Winter, James H. *London's Teeming Streets: 1830–1914*. London: Routledge, 1993.

Wright, Helena E. "Photography in the Printing Press: The Photomechanical Revolution." *Presenting Pictures* 4 (2004): 21–42.

Wynter, Sylvia. "Unsettling the Coloniality of Being/Power/Truth/Freedom: Towards the Human, After Man, Its Overrepresentation—An Argument." *CR: The New Centennial Review* 3, no. 3 (2003): 257–337.

Zangwill, Israel. *Children of the Ghetto: A Study of a Peculiar People*. 3rd ed. London: Project Gutenberg, 1914. http://www.gutenberg.org/ebooks/12680.

INDEX

actor-network theory, 47, 54, 64, 69
affect, 13–14, 35, 39–45, 78, 104, 113

Bazalgette, Joseph, 2, 3, 17, 48, 51–52, 54, 59, 64, 80, 133, 137
Benjamin, Walter, 4, 42
Bertillon, Alphonse, 105, 129
biopolitics, 6, 10–11, 47, 56, 64, 97–98, 103, 107, 109, 114. *See also* governance
Bleak House (Dickens), 83, 132–134
Booth, Charles, 16, 133–36
Burke, Edmund, 17, 25, 33–34, 39, 42, 104, 147n48
Burke, Kenneth, 46

catachresis, 23–24, 37, 40, 44–45, 48, 97, 130, 135
Chadwick, Edwin, 16, 21, 55–58, 60–61
Children of the Ghetto (Zangwill), 68, 89–90, 136–37
cholera, 5, 16, 50, 53–54, 59
circulation, 1, 3–5, 7, 18–19, 65–70, 72–77, 79, 86–88, 91, 95; communication and, 10–13; race and 57, 89–90, 93–94; sewers and, 46, 49–54 58, 64–65; walking and 82–85
cliché, 2–3, 23–24, 45, 130, 135, 138–39
Commercial Street, 13, 65, 67, 70–74, 79–83, 88, 90, 93, 137, 139
communication, 11–13, 17, 28, 43, 45, 47, 52, 66, 71–73, 80, 86, 131–32, 136, 139

crowd, the, 5, 16–17, 38–40, 42–43, 45, 49, 65–68, 70–75, 77–79, 81–84, 86–88, 91–92, 94–95, 126, 133, 135, 137

Daniel Deronda (Eliot), 89
Darwin, Charles, 9, 31, 47, 104, 109
Deleuze, Gilles, 13, 70, 107–109
Dickens, Charles, 14, 16, 57, 83, 131–32, 134, 137
Drury Lane, 17, 28–30, 123

Eliot, George, 89
Ellis, Havelock, 104–5

Fanon, Frantz, 6, 36, 106
Foucault, Michel, 10, 44, 109
Freud, Sigmund, 8–9, 46–48, 115

Galton, Francis, 7, 19, 97–98, 103–9, 111, 114, 119, 129, 136
Guattari, Felix, 70, 107–9
gender, 32, 66–67, 82–86, 114, 116, 123, 135–36; prostitution and, 29, 32, 65, 67–68, 72, 82–86, 90, 93, 115, 133, 135–36. *See also* urban space
genealogy, 3, 4, 6–10, 13–14, 19, 25, 45, 130, 137
Gissing, George, 130, 133, 137
governance, 3–5, 9–10, 16–17, 22–23, 25–26, 35–37, 47, 52, 60, 74–79, 86, 130; aesthetics of, 14, 17, 23, 36; governmentality and, 10–13, 24–28, 33, 36, 43–45, 47, 95, 140; liberalism and, 10, 13,

181

Founded in 1893,
UNIVERSITY OF CALIFORNIA PRESS
publishes bold, progressive books and journals
on topics in the arts, humanities, social sciences,
and natural sciences—with a focus on social
justice issues—that inspire thought and action
among readers worldwide.

The UC PRESS FOUNDATION
raises funds to uphold the press's vital role
as an independent, nonprofit publisher, and
receives philanthropic support from a wide
range of individuals and institutions—and from
committed readers like you. To learn more, visit
ucpress.edu/supportus.